Wait for the LORD with courage;
  be stouthearted, and wait for the LORD. (Psalm 27:14)

THE
PEOPLE
OF
HOPE

The Story Behind the Modern Church

ANTHONY E. GILLES

Nihil Obstat: Rev. Lawrence Landini, O.F.M.
Rev. John J. Jennings

Imprimi Potest: Rev. Jeremy Harrington, O.F.M.
Provincial

Imprimatur: +James H. Garland, V.G.
Archdiocese of Cincinnati
September 14, 1987

Scripture texts used in this work are taken from the *New American Bible*, copyright ©1970 by the Confraternity of Christian Doctrine, Washington, D.C., and are used by permission of the copyright owner. All rights reserved.

Chapter Eleven, "Prophet of Hope: Teilhard de Chardin; Harmonizer of Religion and Science, Church and World," incorporates parts of three articles previously published by the author in *The Teilhard Review*, February 1977; *Spirituality Today*, Summer 1982; and *America*, May 23, 1981.

Book and cover design by Julie Lonneman

ISBN 0-86716-069-1

TO THOMAS FRANCIS SMITH, O.C.S.O.

THE PEOPLE OF GOD—FROM ABRAHAM TO US

A sweeping history of Judeo-Christian thought by Anthony E. Gilles

PREFACE

As I prepared this sixth and final volume in The People of God series, I discovered that writing contemporary history is very different from writing the history of bygone eras.

First, I found I could depart somewhat from my usual approach of providing the political, social, cultural and spiritual context for Church history, since the reader is doubtlessly better informed about this epoch than earlier ones. Thus, in this volume I followed the approach I took in the preceding five volumes only until about the end of World War II. After that I refocused on the development of Christian thought, to the exclusion of such "extraneous" factors as politics and the like (although not ignoring such factors completely). As a result, the focus in the second half of this book becomes modern Protestant and Catholic thinking and, in particular, the documents of Vatican II—which I consider the most important restatement of Christian thought since the early days of the Church.

Second, I found the overall selection of content to be much more difficult than in the previous volumes. When it comes to our own history, we have a tendency to be somewhat possessive, holding on to things we would like to see emphasized and discarding things we feel are less important. I don't pretend to be any less influenced by this tendency than anyone else. So why have I chosen what I have chosen? What are my personal preferences? How would I like to see the story of the Church develop in the future? What do I think the guiding principles should be?

In answering such questions I don't presume to know how the future will unfold. For example, I don't know whether 50 years from now historians will judge that popular devotion to Our Lady of Fatima, which I have ignored, was of more significance to the progress of Christian thinking than liberation theology, which I have discussed in some detail. Nor do I know whether 50 years from now Teilhard de Chardin, one of the main characters in my history, will have been forgotten and Archbishop Marcel Lefebvre, whom I ignore, will be remembered as the preserver of authentic Catholicism. Again, I cannot be certain whether the American bishops' pastoral on war and peace will more strongly influence the shape of the Church to come than devotion to the Sacred Heart.

Yet I think I am in touch with the mind of the Church in the modern world when I choose to focus on liberation theology rather than devotion to Our Lady of Fatima, Teilhard de Chardin rather than Archbishop Lefebvre, and the bishops' pastoral rather than devotional practices which originated in 17th-century France. For those who find value in the three excluded examples and resent my absorption with the topics I have actually chosen, I can only say this: I do not intend to deny the value of those aspects of Christian thought and life which I have excluded. I have simply tried to concern myself with what I consider to be main currents rather than subsidiary channels—but time may prove me wrong.

'To Make All Things New'

In the last analysis I suppose the one criterion which guided my writing in this volume more than any other was Scripture's words, "See, I make all things new!" (Revelation 21:5). In my opinion the Spirit constantly inspires us to move ahead, to make ever greater progress in our personal growth as Christians. And what is true for the individual is true for the Church as a whole. What I have done in the pages ahead is to focus on the Church's growth toward maturity, or toward a state of consciousness in which we learn what it means truly to hope in the promises of the Lord.

I see much of the Church's behavior and thought during the 19th and early 20th centuries as concerned more with preservation of the status quo than with growth toward maturity, and I make no secret of the fact that I prefer what has taken place since Vatican II—mistakes, confusion and all—to the stifling climate of the Vatican I Church. Nor do I make any secret of my preference for such people as John XXIII, Teilhard de Chardin and Dorothy Day over the likes of Pope Pius IX.

If I have any bias in the pages ahead then, it is toward describing the vision of the Church as seen by the bishops at Vatican II, and toward the post-Vatican II Church that is being built today on the thinking of people like Karl Rahner and Pope John Paul II. It seems to me that such people have understood how to blend the old with the new in such a way as to preserve the roots of the Christian past while constantly moving ahead toward that ideal Church which will forever exceed our grasp until the Lord comes again. But even though we fail to live the gospel worthily, even though we fail to make the Kingdom a present-day reality, we nonetheless are constantly pressing ahead as the pilgrim people of God, always seeking, like the Father, to make all things new.

Acknowledgments

I wish to express my continuing indebtedness to the 10-volume *History of the Church* edited by Hubert Jedin (originally *Handbuch der Kirchengeschichte*, English translation, 1965, Crossroad Publishing Co., 1982), on which I rely for much of the discussion in the first half of this book. I wish to thank my wife, Andrea, who has supported me in perseverance and love while I put these six books together. I also wish to thank the staff of St. Anthony Messenger Press, particularly my editors, Karen Hurley, Lisa Engelhardt, Carol Luebering and Father Greg Friedman, whose insights and suggestions have made these books much more interesting and readable than they were in original manuscript form, and Julie Lonneman, whose cover illustrations always managed to capture succinctly the spirit of the books they enclosed. Finally, if there are any readers approaching this volume after having read the first five, I wish to thank you for allowing me to share with you our story, the story of the People of God.

CONTENTS

TIMELINE 1789—PRESENT

Popes

Pius VI (1775-1799)

Pius VII (1800-1823)

Leo XII (1823-1829)
Pius VIII (1829-1831)
Gregory XVI (1831-1846)

Pius IX (1846-1878)

Events

1789: The French Revolution; French National Assembly nationalizes Church property
1790: John Carroll of Baltimore becomes first bishop of United States
1791: First Amendment to U.S. Constitution provides for separation of Church and State
1793: Robespierre outlaws Catholicism in France
1795: Catholicism is restored in France

1800

1800: Napoleon Bonaparte becomes French "First Consul"
1801: Napoleon concludes concordat with Pius VII
1804: Napoleon named Emperor
1809: Napoleon annexes Papal States, takes Pius VII captive
1813: Simon Bolivar gains control of Venezuela; Mexico gains independence
1814: Pius VII returns to Rome
1815: Napoleon is defeated at Waterloo
1816: Pius VII issues *Esti Longissimo*, urging Latin American bishops to support colonial governments
1822: Brazil becomes independent nation
1825: Aristocrats restored in France
1829: Catholic Emancipation Act permits British Catholics to hold public office
1830: July Revolution in Paris, Charles X abdicates; the Blessed Virgin is said to appear to Catherine Labouré
1832: Gregory XVI condemns freedom of religion and press in *Mirari Vos*
       Giuseppe Mazzini founds movement for Italian unification
1834: Pope Gregory condemns Lammenais in *Singulari Nos*
1837: Bishop John England of Charleston, South Carolina, proposes joint lay-episcopal government
       of U.S. Catholic dioceses but is opposed by other American bishops
1843: Queen Isabella II of Spain assumes throne
1846: The Blessed Virgin purportedly appears at La Salette
1848: Wave of revolution sweeps through Europe; Pius IX flees Rome
       Marx and Engels publish *Communist Manifesto*
1849: Italian nationalists declare Rome a republic; nationalists are defeated and Pius IX returns

1850

1851: Pius IX promulgates the "perpetual adoration" devotion
1854: Pius IX proclaims the doctrine of the Immaculate Conception
1856: "Know-Nothing" Party in America drafts anti-Catholic platform
1858: Bernadette Soubirous claims visions of Blessed Virgin at Lourdes
       American priest Isaac Hecker founds Paulist Fathers

History Makers

Bishop John Carroll (1815)

Joseph de Maistre (1821)

Cardinal Ercole Consalvi (1824)
Friedrich Schlegel (1829)

Friedrich Schleiermacher (1834)

Count Louis Bonald (1840)
Bishop John England (1842)

François Chateaubriand (1848)

Felicité de Lammenais (1854)
Søren Kierkegaard (1855)

Robert Owen (1858)

xv

Single dates in parentheses indicate an individual's date of death; dates spanning a number of years refer to time in office.

Individuals	Year	Events	Popes
Cardinal James Gibbons (1921)	1921:	Adolf Hitler organizes storm troopers in Germany	
Louis Duchesne (1922)	1922:	The U.S.S.R. is formally organized	Pius XI (1922-1939)
Franz Schindler (1922)	1923:	Teilhard de Chardin engages in paleological excavations in China	
Baron Friedrich von Hugel (1925)	1924:	Italian voters endorse Mussolini	
Cardinal Désiré Joseph Mercier (1926)			
Adolf von Harnack (1930)	1929:	Italy and the Vatican conclude the Lateran Treaty	
Lucien Laberthonnière (1932)	1931:	Pius XI publishes *Quadragesimo Anno*	
Henri Bremond (1933)	1933:	Adolf Hitler becomes chancellor of Germany, and first concentration camps are built by Nazis	
		Dorothy Day and Peter Maurin found the Catholic Worker movement	
Rudolf Otto (1937)	1937:	Pius XI issues the anti-Nazi encyclical *Mit Brennender Sorge*	
Alfred Loisy (1940)	1939:	World War II begins	Pius XII (1939-1958)
Romolo Murri (1940)			
Henri Bergson (1941)	1941:	Thomas Merton enters Trappist monastery of Gethsemani in Kentucky	
Benito Mussolini (1945)	1943:	Information of the Holocaust begins to reach the Vatican	
Adolf Hitler (1945)		Pius XII issues *Divino Afflante Spiritu*, encouraging modern biblical scholarship	
Dietrich Bonhoeffer (1945)			
Maurice de Wulf (1947)	1950:	Pius XII declares the doctrine of the Assumption in *Munificentissimus Deus*	
Maurice Blondel (1949)			
Joseph Stalin (1953)			
Teilhard de Chardin (1955)			
Albert Schweitzer (1965)	1962:	Vatican II opens in Rome	John XXIII (1958-1963)
Paul Tillich (1965)	1965:	Second Vatican Council closes on December 8	Paul VI (1963-1978)
Karl Adam (1966)	1967:	The Charismatic Renewal is begun at Duquesne University	
Karl Barth (1968)	1968:	Paul VI publishes *Humanae Vitae* prohibiting artificial birth control	
Thomas Merton (1968)			
Reinhold Niebuhr (1971)	1973:	U.S. Supreme Court legalizes abortion	
Jacques Maritain (1973)			John Paul I (1978-1978)
C. H. Dodd (1973)	1979:	John Paul II publishes *Redeemer of Man*; Hans Küng's teachings are censored by the Vatican	John Paul II (1978-)
Rudolf Bultmann (1976)		Latin American bishops at Puebla, Mexico, reaffirm the Church's "preferential option for the poor"	
Étienne Gilson (1978)	1980:	Four American religious women are murdered in El Salvador	
Dorothy Day (1980)			
Jean-Paul Sartre (1980)	1983:	U.S. bishops publish peace pastoral	
Karl Rahner (1984)	1984:	Number of U.S. seminarians has fallen from 47,500 in 1964 to 12,000	
Edward Schillebeeckx	1985:	Extraordinary Synod of Bishops in Rome reaffirms Church's dedication to the principles of Vatican II	
Jürgen Moltmann	1986:	American theologian Charles Curran of The Catholic University is censored by the Vatican	
Hans Küng		U.S. bishops publish economic pastoral	
Gustavo Gutierrez			

1950

2000

INTRODUCTION

'With God' in the World: Maturing Into Hope

From one's initial "yes" to Jesus Christ, one constantly moves forward through new stages of growth. *Hope* propels that growth. For hope is the inner dynamic of faith which completes faith and points it toward fulfillment; it is the power by which one grows toward maturity in Christ. The Apostle Paul says that one who is not possessed by Christian hope is "...without God in the world" (Ephesians 2:12); conversely, to hope in a Christian sense is to be *with* God in the world.

The underlying theme of this book is the growing confidence which we modern Christians have that God is present with us in the world. Modern Christians are "People of Hope" precisely because we are beginning to understand more fully that Christianity is a this-worldly religion, a religion by which "this world" becomes transformed into a *future* world—a world of resurrected life and of peace, justice, forgiveness and joy. While not "seeing" this future world, we People of Hope nonetheless believe that we have been empowered to bring the future age into existence and act as if we so believe.

Hope, then, is a virtue practiced by mature (and maturing) believers. It is a virtue which befits a people who have journeyed through the stages of growth already recorded in the five previous books of this series.

This final volume in *The People of God* series is about the modern Church's struggle to define the boundary line between the Church and the world. By *modern* I mean the period from the French Revolution to the present. The challenge of the Church during this era,

1

particularly the Catholic Church, is to decide which of the world's values to incorporate into its own life, teaching and ministry, and which to exclude.

SHIFTING BOUNDARIES BETWEEN CHURCH AND WORLD

In the Middle Ages, Catholic Christendom had achieved a remarkable synthesis between the respective values of the Church and the world. Following Martin Luther's revolution, however, the medieval Catholic synthesis was severely challenged. In the confusion, cynicism and skepticism of the post-Reformation era, many people, particularly intellectuals, rejected both the traditional Catholic worldview as well as the new Protestant theology. By the late 18th century the intellectuals of Europe had virtually all been lost to the Church—whether Catholic or Protestant.

Meanwhile, Catholicism clung tenaciously to its medieval model of Church and world, while Protestants constructed such an abundance of creeds, traditions and denominations as to make a single, unified Protestant worldview impossible.

Eventually, by the time of the French Revolution, a new secular worldview had replaced the Christian worldview (whether Catholic or Protestant) as the predominant way of understanding human existence. This secular worldview—known as the "Enlightenment"—has been succinctly summarized by one of the leading historians of the period as follows:

1) Man is not natively depraved.
2) The end of life is life itself: the good life on earth instead of the beatific life after death.
3) Man is capable, guided solely by the light of reason and experience, of perfecting the good life on earth.
4) The first and essential condition of this...is the freeing of men's minds from the bonds of ignorance and superstition, and of their bodies from the arbitrary oppression of constituted authority [in Church and civil state].
5) Man is natively good, easily enlightened, disposed to follow reason and common sense; generous, humane, and tolerant, more willing to be led by persuasion than compelled by force.[1]

Much of this Enlightenment worldview came to be characterized as *liberalism*, so that in the pages ahead when I refer to "liberalism" or "liberal ideas," I am referring roughly to the five propositions listed above, and not to liberalism as we may think of it today.

We will find that from the early 19th century to the late 20th century the Church's attitude toward liberalism changed drastically. This book tells the story behind that change.

Until roughly the mid-20th century, the Catholic Church tolerated no dialogue with this Enlightenment liberalism. The Church's only response to liberalism's quest for human progress was one of denial, or an attitude which saw danger and evil in everything new and unfamiliar.

Protestantism, on the other hand, beginning early in the 19th century did initiate a dialogue with liberalism, seeking to incorporate helpful insights of liberalism into the Church's mission. By the late 19th century, after a series of political revolutions, many Christians began to feel that the essential thrust of liberalism—its desire for human progress based on reason—could be accommodated to the gospel. They began to see a relationship between the liberals' call for the improvement of earthly existence and the gospel's call to build the Kingdom of God. To be sure, most Christians realized the implicit incompatibility between the *entirety* of liberalism and the gospel, but they nonetheless sensed that some good could be gleaned from liberalism.

The essential issue at stake was the distinction between that which is "Church" and that which is "world." We could depict the various opinions on this issue by means of the set-theory diagrams on pp. 4-5.

In the Conclusion of this book (see pp. 189-191) we will construct a set-theory diagram which represents the position toward which the modern Church is now moving. In the pages ahead, then, we will follow the story of how the Church has moved from the positions represented by the four diagrams here toward a radically new synthesis and worldview. In the previous volume in this series, *The People of Anguish: The Story Behind the Reformation*, we watched the medieval synthesis unravel as Christians split into hostile factions; in this concluding volume we will begin our story with the Church's struggle to repulse the new secular religion of liberalism. But we will see the Church gradually grow up and enter into dialogue with the new age.

TEACHING THE WORLD TO HOPE AGAIN

By the time of Vatican II, the world itself had changed its evaluation of liberalism's belief in unlimited human progress apart from God. The horrors of 20th-century warfare and the establishment of totalitarian governments led modern people to reexamine their spiritual roots. In the face of compulsive materialism, the breakdown of many traditional values, the ever-increasing reliance on weapons of

3

The Medieval Catholic Worldview
Here the world's values are completely subordinated
to the Church's mission of salvation.

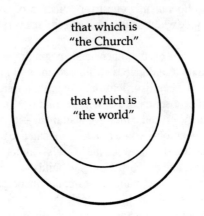

The Enlightenment Liberal Worldview
Here the Church's mission is completely subordinated
to the values of liberalism.

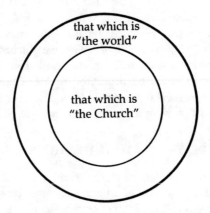

The 19th-Century Liberal Protestant Worldview

Here an attempt is made to reconcile
certain aspects of liberalism with the gospel.

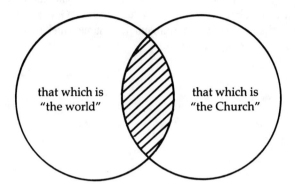

that which is
"the world"

that which is
"the Church"

The Catholic Worldview Until Well Into the 20th Century

Here there is "no compromise" between liberalism and the gospel.

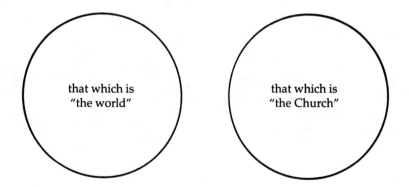

that which is
"the world"

that which is
"the Church"

destruction, the growing disparity between rich and poor, and the cheapening of human life in all stages of its existence, liberalism's belief in the perfectibility of the human race apart from God has become an idea that is no longer credible.

The principal challenge for today's Christian, then, is to teach the world how to hope again, to teach the world that God is with us in the world, that Jesus is called Emmanuel, "a name which means 'God is with us'" (Matthew 1:23).

CHAPTER ONE

REVOLUTION AND REACTION

From the Old Regime
to a Post-Revolution World (1750-1820)

Beginning about the middle of the 18th century, the states of
Europe and their colonies entered a period of political upheaval and
transformation. The "Old Regime"—the nickname given to the
established order throughout Europe—came under attack from every
quarter. In many parts of Europe the Old Regime was characterized by
the medieval Church-State relationship. Consequently, as the
established political order became threatened by revolution, so too were
the Church's traditional prerogatives put in jeopardy.

THE FRENCH REVOLUTION'S EFFECTS ON THE CHURCH

The pinnacle of revolutionary fervor was reached in France. For
two centuries the kings of France had bled their people white with
taxation. Yet by 1786 the government was virtually bankrupt. King
Louis XVI, hoping to stave off the nation's collapse, convened the
French legislature, known as the Estates-General. This was a fateful
step since this body intended to seize power for itself. The
Estates-General renamed itself the National Assembly and in 1789
declared its independence from the crown. The French Revolution had
begun.

In 1792 radical elements gained control of the Revolution,
declared France to be a republic and, in 1793, sent Louis XVI to the
guillotine. Throughout Europe aristocrats (from whose ranks most
Catholic bishops were drawn) shuddered at the prospect of losing their

7

privileges and thus united to combat the Revolution.

Yet people in one country after another were encouraged by the French Revolution, with its ideals of "liberty, equality, fraternity," to throw off the yoke of aristocratic oppression. In 1799 Napoleon Bonaparte gained control of the revolution in France and attempted to turn all of Europe into a colony of the Revolution. Wherever he went, Napoleon spread revolutionary ideas and established new political and legal institutions based on revolutionary principles.

As we shall see, Napoleon was finally defeated in 1815 by the traditional European power structure, but he nonetheless concretized the Revolution's ideals in much of European society. As a result, the year 1815 becomes something of a watershed; henceforth European society would be divided into factions which either favored or opposed the principles of the French Revolution.

The Eve of the Revolution

When the French Revolution began, the French Church was very much a part of the Old Regime and, in many respects, internally corrupt. Christianity in general and Catholicism in particular had been superseded in the minds of many educated French people by Enlightenment liberalism (see Introduction, p. 2). And since Rome generally assumed a purely defensive posture in response to the new currents of thought, the Catholic Church in the minds of many had become the very symbol of the old order.

As in the Middle Ages, French nobles still controlled Church "benefices"—that is, ecclesiastical offices such as bishoprics or abbacies—by appointing their sons or nephews to these posts. Thus the most important offices in the French Church were filled on the basis of birth rather than merit. Further, both the French monastic orders and the secular clergy had in many cases earned notorious reputations for immorality.

In Rome, Pope Pius VI (1775-1799) hardly set an example for the Church's clergy. Like the worst of the Renaissance popes, Pius cared more about his good looks and the careers of his relatives (whom he regularly appointed to Church positions) than he did about the Church's spiritual welfare. As an indication of Pius's true interests, he once spent the better part of a year embroiled in a heated controversy with the king of Naples over the king's refusal to follow through on his promise to give the Pope a prized white horse.

France, as the nation with the largest Catholic population in Europe, was extremely important to the papacy. Thus Pius VI had willingly acquiesced to many of King Louis XVI's policies affecting the Church, even when such policies violated the reform principles established by the Council of Trent. The Pope's conciliatory attitude toward the king's attempts to control the French Church assured Catholicism of its status as the official State religion, but it also meant that, as the State began to crumble, the Church lost its royal patron and defender.

The roughly 50,000 French priests, 25,000 monks and 35,000 nuns were overwhelmingly aristocratic in sympathy if not noble by birth. In their eyes, what was good for the nobility was good for the Church. The Church owned at least 10 percent of all French land and received an annual tithe from French Catholics made obligatory by the crown. When the Revolution began, therefore, many revolutionaries regarded the French Church as a constituent element of the political system which they intended to overthrow.

The National Assembly Confronts the Church

In a monumental decision, the French National Assembly voted on August 4, 1789, to abolish the Church's ancient prerogatives, including the hated tithe. On November 2 the Assembly confiscated all Church lands, and on February 13, 1790, it decreed the dissolution of most monasteries and forbade French citizens from taking monastic vows. Two years later all other religious congregations in France were abolished.

In a "Civil Constitution of the Clergy," the revolutionaries attempted the complete takeover of the French Church. This document reshaped French dioceses in congruence with the boundaries of the Revolution's new "Departments" (provinces), specified that bishops were to be elected rather than appointed and decreed that clerical salaries were to be paid by the State, thus solidifying the Revolution's control over the clergy.

Toward the end of 1790, the Assembly required all French bishops and priests to take an oath of loyalty to the new Constitution. About two-thirds refused, thereby splitting the French clergy into two factions: the "refractory clergy" who refused to take the oath and the "constituent clergy" who did take the oath. The latter assumed the leadership of the French Church.

The Radicals Take Control

On September 21, 1792, under Maximilien Robespierre and the Jacobin party, radical forces gained control of the Revolution. Thus began the infamous "Reign of Terror." Priests were forbidden to wear clerical dress and were required to take a new oath in support of

9

revolutionary ideals. Because Pope Pius VI had already condemned the "Declaration of the Rights of Man and of the Citizen"—the Revolution's charter of individual liberties—hundreds of refractory priests were deported and 300 more were executed.

The National Assembly had attempted to unite Church and State under its leadership, but Robespierre and his supporters attempted to do away with the Church altogether. Churches were sacked, looted and closed all over France. Robespierre hoped to replace the traditional alliance between throne and altar with a humanistic "republic of virtue."

The Church Under Napoleon

Robespierre's Reign of Terror came to an end in 1794 when he was assassinated. A new constitution adopted in 1795 placed executive power in the hands of "The Directory," a ruling council of five men who proved to be ineffectual in directing the Revolution. Meanwhile General Napoleon Bonaparte began his extraordinary rise to power. On November 9, 1799, Napoleon successfully overthrew the five directors. He established himself as "First Consul" until 1804 and then as Emperor until 1814.

Prior to Napoleon's takeover, French armies had invaded Italy and sympathetic Italian Jacobins had proclaimed the end of papal sovereignty. Pope Pius VI was deported to France, where he died on August 29, 1799, and the College of Cardinals was disbanded. Many Italians believed they were witnessing the abolition of the papacy.

Yet as soon as Napoleon gained power, he reversed the direction taken by the Jacobins. Napoleon observed that by and large the peasantry throughout Europe had resisted revolutionary ideals and clung to their Catholic faith. He astutely realized that an alliance with the papacy would make his task of ruling a largely Catholic empire much easier. Thus, on July 15, 1801, Napoleon concluded a "concordat" with the new pope, Pius VII (1800-1823).

According to Article 1 of the concordat, Catholics in France were guaranteed freedom of worship, provided their religious practices "agree with police regulations which the government might pass in the interest of maintaining public peace."[1] In order to remove the problem created by France's dual episcopacy (constituent and refractory), Article 3 of the concordat required the resignation of all French bishops in favor of an entirely new episcopate. Napoleon retained the right to appoint the new bishops (and all subsequent bishops), and the pope was granted the right to confirm Napoleon's appointments.

By concluding this agreement directly with the pope rather than with the French episcopate, Napoleon emphasized the pope's spiritual supremacy over the French Church. Thus the concordat marked the beginning of the end of French *Gallicanism*. This term, from "Gaul," the ancient name for the regions of France, had come to refer to episcopal independence from Rome. The concordat also precipitated a corresponding resurgence of French *ultramontanism*. This term, meaning literally "beyond the mountains," was used in this context to refer to the subordination of the French bishops to the pope who was far "beyond the mountains" rather than right "in Gaul."

Bonaparte's State-supported Church was simply a tool by which he intended to pacify and control the masses while he carried out his military conquest of Europe (see map I, p. 12). Despite his opportunistic intentions, however, Napoleon indirectly contributed to the partial re-Christianization of those parts of Europe where revolutionary ideas had captured the popular imagination.

Indeed, many people were by now disillusioned with the Revolution, and Catholicism began to make something of a comeback. Yet, on the whole, the decline of Christianity had outstripped its revival. Among the thousands of dying soldiers whom Napoleon left in Moscow in 1812, only a handful requested a priest for the administration of the sacraments.

Napoleon's domination of the Catholic Church is well illustrated by an oath which he had printed in the official catechism used in Catholic schools throughout his empire. The oath demanded of all Catholics "love, respect, obedience, and loyalty toward Napoleon our Emperor, service in the army, and payment of the taxes necessary for the defense and maintenance of the fatherland and its throne."[2]

In 1809, Napoleon annexed the Papal States and confined Pope Pius VII in a lush prison on the Italian Riviera. After unsuccessfully trying to force new religious policies on the French bishops, Napoleon moved Pius VII to France and cajoled him into signing a document granting the emperor extensive privileges over the Church.

By now, however, the dictator's tactics had alienated many of his Catholic subjects. Some of them formed secret counterrevolutionary societies, such as the Knights of Faith, in which Catholic interests were linked not to the Revolution but to the cause of restoring the Old Regime.

AFTER NAPOLEON: LIBERALS VERSUS REACTIONARIES

In 1815 Napoleon was defeated by an alliance of European powers led by Austria, Britain, Prussia and Russia, and his empire came to an end (see map II, p. 13). At the Congress of Vienna the great powers met to restore the "legitimate order"—that is, to return the Old

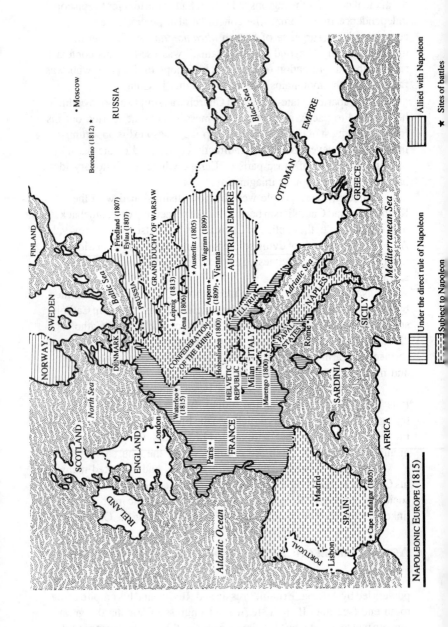

NAPOLEONIC EUROPE (1815)

Under the direct rule of Napoleon

Subject to Napoleon

Allied with Napoleon

★ Sites of battles

Moscow
RUSSIA
Borodino (1812) ★

Black Sea
OTTOMAN EMPIRE
GREECE
Mediterranean Sea

FINLAND
Baltic Sea
Friedland (1807) ★
Eylau (1807) ★
PRUSSIA
GRAND DUCHY OF WARSAW
Austerlitz (1805) ★
Wagram (1809) ★
AUSTRIAN EMPIRE
Aspern (1809) ★ · Vienna
Leipzig (1813) ★
Jena (1806) ★
CONFEDERATION OF THE RHINE
Hohenlinden (1800) ★
ILLYRIA
Adriatic Sea

NORWAY
SWEDEN
DENMARK
North Sea
Waterloo ★ (1815)
HELVETIC REPUBLIC
Milan ·
ITALY
Marengo (1800) ★
PAPAL STATES
· Rome
NAPLES
SICILY
SARDINIA

SCOTLAND
IRELAND
ENGLAND
· London
· Paris
FRANCE

Atlantic Ocean
· Madrid
SPAIN
PORTUGAL
· Lisbon
★ Cape Trafalgar (1805)
AFRICA

12

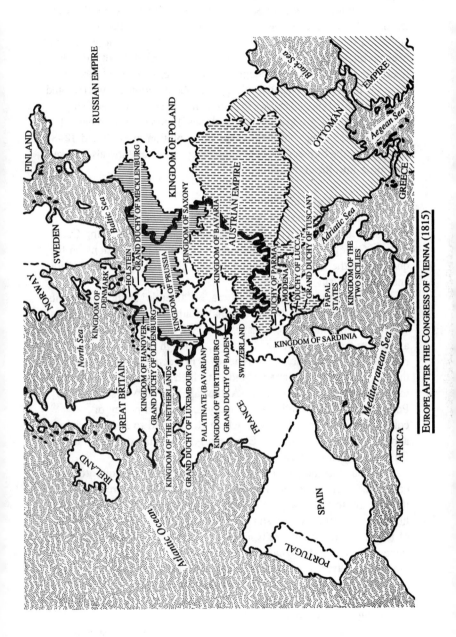

EUROPE AFTER THE CONGRESS OF VIENNA (1815)

Regime to the position it had occupied prior to the French Revolution.

Although the Congress of Vienna reestablished the old order temporarily, Europeans were still deeply divided over the principles advanced by the French Revolution. On one side were those who had been permanently converted to the revolutionary principles of individual liberty and equality for all people. On the other side stood those who regarded the Revolution and its ideals as an abomination and who wanted to restore the privileged classes to their former positions of leadership.

The latter group (the "reactionaries") momentarily regained power in 1815. But resurgent waves of revolution in 1830 and 1848 would bring the former group (now lumped together as "liberals") more and more into the forefront.

At the Vatican

This divisiveness between reactionaries and liberals was replicated in the inner councils of the Vatican. After 1815 the Curia and the College of Cardinals gradually separated into factions on the question of the Church's role in a Europe changed by the Revolution and by liberalism.

One faction, contemptuously called "liberals" by their opponents so as to associate them with freethinking atheists and revolutionaries, was led by Cardinal Ercole Consalvi (1757-1824), a layman not ordained a priest until his later years. Consalvi, although hardly a supporter of revolutionary ideals, nonetheless believed in practical compromises with the new European governments, most of which would eventually come to be guided by liberal principles. As the papal secretary of state under Pope Pius VII, Consalvi pragmatically promoted a policy of concordats—that is, a policy in which Rome tried to secure written agreements from the various European governments defining the Church's rights vis-a-vis the State.

The other hierarchical faction, nicknamed the "zealots," took a completely defensive and inflexible position on the Church's relationship to the new post-Revolution governments. For the zealots, liberalism was simply Protestantism in disguise. According to their way of looking at things, liberalism and Protestantism each promoted the same evil: freethinking independence and individual discernment of moral issues free of control by an absolute authority such as king or pope. The zealots ardently promoted the old alliance between the hierarchy and the aristocracy which had characterized life in prerevolutionary Europe.

We get a good picture of how these two differing schools of thought in the Church (liberals versus zealots, or reactionaries) exerted themselves by examining Church-State relations in various postrevolutionary countries.

In France

Both before and after 1815, France was the bellwether for the rest of Europe. Thus it provides a good example of how the Church gradually realigned itself with the old guard or, to put it another way, how the reactionary element within the hierarchy gained the upper hand over the liberal element.

In 1814, as Napoleon's empire began to dissolve, King Louis XVIII, younger brother of the guillotined Louis XVI, ascended the restored French throne. All of royalist, reactionary Europe dreamt of the reestablishment of the Old Regime. Louis himself favored the complete restoration of the old way in France. Yet he owed his crown to men who favored a monarchy controlled by an elected assembly, as in England, and thus he could not completely do away with Napoleon's Concordat of 1801 or otherwise restore the hierarchy to its old privileges. Louis nonetheless made Catholicism the official State religion once again. Gradually the "Ultra" party (so named because its members were "ultra-reactionaries") gained more influence in the government. One sign of the Old Regime's resurgence is this: Out of 90 bishops installed by the crown between 1815 and 1830, 70 were taken from France's oldest aristocratic families.

The French Church's struggle to regain its ancient prerogatives, however, largely alienated the young middle-class professionals in France. Most of them had been converted to revolutionary principles and had grown increasingly anticlerical and hostile to Catholicism. Among the peasants and the aristocracy on the other hand, Catholicism held its own, although sincere religious belief was widely lacking. By all accounts, religious ignorance and indifferentism gripped even those portions of French society which supported the reactionaries.

The French Church's alliance with the restored monarchy gained it a few institutional advantages—such as Church control of all elementary school education. But on the whole, this alliance irreparably damaged the French Church's reputation in the eyes of liberals. And since the liberals would eventually come to power in France, the French Church would gradually come to be regarded by many as a throwback to prerevolutionary times.

In Italy, Spain and Portugal

In Italy, too, reactionaries within the Church gained the upper hand. Jesuit and Redemptorist pamphleteers assaulted modern ideas and linked them to Protestantism. Pope Leo XII (1823-1829) persecuted Italian Jews and forbade the formation of the popular new lay Bible-study societies. The pope also attempted to repress the Carbonari, secret societies of men who advanced liberal political ideas and sought the political unification of Italy.

In Spain and Portugal, the clergy and the forces of political reaction likewise became reunited. And in all three countries the Church's alliance with old-guard reactionaries motivated a large portion of the educated middle classes to embrace liberalism and to distance themselves from the Church.

In Germany

Germany after 1815 was still a nation of mixed religious denominations and mixed sentiment toward the Revolution, with the exception of Catholic, old-guard Austria. Rome thus had to negotiate with the various German principalities individually in order to arrange concordats. Generally speaking, most of the German principalities adopted agreements similar to Napoleon's Concordat in 1801.

In those principalities which refused to enter into concordats with Rome and which attempted to dominate the Church completely, Catholics had to look south of the Alps for leadership. As a result, in many principalities ultramontanism began to exert a growing influence on the Church, as it had in France (see p. 19).

In Latin America

In the Americas a somewhat different picture emerged. Before 1815 the relationship between Church and State had been governed by the same principles which guided the colonies' mother countries of Spain and Portugal. Pope Pius VII thus hoped to continue in Latin America the policy of alliance between throne and altar which the Church was otherwise pursuing in Europe. In 1816 the Pope issued a reactionary encyclical, *Esti Longissimo*, in which he urged Latin American bishops to resist liberalism and support "legitimate" colonial governments.

As in Europe so in the New World, the Church's policy of associating itself with the Old Regime would eventually be recognized as a great blunder. Eight years after the Pope's encyclical, Simon Bolivar's revolution toppled one colonial government after another. In the eyes of the revolutionaries, the Catholic Church was simply a tool of repressive colonial governments. Thus, as in Europe, many members of the middle and educated classes dissociated themselves from Catholicism.

16

Rome eventually realized that it faced a new situation in Latin America and, as it had done in Europe, began to make concordats with the new republican governments. Bolivar and other revolutionary leaders, for their part, realized that the masses of the people were still tied to the clergy and the Catholic faith, and thus most of the new governments made Catholicism the official State religion. Yet this policy was a two-edged sword: As with the restored monarchies of Europe, Latin American republics likewise exerted a great deal of control over the State-sponsored Churches.

THE CHURCH IN A DEMOCRATIC REPUBLIC

The situation in the United States of America differed radically from that in Europe and the former European colonies of Latin America. In 1787 the framers of the Constitution of the United States had adopted an entirely new and unique principle by which to govern Church-State relationships. In its First Amendment the Constitution provided, "Congress shall make no law respecting an establishment of religion or prohibiting the free exercise thereof."

Thus in the United States, unlike in Europe or Latin America, the Catholic Church never possessed the opportunity to ally itself with the civil government. Even without the Constitution, however, Catholics in America could hardly have exerted any significant influence on government policy; in 1815 there were only 150,000 Catholics in a population of some 6,000,000. Further, several state legislatures in America passed laws which openly discriminated against Catholics. In some states, for example, Catholics were denied the right to hold public office.

Perhaps precisely because of its minority status and the hardships it suffered, the Catholic Church in the United States, unlike its European counterpart, had to accommodate itself to democratic principles. Gradually, American Catholics won the repeal of discriminatory legislation and proved themselves loyal to a republican form of government.

The first American Catholic bishop, John Carroll (1735-1815), observed, "America may give proof to the world that general and equal toleration, by providing a free climate for fair argument, is the most effectual method of bringing all denominations into a unity of faith."[3] Carroll's bold and tolerant vision was not shared by Rome, however, which frequently looked upon the Church in the world's truest democracy with great suspicion.

Rome's suspicions about American Catholics' democratic spirit seemed justified when the laity in some parishes insisted on governing their own congregations through a board of lay trustees which held legal title to Church property. Trustees in some parishes virtually declared their independence from all episcopal supervision. In Norfolk, Virginia, for example, lay trustees attempted to install their own popularly elected bishop. Bishop John England of Charleston (1786-1842), who believed that a new style of Church governance was appropriate to a democratic republic, attempted to settle the lay trusteeship controversy when he proposed to his brother bishops that the laity and the bishops govern their dioceses together. (There were 24 American dioceses by 1837.)

The other American bishops, however, rejected England's solution. In a series of episcopal meetings in Baltimore, the bishops forbade the foundation of new parishes unless legal title to Church property was first placed in the name of the bishop. This policy put an end to the trustee system and, to this day, each American bishop owns his diocesan property as a "corporation sole."

American Catholicism might exist in a land dedicated to democratic principles, but it governed its own house according to medieval ideals championed by Rome. It would take more than a century before the hierarchy would begin to allow laypeople some share of responsibility in the governance of their Church.

CHAPTER TWO

THE PAPACY RISES AGAIN

From Post-Revolution to Pius IX (1820-1846)

After the Reformation of the 16th century, the popes' influence in affairs of State was greatly reduced. In Protestant countries like England and in much of Germany and the Low Countries, the medieval notion of papal supremacy was dealt a death blow. But even in Catholic countries like Spain and Austria, and especially in France, the post-Reformation popes often found themselves at odds with strong Catholic monarchs and independent-minded bishops.

In 17th-century France, for example, King Louis XIV ruled the French Catholic Church; his handpicked bishops looked to him as their sovereign rather than to the pope. Such Gallicanism (see pp.10-11) gradually gave way after the French Revolution, for reasons we shall discuss in this chapter, to its opposite—ultramontanism, or the belief in the papacy's supremacy over national Churches. This change resulted in large part from the ongoing battle between liberals and reactionaries.

THE RISE AND FALL OF CATHOLIC LIBERALISM

In 1820 reactionary governments were in ascendance throughout Europe, and the Church had reached an accommodation with most of them through Cardinal Consalvi's concordat policy (see p. 14). France, for example, had come to be ruled by the reactionary King Charles X. When French liberals pressed for governmental reforms, Charles grew increasingly inflexible, censoring the press, dissolving the legislature and gerrymandering the electoral system in favor of the Ultras (see p. 15).

On July 28, 1830, Parisian liberals revolted, barricaded the city and drove Charles from power. Many Catholics and some priests participated in this "July Revolution." For several years Catholic thinkers had been questioning the Church's alliance with the forces of reaction. Such persons argued that the ideals of the Revolution of 1789—individual liberty, political freedoms for the middle and lower classes, freedom of the press and freedom of religion—were not only compatible with the gospel but mandated by the gospel.

This impulse toward Catholic liberalism got a strong shot in the arm from certain events taking place in Belgium.

Belgium: Center of Liberal Ferment

As was the case everywhere else in Europe, the Belgian Church in 1815 was strongly reactionary. The Belgian bishops, for example, forbade Catholics from taking an oath of allegiance to the new Belgian constitution because it guaranteed freedom of the press and of religion. By 1825, however, Catholic laymen, principally journalists and legislators, began to call for the separation of Church and State in traditionally Catholic countries, freedom of education (uncontrolled by the Church) and freedom of the press. By 1826 Catholic newspapers in Belgium were regularly promoting such ideas.

Non-Catholic liberals urged their Catholic confreres to form with them an alliance in which the latter would demand liberal political reforms from the Belgian government while the former would agree not to limit the Church's freedom in Belgian society (which was largely Catholic). By 1828 the two groups of liberals had agreed to this union and were jointly pursuing their goals.

The Vatican nuncio to Belgium referred to this situation as a "monstrous alliance."[1] Nevertheless, the bold move by Catholic liberals in Belgium to support the principles of the Revolution greatly encouraged Catholic intellectuals in France, particularly the man who would soon become Europe's leading spokesman for Catholic liberalism.

The Strange Case of Lammenais

Félicité de Lammenais (1782-1854) was born into a wealthy French Catholic family. In the first of four major conversions in his thinking, he renounced his faith after studying the writings of Jean-Jacques Rousseau. At age 22, however, Lammenais returned to the Catholic Church, became a college professor and in 1808 wrote *Reflections on the State of the Church in France*, a work in which he criticized reason as a means of arriving at truth. In another essay he condemned Napoleon's Church-State policies, and he was subsequently forced to flee to London.

After Napoleon's defeat, Lammenais returned to France, became a priest and wrote his *Essay on Indifference Toward Religion*, in which he criticized the French government for not promoting Catholicism as the only true religion. By this time Lammenais had come to be regarded as the darling of French reactionaries. Lammenais's writings were so brilliant that they gained mass appeal; Louis XVIII's minister of religion once said that Lammenais's writings "could bring the dead back to life."[2] By 1826 Lammenais had become the most famous advocate of reactionary Catholicism in all of Europe.

In 1828, however, Lammenais startled everyone, making yet another major conversion in his thinking by abandoning his previous views and embracing liberalism. In *On the Progress of the Revolution and the War Against the Church* (1829), Lammenais showed the influence on his thought of both American and Belgian thinkers by endorsing freedom of the press. Meanwhile, liberal Catholic journalists in France had begun to support the same principles as their Belgian counterparts. After the July Revolution, several of these Catholic liberals started a newspaper, *L'Avenir* ("The Future"), and persuaded Lammenais to write the inaugural editorial.

Under Lammenais's leadership, *L'Avenir* supported such liberal causes as the right of national minorities to self-determination, the universal franchise, separation of Church and State,* military disarmament and the political unification of Europe. *L'Avenir* also urged the Church to accept new developments in science and the arts and to promote social democracy. Lammenais himself wrote numerous articles for the newspaper in which he condemned sacred cows such as the prevalent system of Catholic seminary education.

A contemporary bishop described Lammenais as "the idol of the young priests...but a vexation to all old clergymen and pious believers."[3] Bishops everywhere ordered their priests to stop reading *L'Avenir*, and by October 1832 Rome's negative reaction to the newspaper had forced Lammenais and his associates to close down the paper.

Lammenais traveled to Rome to persuade Pope Gregory XVI (1831-1846) to allow *L'Avenir* to continue operating, but he was unprepared for the hostile reaction awaiting him. One cardinal publicly accused Lammenais of being an "arrogant spirit,"[4] and an official in the Curia charged Lammenais with "preaching revolution in the name

---

* In Catholic countries the Catholic Church wanted not separation but integration of Church and State.

of religion."[5] When the foreign ministers of the leading states of Europe joined the crusade against Lammenais, Gregory XVI could no longer refrain from condemning his ideas

In the encyclical *Mirari Vos* (1832), Pope Gregory characterized liberalism as "this false and absurd maxim, or better this madness, that everyone should have and practice freedom of conscience"[6] (a far cry from Vatican II's *Declaration on Religious Liberty*, which would appear in 1965!). The Pope spoke of freedom of the press as "this loathsome freedom which one cannot despise too strongly,"[7] and he condemned popular democracy and separation of Church and State. When reactionaries complained that the Pope had not condemned Lammenais by name, the Pope obliged by issuing another encyclical, *Singulari Nos* (1834), in which Lammenais's writings were explicitly condemned.

In the meantime, Lammenais had publicly condemned the Pope's rejection in June 1832 of the legitimacy of a Polish uprising against the Russian czar by writing *Words of a Believer*, in which he criticized both the papacy and all European monarchy. Then, when he received news of *Singulari Nos*, Lammenais renounced what he called "Christianity of the Pontificate" in favor of "Christianity of humanity,"[8] and left the Catholic Church for good—his fourth and final "conversion."

Lammenais was obviously a somewhat unstable character. But by condemning him out of hand without giving him an opportunity for a fair hearing, the Vatican put the world on notice that it had soundly rejected liberalism and given its wholehearted support to the reactionaries. The Lammenais affair had tremendous symbolic importance: It solidified in the minds of most educated people the belief that the Catholic Church stood for oppression against freedom, for obscurantism against free thinking and open inquiry, and for regression against progress.

CATHOLIC CONSCIOUSNESS BEFORE VATICAN I

In this period as in every epoch in the Church's history, there was much more going on than Vatican politics. For example, the period after the French Revolution witnessed a tremendous revitalization in Catholic circles of both spirituality and theology. One could assert, in fact, that because of the French Revolution many Catholics for the first time felt their faith sufficiently threatened to take the initiative to strengthen it. In some areas of Europe the Catholic Reformation* of

---

* See the preceding volume in this series, *The People of Anguish: The Story Behind the Reformation*.

the 16th century was implemented only now. As necessity is the mother of invention, so the French Revolution was in many ways the mother of 19th-century spiritual rejuvenation.

The Romantic Movement

At the turn of the 19th century, Christians throughout Europe were reacting to the Enlightenment's overemphasis on rationalism. This reaction manifested itself most notably in the movement named *Romanticism*. Whereas the Enlightenment had emphasized the individual and reason, Romanticism focused on communal values, feeling and tradition. Whereas the philosophes (the Enlightenment's critics of Catholicism and traditional authority) had criticized the Middle Ages as the source of authoritarian dogma, the Romantics saw the Middle Ages' emphasis on faith and mysticism as an attempt to create human wholeness.* And whereas the philosophes considered the Catholic Church merely an absolutist institution, the Romantics looked upon the Church as an organically evolving body which preserved the memory of the past and brought that memory into the present.

Romanticism cut across denominational lines, but it should come as no surprise that many Protestant Romantics—because of Romanticism's reverence for the Middle Ages and tradition—eventually converted to Catholicism. In 1800, a famous Lutheran prince, Count Friedrich Leopold Stolberg (1750-1819), caused quite a stir when he and several of his pietist associates became Catholics. Stolberg wrote a famous treatise, *History of the Religion of Jesus Christ*, which reawakened Europe's interest in and reverence for the medieval past.

Another German Romantic, Friedrich Schlegel (1772-1829), became a staunch defender of the medieval worldview in opposition to the Napoleonic concept of the rational State. The greatest exponent of Romanticism was François Chateaubriand (1768-1848). In *The Genius of Christianity*, he convinced many Europeans that Christianity, far from being the bane of civilization, had in fact preserved civilization from collapse.

The Romantics' emphasis on the past and on communal values, in opposition to the Enlightenment's emphasis on the individual, inspired Catholics throughout Europe to look toward the papacy as the unifying force of a Church which unites all peoples into a spiritual community. Hence, Romanticism came to be a principal impulse behind the development of ultramontanism which, in the latter part of the

---

* See *The People of Faith: The Story Behind the Church of the Middle Ages* for a fuller discussion of this theme.

century, culminated in the first Vatican Council's definition of papal infallibility (of which we shall say more later).

The Laity's Influence

The emphasis which the French Revolution placed on equality and fraternity had one positive effect on the Church's spiritual life: It recalled many laypeople into the service of the Church. Since the Middle Ages the laity were thought to occupy the bottom rung of a pyramid, the apex of which was reserved for the clergy. Although clericalism and hierarchical elitism certainly did not disappear during the post-Revolutionary era, a substantial minority of the laity nonetheless began to consider themselves as co-apostles with the clergy.

The laity's rediscovered enthusiasm for apostolic activity came to be summarized under the general heading of "Catholic Action." Catholic Action primarily expressed itself in societies known as "congregations," or groups of laypeople organized in local communities for the purpose of performing a particular aspect of apostolic service—such as hospital and prison visitations, or catechetical instruction for the young. Some priests resented these intrusions into what had previously been thought of as exclusively priestly ministries, and the laity at times clashed openly with clerical authorities over the question of lay participation in the Church.

Perhaps the most influential lay ministry in the early 19th century was that of writing. We have already seen the role that Catholic journalism played in Belgium and France (see pp. 20-22). In addition to journalists, other Catholic writers helped to define the shape of post-Revolution Catholicism. Count Louis Bonald (1754-1840), for example, was a staunch advocate of royalist values and a critic of popular democracy. His political theories helped popularize the Church's reaction to the Revolution. Bonald's colleague, Joseph de Maistre (1753-1821), became a leading theorist for ultramontanism; in 1819 he wrote *On the Pope*, a book which did much to promote the theory of papal infallibility. And, finally, there were poets like Alphonse Lamartine (1790-1869) and novelists like Victor Hugo (1802-1885), who popularized the beauty of the Church's tradition and its positive influence on human society.

Ultramontanism

Many Catholics had already been predisposed toward the reactionary tendencies of the hierarchy in the post-Revolution era. The upheaval of 1830 (see map III, p. 25) and the spread of Lammenais's liberalism further turned conservative Catholics away from liberal

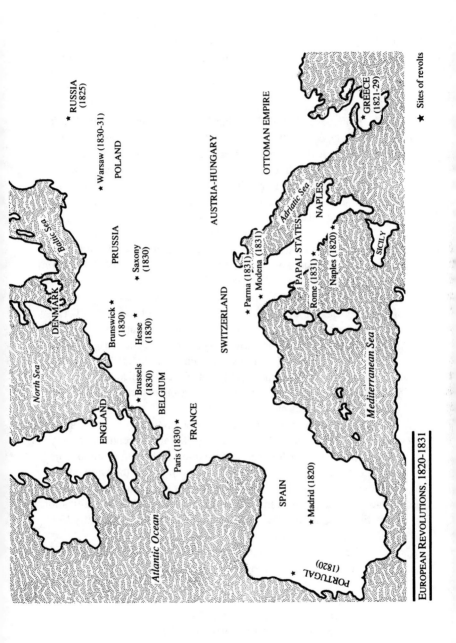

EUROPEAN REVOLUTIONS, 1820-1831

★ Sites of revolts

25

93-272

developments in their own countries and toward the papacy as the bastion of absolute authority. Hence, from 1830 on, ultramontanism steadily gained influence in the Catholic world; once again the papacy came to be regarded as a supranational institution uniting Catholics throughout the world.

Although the spirit of ultramontanism was growing everywhere, it developed differently in different countries.

In France, where Gallicanism had once made the French Church virtually independent from Rome, ultramontane ideals were now predominant. A contemporary historian, René Montalembert (1810-1870), wrote, "I would wager that among the 80 French bishops there are not three supporters of the Four Articles."[9] (The Four Articles were guarantees against papal interference in the French Church which had been wrested from the papacy by Louis XIV in the 17th century.)

Several factors accounted for the growth of French ultramontanism: (1) After 1830 there was no longer a strong monarchy in France, and thus the focal point of absolute authority shifted from the king to the papacy. (2) Priests who were vilified by the virulently anticlerical "July Revolutionaries" (see p. 20), especially in urban areas, naturally turned to the papacy as a source of unifying support. (3) Writers like Montalembert, who started the newspaper *L'Univers Religieux* after *L'Avenir* shut down, successfully promoted ultramontane ideas among educated Catholics. (4) The lower clergy, after centuries of submission to sometimes tyrannical bishops, welcomed the opportunity to appeal directly to Rome, a phenomenon which was encouraged by papal nuncios to France.

In German-speaking lands ultramontanism grew more slowly than in France. The ancient electoral city of Mainz in central Germany became a focal point for the dissemination of French ultramontane thought. German theorists wrote treatises in which they argued that Germany's traditional divisiveness no longer served any useful purpose; ultramontanism, they said, was a useful tool for German unification. As in France, Catholic newspapers played a key role, particularly *Der Katholik*, founded in 1824.

Austria resisted the ultramontane trend until late in the pontificate of Gregory XVI. As late as 1842, for example, three out of four Austrian bishops were still opposed to permitting Austrian seminarians to study in Rome. Austria had developed its own version of Gallicanism, known as *Josephinism* for Emperor Joseph II (1765-1790).

Josephinism was an attempt to subordinate the Austrian Church to the State by eliminating Rome's jurisdiction over Austrian ecclesiastical affairs. In its heyday in the late 18th century, Josephinism had resulted in an edict of toleration for non-Catholics (the most liberal edict of its kind in Europe), dissolution of certain religious orders, state ownership of some Church property, government censorship of papal publications, and state control of seminaries and other religious schools.

This most independent of all Catholic nations, however, gradually joined the ultramontane movement. In 1833, for example, the Austrian government agreed to prohibit the use of school texts which for years had been on the papal Index. Perhaps the most important factor in changing Austria's policy toward Church-State relations was the French example. Austrian foreign minister Klemens von Metternich, the leading spokesman for European reactionaries, was alarmed by the growing French influence in the Curia; so he began to urge the emperor to move Austria in the same direction taken by France.

National Churches Give Way to Centralized Catholicism

When Austria eventually relaxed its policy of Josephinism, it meant the final blow to the independence of national Churches. From the time of Pope Pius IX (whom we discuss in the next chapter), national Catholicism steadily declined and was replaced by a more homogeneous and centralized universal Catholicism.

The net effect of this development was a resurgence of papal supremacy. After several centuries of decline in papal influence on nearly autonomous national Catholic Churches, Rome's supremacy over these national Churches was about to reach a level never before achieved. The papal infallibility and strict Vatican control over national Churches which Catholics today take largely for granted are products of the age of Pius IX (1846-1878).

So complete is the popes' control of the Church from the mid-19th century onward that it becomes necessary to organize our treatment of Church history from the age of Pius IX until the era of Vatican II according to the various popes' reigns. In a very real sense, the popes virtually *became* the Church, so much so that in the pages ahead we must structure much of the discussion in terms of papal personalities, politics and policies.

CHAPTER THREE

THE AGE OF PIUS IX

From Pius's Election to Vatican I (1846-1869)

Giovanni Maria Mastia-Ferretti, elected by the Conclave of Cardinals on June 16, 1846, as Pope Pius IX, served as pope longer than any other man in history (1846-1878). Because of his long pontificate and because of his uniquely reactionary attitude to the problems faced by the Church in an age of liberalism, Pius IX—if only negatively—ranks as one of the most influential popes of all time. He is counted, along with Leo the Great (440-461), Gregory the Great (590-604) and Innocent III (1198-1216), as one of the four popes who definitely shaped an entire era of Catholic history.

THE REIGN OF 'PIO NONO'

Catholic liberals watched hopefully for a sign of Pius's attitude toward the liberal political and social movements stirring European society. At first it appeared that Pius would turn the Church away from the reactionary policies of his predecessors. Within a month of his election he declared a general amnesty for political radicals in the Papal States. He also held audiences with liberals where he made laudatory remarks about the movement for Italian political unification.

Such pro-liberal inclinations raised the hopes of Catholics and non-Catholics alike. Fredrick Ozanam, a leading Catholic progressive in France, summarized the new euphoria when he called Pius "a messenger of God sent to complete the great work of the 19th century, the alliance between religion and liberty."[1] Ozanam's optimistic remark, however, turned out to be nothing more than a naive expression of hope for a new papal attitude which was never to materialize.

On November 8, 1846, Pius began to reveal his true colors by issuing the encyclical *Qui Pluribus* in which he made the standard papal denunciation of liberal ideas. The honeymoon between Pius and the liberals ended for good when—in response to calls to the contrary—the Pope announced that he would neither make reforms of the curial bureaucracy nor allow laymen to participate in the government of the Papal States.

As an Italian bishop Pius had been strongly attracted to the *Risorgimento* (the movement for the political unification of Italy). But as pope he increasingly came to feel threatened by the prospect of a strong and unified secular state in Italy. He thus modeled his behavior on medieval popes who jealously guarded their papal fiefdoms. Eventually the world came to realize that *Pio Nono*, the Latin for "Pius IX," was an appropriate name: He said "No! No!" to virtually every attempt to reconcile the Church with modernity.

A Third Wave of Revolution

A new wave of revolution swept through Europe in 1848 (see map IV, p. 25) and snuffed out once and for all any liberal tendencies Pius may have harbored. As in the revolutions of 1789 and 1830, the new revolutionary fervor broke out in France. In February 1848 radicals seized Paris and forced King Louis-Philippe to abdicate his throne. In March archconservative Vienna itself felt the sting of rebellion, and the architect of post-Napoleonic, reactionary Europe, Foreign Minister Metternich, took the path of exile. In Germany the call for national unity inspired the convening of a national assembly in Frankfurt, where liberals hoped to construct a constitutional republic that would put an end to the factionalism and tyranny of rule by princes.

Yet almost as soon as these revolutions had begun, they were extinguished. Unlike the earlier uprisings, this time the revolutionaries lacked mass support. The peasantry and the aristocrats were weary of revolution and fearful of the new socialist ideology (discussed in Chapter Five) that seemed to have captivated many European intellectuals. In cities the Industrial Revolution had spawned a large population of oppressed workers, but this new "proletariat" was as yet unaware of its power to influence the political system. In France, as a symbol of the restoration of the status quo everywhere, Napoleon Bonaparte's nephew, Louis-Napoleon, was elected president of the "Second Republic," and the revolutionary uproar quickly came to an end.

Pius IX was horrified to learn that many priests and several

REVOLUTIONS OF 1848

★ Sites of revolts

bishops had encouraged a national uprising against Austrian rule in the Piedmont region of Italy. Thus on April 29, 1848, the Pope issued an encyclical which disavowed papal support for the revolutionaries. In the eyes of progressive Italians, the "liberal" pope had now become the "antinational" pope.

When a popular revolutionary leader, Count Pellegrino Rossi, was assassinated, Italian radicals took out their frustration on the Pope, holding him hostage in his palace. On November 24, 1848, Pius assumed a disguise and escaped south to the kingdom of Naples, ruled by a reactionary king who gave the Pope refuge for 17 months. With Pius safely away from Rome, the papal secretary of state Cardinal Giacomo Antonelli (1806-1876) fulminated over the evils of liberalism and took control of affairs in Rome. He exhorted the old-guard powers of Europe to intervene in the Italian revolt.

Antonelli's policy and the Pope's flight turned Italian liberals irrevocably against Pius. When a revolutionary assembly in Rome convened to form a new republican government, it voted to strip the Pope of all temporal power in the Papal States. Antonelli's plea for help was answered by the armies of Austria, Spain, Naples and France, and the short-lived Roman Republic of 1849 was quickly eradicated.

Pius IX returned to Rome in September 1849, thoroughly convinced that liberalism was completely opposed to the welfare of the Catholic Church. In this suspicious and defensive state of mind, he proceeded during the rest of his papacy to segregate the Church as much as possible from the modern world.

The Pope's Temperament

By temperament Pope Pius IX was affable and cordial. Yet he was emotionally unstable, often flying into fits of rage that terrorized his subordinates. In addition to this limitation, he was neither intelligent nor well educated enough to cope with a quickly changing world. Pius looked upon complex issues as if they were either black or white, with no shades of gray. Further, he relied too heavily on curial politicians (most of them conservative Italians) for counsel. His ill-advised decisions often had drastic consequences for the universal Church in an age light-years away from the medieval world dominating Pius's consciousness.

A deeply spiritual and unquestionably moral man, Pius was nonetheless prone to an almost superstitious belief in divine intervention in human affairs. Frequently during the midst of crises, Pius would promise his advisers that God would deliver the Church from whatever disaster was threatening at the moment. As another indication of his irrational approach to papal politics, Pius insisted throughout his pontificate on the absolute freedom of the Church from secular control, while paradoxically urging the Catholic states of Europe to guarantee Catholicism's status as the supreme, State-sponsored religion.

Pius appointed a large number of non-Italians to the College of Cardinals, but then virtually ignored the college as a body altogether, preferring to rely on his friends who, in the words of one observer, "favored everything that was old, from dress to opinions, from labels to theology."[2] The Pope's cabinet of advisers looked on everything that had happened in the world since the Reformation—all the advancements in science, philosophy and theology—as works of the devil.

Pius himself frequently remarked that liberalism, with its emphasis on individual liberties, was a weapon being used by Satan to destroy the Church. The Pope's outlook on life was dominated by an apocalyptic vision in which the forces of good (led by him) warred with the forces of evil. As he saw it, his duty was to defend the Church against the satanic attacks of free press, free speech, constitutional governments, religious tolerance and separation of Church and State.

For most old-guard, reactionary Catholics (who by now constituted the majority among European Catholics), Pius was a great hero who would roll back the tide of history. To Catholic liberals, Pius was at first a disappointment and then, increasingly, an embarrassment. As for non-Catholics, Pius proved their point that the Catholic Church was simply a medieval institution, inimical to progress and of no relevance to the modern world.

The most famous achievement of Pius's pontificate was the decree of the First Vatican Council in 1870 declaring the pope to be infallible in matters of faith and morals. In order to gain some preliminary perspective on that momentous decision and on the achievement of Vatican I generally, let's take a brief "tour" through the Catholic world in the age of Pius IX.

THE CATHOLIC SCENE ON THE EVE OF VATICAN I

France
Pius IX encouraged the ultramontanist movement which was growing in popularity everywhere in Europe, and especially in France. Pius saw ultramontanism not only as the means to centralize ecclesiastical authority in the hands of the pope but also as the most efficient means to coordinate a united assault on liberalism. The Pope's ultramontanist zeal, however, renewed old suspicions in France of papal pretensions in affairs of State.

Pius's nuncio to France, for example, brazenly proclaimed the virtues of Church control of education and otherwise witlessly alienated officials in Louis-Napoleon's government. As a result the new French ruler (now known as "Emperor" Napoleon III) returned to the policies of his predecessors by appointing French bishops himself, carefully selecting men who opposed curial domination. The government also discouraged the growth of religious congregations, encouraged public education at the expense of Catholic schools and took a blase approach to the increasing number of anticlerical attacks appearing in the French press.

After 1867, however, as Napoleon III's administration became threatened by political opposition, the emperor increasingly looked upon the Church as a conservative foil against liberal agitation. Thus the status of the French Church temporarily improved. Priestly vocations rose from about 47,000 in 1853 to about 56,000 in 1869. Nearly 2,500 of these priests were employees of the government, serving in such State offices as the Ministry of Religion or the Ministry of Education. This revived marriage between Church and State continued to alienate liberals and to further concretize their belief that the French Church was little more than the arm of the conservative government.

During this period the French clergy, especially priests seeking freedom from despotic bishops, became more and more ardently ultramontanist. In a nation where the press, the intelligentsia and most of the urban middle class were vehemently anticlerical, Rome seemed like the only haven of refuge to the unpopular French clergy.

Although the State-appointed bishops did little to promote spiritual vitality, religious orders did encourage a rebirth of popular piety and apostolic zeal. From 1851 to 1861 the number of religious sisters rose from about 35,000 to about 90,000—a huge increase—and the number of male religious likewise grew enormously—from about 3,000 to over 17,000. Many of these dedicated women and men staffed Catholic schools—a mixed blessing since they allowed Catholicism access to young minds but, in the process, embittered many progressives who opposed State-supported Catholic education.

Popular piety in France on the eve of Vatican I was dominated by a return to medieval devotions. Pilgrimages once again flourished; great throngs of French Catholics visited the sites of Marian apparitions, such as La Salette (1846) and Lourdes (1858). Devotions to the Sacred Heart of Jesus and the Immaculate Heart of Mary were enormously popular. A religious congregation known as the Assumptionists, approved by Pius IX in 1864, did much to win back the lower classes to Catholicism.

Yet religious indifferentism predominated in the cities, especially among artisans, industrial workers and intellectuals. The French Church scarcely noticed the rising industrial population, largely because the Church's mostly rural and small-town clergy felt itself inadequate to minister to the new laboring poor. French industrial workers, by and large having no priests to minister to them, drifted toward radical communist and socialist ideologies and away from Christianity.

The clergy likewise failed to acknowledge the great need for lay participation in Church leadership and especially in evangelization efforts. Most of the clergy nursed bruised feelings over the press's anticlerical attacks, and many priests treated their parishioners like children, warning them against liberal threats such as a free press and public education.

On the eve of Vatican I, then, the French Church, with a few notable exceptions, was comprised largely of people who feared the future and clung to the past. To such people Pius IX's denunciation of modern times was a welcome relief, and his proposed decree on papal infallibility was seen as a nostalgic reawakening of the Church's medieval grandeur.

Germany and Austria

In Germany Catholics had seen the revolutions of 1848 (see pp. 30-32) not as threats to order but as an opportunity to regain a measure of freedom for local Churches frequently oppressed by Protestant princes. In Prussia, for example, Catholic leaders were successful in promoting passage of a new constitution in which the State relinquished the right to appoint bishops and other clerical offices and lessened its control over religious orders.

Encouraged by Prussia's example, Archbishop Johannes von Geissel of Cologne spearheaded a drive to unite the various regional Churches throughout Germany into a single German Catholic Church. Pius IX, however, squelched the idea. Pius and the Curia felt threatened by the concept of a centralized German Church; for too long German theologians and bishops, in Rome's eyes, had demonstrated a suspicious proclivity for independence.

Eventually the Prussian government reversed itself and began to pursue anti-Catholic measures, leading to the formation of a minority "Catholic Faction" in the Prussian assembly. But by 1867 this party had lost all influence and the Prussian government once again dominated the Church.

In Austria a national bishops' conference in 1849 persuaded

Emperor Franz-Joseph I (1848-1916) to terminate many of the Josephinist policies of his predecessors (see pp. 26-27). And in 1855 the papal Curia successfully negotiated a concordat with the Austrian government in which the old State-run Church was virtually abolished. The concordat gave the emperor the right to nominate (though not to appoint) bishops and guaranteed that Catholic doctrine would be taught in Austrian schools. The State also agreed to enforce the Church's ban on liberal and heretical books. The concordat was essentially a marriage between conservatives and, as in France, alienated a large portion of the educated classes.

England
Since the Reformation, Catholics in England had suffered from many legal infirmities imposed on them by the Protestant Parliament. In 1829, however, England, the most liberal and open-minded of European states, removed virtually all anti-Catholic legislation from its books, and Catholics once again entered into the mainstream of English society.

Pius IX named Nicholas Wiseman (1802-1865) first archbishop of Westminster in a newly restored Catholic hierarchy. Wiseman imprudently made grandiose proclamations about restoring "authentic Church authority" in England, agitating the waters of antipapal sentiment. As a result, Parliament passed a law in 1851 prohibiting anyone from acting as bishop in any other see than one recognized by the Anglican Church. When Wiseman toned down his rhetoric and pledged his loyalty to the crown, the law died on the books.

The greatest challenge for the English Catholic Church during this period became how to minister to the large numbers of Irish Catholics who had immigrated to England following a disastrous famine in 1847. This Irish immigration greatly increased the number of Catholics living near industrial Liverpool (northwest England). Wiseman and his provost, Henry Manning (1808-1892), devoted a great deal of their attention to the training of priests to serve in such newly Catholic industrial areas.

Manning, a convert from Anglicanism and a staunch ultramontanist who succeeded Wiseman as archbishop of Westminster in 1865, had very complex views. Firmly dedicated to raising the industrial workers' standard of living, he may be thought of as one of the first modern champions of the social gospel. At the same time, however, he was fervently dedicated to isolating Catholicism from the modern world; for example, he forbade Catholics to study at Cambridge or Oxford so that they would not be exposed to Protestant liberalism.

Ironically, Manning had himself been a leader of the "Oxford Movement" which sought to return the Anglican Church to more traditional practices. The leaders of this movement wrote *Tracts for the Times*, pamphlets intended to win intellectuals back to Anglicanism and away from "popery and dissent."

The first such tract was written by a young Anglican vicar named John Henry Newman (1801-1890). Newman's thesis in most of his 24 tracts was that Anglicanism was the only religion which successfully mediated between the excesses of "Romanism," on the one hand, and liberal Protestantism, on the other. Eventually, however, as Newman continued to prepare tracts, he wrote himself out of the Anglican Church and into the Roman Catholic Church.

When the newly ordained and controversial Newman published a negative review of a book Manning had written, the two Catholic converts became foes. Whereas Manning supported ultramontanism and an inflexible theology which gave absolute answers to every question, Newman favored collegiality among national Catholic Churches and the presentation of doctrine so as to fit the changing needs of the times.

Newman was viewed with great suspicion in Rome, but his writings nonetheless made him the most famous and influential Catholic thinker of his day. In such works as his *Apologia Pro Vita Sua* and *Grammar of Assent*, Newman proved that one could be both a Catholic and an intelligent spokesperson for progress and reason at the same time.

Because of his success as a Catholic apologist, Rome feared silencing Newman, even though one of Pius IX's spies in England told the Pope that Newman was "the most dangerous man in England."[3] In 1879, Newman's devotion to the pursuit of truth in the face of obscurantist pressure from Rome was finally rewarded when Pope Leo XIII made him a cardinal.

The United States

The Irish immigrations greatly affected the American Church as well. Between 1840 and 1860, the Catholic population in the United States grew from two-thirds of a million to three million, and by 1870 to 4.5 million—about 11 percent of the total population. The influx of immigrant Catholics (from 13 other countries besides Ireland) gave rise to the "Nativist Movement," led by persons opposed to the growth of American Catholicism.

In the 1850's Nativists organized themselves into the Know-Nothing Party, a secret society opposed to the influx of Catholic immigrants. As it became increasingly powerful, the party's members could no longer claim to "know nothing" about its existence, and thus it took on a more public demeanor. In 1856 the party's national platform endorsed the suppression of Catholics and stirred up anticlerical violence and looting of churches in areas of small Catholic population. The Know-Nothings' most significant achievement was their successful campaign to prohibit Pius IX's proposed apostolic delegate to Washington from taking up residence in the United States.

With the start of the Civil War, the Know-Nothings passed into oblivion, but a new challenge confronted the American Church—namely, the proper response Catholicism should make to the slavery issue. In a nation where accusations of "popery" always lingered just below the surface of politicians' rhetoric, the Catholic bishops decided not to take a united stand on slavery, leaving the Catholic response to the conscience of the individual (the one area of life where such freedom of conscience was allowed).

Although momentary accusations of papal interference in the political process were prevented, the Church nonetheless lost a historic opportunity to gain moral credibility. After the war, most emancipated blacks formed their own black Churches under the leadership of Protestant pastors. The black population in the United States was thus almost totally lost to the Catholic Church.

After the Civil War the Catholic bishops steered the American Church into something of a "denominational ghetto." Fearful of allowing Catholics to come too close to Protestantism, religious indifferentism or liberalism, the Catholic bishops undertook a massive campaign to establish parochial schools in every diocese. The slogan of the day became "school before church"—that is, it was believed that only Catholic education could keep Americans Catholic.

Thus began a century-long process by which American Catholics walled off their educational and cultural life from Protestant America. In the process—since there existed at this point little opportunity for widespread Catholic higher education—American Catholics, particularly in the large cities of the Northeast, found themselves educationally and culturally deprived in comparsion to their Protestant neighbors. Well into the 20th century, to be Catholic in America meant to be a member of a lower social and economic class.

Since few bishops and priests were American-born until after the Civil War, the Catholic Church in the United States often took on a missionary demeanor. And the prevailing mentality in Rome was often one of aristocratic European condescension to crude American tastes. The Curia in particular never understood the American temperament. The American Church was often regarded as a backwater of vulgarity which served little useful purpose other than to funnel money to Rome.

Spain and Spanish America

In the 1830's and 1840's, as revolutionary ideas finally took hold in Spain, anti-ecclesiastical sentiment came to the fore. Waves of anticlerical violence in this previously devout Catholic nation led to the murder of priests, the sacking of monasteries and State appropriation of Church property. In a land with more priests and religious per capita than any other country in the world, religious vocations for the first time began to fall.

When Queen Isabella II came of age and assumed control of the government in 1844, State-sponsored repression of the Church ended. Isabella was an archconservative who detested the progressive ideas circulating throughout the educated classes of Spanish society. The queen promptly reversed all of the anti-Church measures of the previous decade. In 1851 Church and State entered into a concordat which guaranteed the supremacy of the Catholic faith in Spain and allowed the Church a measure of autonomy it had never enjoyed under Isabella's predecessors.

The Church-State entente drove a wedge between the educated middle class and the hierarchy. Queen Isabella's repressive policies and scandalous personal life (she named her lover, an actor with no credentials, as minister of state) stirred liberals to rebellion. In 1868 the Queen was driven from the throne and a liberal constitutional monarchy was established.

Once again religious orders in Spain were abolished. The establishment of universal suffrage and a free press ended the Church's alliance with the government and broke the Church's hold on education. As Isabella fell, much of the Spanish Church's credibility and prestige fell with her.

So, to the horror of Pius IX, even Catholic Spain joined the ranks of liberal nations. The Pope became ever more reclusive and morbid, convinced that only a policy of absolute segregation from the modern world could save the Catholic Church from ruin.

Although the new republican governments in Spanish America had thrown off Spain's control, they kept the old Spanish custom of patronage—control of the Church through appointment of bishops and supervision of certain aspects of Church discipline. Although Rome had tolerated *royal* patronage, it vehemently resisted *republican* patronage. Consequently the relationship between the Church and the new governments in Latin America was frequently marked by conflict. Most of the new republics did not even maintain official diplomatic relations with Rome, although the Church did manage to execute conciliatory concordats with seven of the new governments.

The Guatemalan dictator Rafael Carrera (1839-1865) initiated a new era in Latin American Church-State relations. He restored many of the Church's privileges simply to keep the masses under control. Although opportunistic arrangements such as this gained the Church short-term improvements in its relationship with some of the new governments, the policy of State protectionism lost the Church much of its moral credibility in the long run.

Here was the beginning of a long line of marriages between the Latin American Church and dictatorial-military regimes which, until recent times, placed the Church squarely behind repressive tyrants and, thus, against the poor. In Chile, for example, Archbishop R. V. Valdivieso (1847-1878) maintained close relations with a dictatorial government which frankly acknowledged Catholicism's utility in maintaining order among the masses. Until recent times, then, life in most of Spanish America (as well as in Brazil, Portugal's former colony) was characterized by a marriage of utility between Church and State which often worked to the detriment of the poor.

Eventually the Latin American Church reevaluated its policy of cooperating with dictatorial regimes and, in recent times, has adopted a "preferential option" for the poor. But on the eve of Vatican I such an option was the farthest thing from any churchman's mind.

CHAPTER FOUR

THE VATICAN I CHURCH

The Spiritual and Theological Milieu: Saying 'No' to the World

Since there was so much diversity and variety from country to country, it is difficult to capsulize ordinary Catholic life on the eve of Vatican I. The best that we can do is to summarize major trends.

EVERYDAY CATHOLIC LIFE ON THE EVE OF VATICAN I

Priestly Spirituality

One of Pius's positive achievements (and one of his greatest personal concerns all during his pontificate) was an improvement in priestly spirituality. Pius saw the parish priest as the focal point of Catholic life and, of course, given the Pope's negative assessment of lay responsibility in the Church, his judgment was accurate.

The Pope implemented a program of seminary reform which, in his eyes, dramatically improved priestly training. This program based seminarian education on the method developed in the 17th century by the religious Society of Saint-Sulpice. The Society's educational philosophy was entirely Thomistic (that is, based on the theology of Thomas Aquinas) and its spirituality was French in flavor (that is, highly personalistic and emotional and not unaffected by Jansenist* zeal and scrupulosity. See *The People of Anguish*, Chapter 10).

---

* The Jansenists, declared heretical by Rome, nonetheless influenced an entire age of Catholic spirituality. By overemphasizing sinfulness and degradation, they fostered a mentality of suffering and negativity in Catholic devotions.

Because of this twofold thrust in seminarian education, priests in the era of Pius IX were increasingly cut off from intellectual currents that had superseded Thomism, and they generally adopted a spirituality that was other-worldly rather than this-worldly. As Pius IX reacted against the incursions of modern thought, so too the priests for whom he served as a role model tended to segregate themselves from the real world. The ideal parish priest became the solitary man of prayer, living a life of self-denial and mortification while serving on defensive alert against the inroads of modern culture.

Priests had few friends, either among themselves or least of all with the laity. Just as Pius IX was characterized by a contemporary catchphrase as "the prisoner of the Vatican," so too was the parish priest a prisoner of the sanctuary and the rectory. In an analogy drawn by the historian Hippolyte Taine (1828-1893), the attributes of the good priest were "loyal sentry duty in a guardhouse, obeying the watchword, and standing a lonely and monotonous guard."[1] Only rarely did this self-imposed priestly seclusion allow for contact with modern life.

Yet there were notable exceptions. In 1859 the Italian John Bosco (1815-1888) founded the Salesian Order, which undertook an active ministry to the new working-class poor and especially to young boys. Many bishops also called on their priests to escape the confines of the parish and take the gospel out into the world. One of the most notable of these was Felix Dupanloup, bishop of Orleans in France from 1849 to 1878.

Like Bosco in Italy, Dupanloup became a promoter of Catholic education for the lower classes. He also encouraged his priests to think of their vocations in more imaginative terms, urging them to take on social and educational apostolates. Ahead of his time, Dupanloup may be regarded as the forerunner of the activist priests of the 20th century.

Lay Spirituality

Generally speaking, the rule of thumb in the Catholic world during this era was "As the priest goes, so goes the Church." And since the great majority of priests had developed a defensive mentality about the position of Catholics in the modern world, many lay Catholics shared this attitude. One's Catholicism and one's work in the world were increasingly thought of as two separate realities which should never commingle. More and more Catholics thought in terms of "us versus them"—that is, in terms of a subtle and persistent battle between Catholic truth and worldly error. The few forays which Catholics made into the world were made solely for the purpose of winning others to the Catholic view. True dialogue with others was rare.

As one might expect in an era when pope and priests looked back to the medieval heyday of Catholic supremacy as the model for all that was good and noble, everyday Catholic spirituality on the eve of Vatican I turned back to the Middle Ages for guidance. Pius IX himself encouraged this renaissance in medieval spirituality by restoring indulgences to new life and by revivifying devotion to Mary. Although Marian spirituality had never lost its hold on Catholicism, the Church during the Reformation had been more concerned with debate over Christocentric issues, such as justification by faith.

Another spur to the rebirth of medieval spirituality in Pius IX's day was the impact of the Romantic movement on the ordinary believer. Romantic literature, music and art* stimulated a renewed popular interest in relics, pilgrimages, the saints and, above all, devotions to Mary. The Romantic flavor of spirituality made Catholic piety increasingly sentimental and emotional. Devotions to the Sacred Heart of Jesus and to the Immaculate Heart of Mary were enormously popular. Along with the good effect of this renewed interest in things medieval, there was also some neo-medieval excess, characterized by a sickly sentimentality which at times turned Jesus, Mary and the saints into little more than characters in a syrupy French love story.

As the Church itself turned away from the real world, it simultaneously denied real human attributes to its founder and his mother. And as papal and priestly exemplars became increasingly solitary in their piety, so too did everyday spirituality become almost exclusively individualistic. Frequent Holy Communion became the center of Catholic life, yet the Eucharist, as in the Middle Ages, was seen not as a communal celebration of the Lord's presence but as the means of accumulating grace and earning good standing in God's eyes.

The individualistic thrust to Eucharistic spirituality was especially noticeable in devotions to the Blessed Sacrament. In 1851 Pius IX promulgated the "perpetual adoration" devotion in which the faithful venerated the consecrated host around the clock. The focus of such devotions was the individual's spiritual enrichment through contact with Jesus in the sacrament of the altar—that is, an individualistic "Jesus-and-me" spirituality which ignored the liturgical and communal dimension of the Eucharist.

---

* In the field of literature, one thinks, for example, of the lyrical poetry of Goethe in Germany, of Lamartine in France, and of Lord Byron and Wordsworth in England; of the nature poems of the American William Cullen Bryant; of novelists such as Sir Walter Scott, George Sand and Victor Hugo; and in music, of Franz Schubert, Robert Schumann, Hector Berlioz and Frédéric Chopin; and, in art, of Goya, Constable, Turner and Delacroix.

This overly individualistic spirituality turned the eyes of the faithful almost exclusively to the suffering Jesus with whom one commiserated in the Eucharist and virtually ignored the image of the victorious risen Savior. Consequently, Catholic life was often burdened by a morbid fascination with suffering for its own sake. Little was said or thought of the "full life" (see John 10:10) which Jesus had promised.

The Immaculate Conception

Without doubt the most popular aspect of Catholic spirituality on the eve of Vatican I was the renewed devotion to Mary. One cannot understand this phenomenon without taking into account the number of Marian apparitions which stirred the Catholic world. In 1830 the Blessed Virgin was said to have appeared to Catherine Labouré to promote a devotion to the miraculous medal which the Virgin gave to Catherine; in 1846 Mary purportedly appeared at La Salette in southeastern France; and in 1858, at Lourdes. Every year witnessed the birth of at least one and often several new congregations dedicated to Mary.

The crowning achievement of Marian spirituality was Pius IX's dogmatic definition in 1854 of the Immaculate Conception. In actuality Pius did not initiate the movement toward the doctrinal definition, though he was already personally convinced of the truth of the dogma. Rather, he responded to numerous petitions for a definition coming to him from every sector of the Church. In 1840, for example, 51 French bishops had petitioned Pope Gregory XVI to define the doctrine. And when Pius IX had polled the world's bishops on the issue in 1849, 90 percent urged the Pope to proceed with a doctrinal definition. In the bull *Ineffabilis Deus* (December 8, 1854) Pius thus declared, "From the first moment of her conception the Blessed Virgin Mary was, by the singular grace and privilege of Almighty God, and in view of the merits of Jesus Christ, Savior of mankind, kept free from all stain of original sin."

Although the faith of the Church unquestionably supported Pius's dogmatic definition, there was more to the Pope's action than simply the promotion of Marian devotion. Pius looked upon the Immaculate Conception as a testing ground for his plans to promote the doctrine of papal infallibility. In *Ineffabilis Deus* a pope, for the first time in history, defined a dogma of the faith solely on his own authority and not in cooperation with his brother bishops convened in council.

Further, Pius decreed that the Immaculate Conception was revealed by God and therefore was binding on all Catholics as an infallible truth of Catholic faith Since the concept of the Immaculate

Conception was so universally popular in Catholic circles, Pius's bull raised scarcely a whimper of protest. Thus, after 1854, Pius and his ultramontane supporters became irrevocably dedicated to an explicit promulgation of papal infallibility.

CATHOLIC THEOLOGY ON THE EVE OF VATICAN I

As might be expected, Catholic theology during the era of Pius IX was generally stagnant and unoriginal. This was the case virtually everywhere but in Germany where a few theologians braved the hazard of departing from Tridentine theology and Thomism.

Johann Dollinger

The leading name in German theology was Johann Dollinger (1799-1890). Ordained a priest in 1822, Dollinger taught canon law and Church history at the Universities of Munich and Tubingen. The faculty at these two universities initiated a German theological renaissance in which Catholic theologians departed from the traditional Scholastic concerns with metaphysics and speculative analysis in favor of a historical approach to the definition of doctrine.

This historical approach owed much to the work of the Protestant theologian Ferdinand Bauer (1792-1860), frequently called the father of modern Church history. Bauer applied his historical-critical method to the Bible and drew conclusions about New Testament authorship which are still the basis of a good deal of 20th-century biblical scholarship. At the time, however, Bauer's conclusions startled many Protestants and were simply condemned out of hand by most Catholic theologians. Dollinger, on the other hand, realized the value of Bauer's work and used Bauer's historical method in his own writings.

Dollinger and several other German Catholic theologians hoped to preserve Catholic theology from collapse in the face of the impressive development of Protestant theology. This development began in 1821 when Fredrich Schleiermacher (1768-1834) published *The Christian Faith*, a work which gave birth to modern Protestant liberal theology. In America Horace Bushnell (1802-1876), in England Fredrick Maurice (1805-1872), and in Denmark Søren Kierkegaard (1813-1855) all continued the Protestant theological revival, producing works of great originality. (We will say more about Protestant theology in Chapter Nine.)

In contrast to the Protestant theological revival, Catholic bishops in Germany and elsewhere zealously prevented any Catholic theology other than Thomism from penetrating the walls of Catholic universities and seminaries. One historian has characterized the theological education received in Catholic seminaries as "a coldly didactic method of interpreting eternal truths [which] replaced original and subjective thought," an atmosphere in which "universal openness to all currents gave way to defense and polemicism."[2]

The Syllabus of Errors

When Dollinger and other creative theologians tried to penetrate this atmosphere, they got into trouble with Rome. Pius IX at first simply admonished the German bishops to exert more control over their theologians, but in the end he listed some of Dollinger's teachings on the infamous *Syllabus of Errors* (1864).

The *Syllabus* was an appendage to the encyclical *Quanta Cura* (December 8, 1864), a general assault on liberalism. The *Syllabus* listed 80 propositions condemned by Pius as erroneous. It covered everything from pantheism to freemasonry, which most people already knew to be in conflict with Catholic belief, as well as many other propositions which were much less clearly a threat to the gospel.

Among the propositions which Pius condemned *as erroneous* in the *Syllabus* were the following:

> The whole governance of public schools wherein the youth of any Christian State is educated...may and should be given to the civil power (#45);

> The Church should be separated from the State, and the State from the Church (#55);

> In this our age it is no longer expedient that the Catholic religion should be treated as the only religion of the State... (#77);

> ...The Roman pontiff can and ought to recognize and harmonize himself with progress, with liberalism, and with modern civilization.(#80)[3]

Along with these "errors," the *Syllabus* also condemned freedom of the press and other tenets of modern civilization simply taken for granted by Catholics today as developments compatible with the gospel. As the *Syllabus* circulated throughout the secular press, it was lampooned as a throwback to the Dark Ages. Theologians such as Dollinger were embarrassed by the document, while progressive bishops like Dupanloup (see p. 42) tried to divert attention from it by downplaying its significance.

THE FIRST VATICAN COUNCIL

The First Vatican Council, convened by Pius IX on December 8, 1869, did not proclaim new Catholic doctrine. The Council simply summarized and concretized the spiritual and theological trends already discussed above. In that sense the Council represented Pius IX's ultimate statement on the modern world. The Pope saw the Council as the supreme opportunity to define fundamental Catholic doctrine in response to liberal principles. As it turned out, however, the Council actually defined little else than papal infallibility.

Some 700 bishops attended the opening of the Council. Aside from the 49 American bishops who came, the Council was almost entirely a European event; even most missionary bishops who attended the Council were Europeans. In fact, 35 percent of the delegates at Vatican I were Italian, and over 50 percent were either Italian or French. Thus German, American, Canadian, Latin American and Asian delegates all taken together were in the minority. Further, Pius's 96 handpicked consultants, whom he placed in charge of drafting conciliar decrees, were hard-line ultramontanists and conservatives.

From the outset it was impossible to consider Vatican I a council in which the voices of Catholics the world over would be heard. In that sense Vatican I was but one more triumph for the medieval conception of the Church, since the councils convened in the Middle Ages were seldom "catholic," or universal, in their representation.

Pius appointed four commissions to debate and define the key issues to be considered by the Council. On April 24, 1870, the Council approved the work of one of the commissions by issuing the constitution *Dei Filius*, a predictable attack on modern liberalism as well as a clear and up-to-date description of Catholic doctrine.

The Decree on Papal Infallibility

The debate over infallibility was the work of another commission from which any delegate hesitant about infallibility was excluded—thanks to political maneuvering by Archbishop Manning of England. This tactic was unnecessary since a clear majority of the bishops was known to favor infallibility in principle. The only real issue was how the decree would be worded.

Some conservatives, who had urged the Pope to have the Council declare the entire *Syllabus of Errors* binding on Catholics as a matter of dogma, wanted a decree declaring the pope infallible not only in matters of faith but even in matters of scientific or historical fact. The majority, however, was clearly opposed to such a definition. The Dominican Cardinal Guidi suggested a definition of infallibility which bound the pope to Catholic tradition. Pius rejected this out of hand, as when he screamed at Guidi, "Tradition! *I* am tradition!"

In this atmosphere of "fraternal charity and unhindered dialogue," the Council fathers proceeded to vote on the draft of the decree on infallibility, even though 136 delegates—one-fifth of those in attendance—circulated a last-minute petition urging Pius to drop his insistence on the decree. When this attempt failed, 60 bishops left Rome under cover of darkness so as not to be forced to oppose the decree publicly. The final vote was 522 for the decree and only two against (one of these being the bishop of Little Rock, Arkansas).

On July 18, 1870, in the constitution *Pastor Aeternus*, the Council decreed:

> ...That the Roman pontiff, when he speaks *ex cathedra*, that is, when in discharge of his office of pastor and doctor of all Christians, he defines, in virtue of his supreme apostolic authority, a doctrine of faith or morals to be held by the universal Church, is endowed by the divine assistance promised to him in blessed Peter, with that infallibility with which our divine redeemer willed that the Church should be furnished in defining doctrine of faith or morals; and therefore, that such definitions of the Roman pontiff are irreformable of themselves and not in virtue of the consent of the Church.[4]

The turgid, legalistic, contorted wording of the constitution perfectly symbolized both the Pope's state of mind and the state of mind of the majority of the Catholic world in 1870. In contrast to the brief, pithy words spoken by Jesus in the Gospels—the language of love as opposed to the Council's language of law—the decree on papal infallibility exuded fear, defensiveness, closed-mindedness and insecurity—all the qualities which post-Reformation, post-Revolution Catholicism had subconsciously imbibed. It was as if the Catholic Church, through Vatican I's constitution on papal infallibility, stood stiffly and rigidly before the world with arms folded, shouting, "No!" to all progress and change—hardly a posture consistent with the attitude of an all-accepting Savior who had said, "Come to me all you who are weary and I will give you rest."

On September 20, 1870, Pius ended the Council in the midst of the turmoil caused by nationalist soldiers invading Rome to establish the new Kingdom of Italy (see map V, p. 50). The infallibility decree was the Council's only significant achievement. The bishops of the world had adopted a doctrine which would serve as one of the greatest future obstacles to the reunification of Christians.

The Fallout From 'Pastor Aeternus'

Notice that the decree virtually put the pope at odds with the Church, or at least *above* the Church, by proclaiming his infallible definitions to be "irreformable of themselves and not in virtue of the consent of the Church." But if the pope is the vicar of Christ, and if the Church is Christ's body, how can the pope's judgment be superior to that of the body as a whole? This was at least one of the objections raised by theologians to *Pastor Aeternus* then and now.

Perhaps if the wording had been different, more people would have been convinced of the wisdom of the underlying doctrine. If, for example, the Council had said something like, "Since Jesus has promised to be with his Church always, even to the end of time, we can be assured that Peter's successor cannot err when it comes to defining faith and morals," the entire reaction might have been different.

But with its rigidly worded definition on papal infallibility, the Catholic Church was quickly scorned by commentators around the world as the bastion of authoritarianism and backwardness. So embarrassed was the Austrian government to be associated with the Vatican's newly proclaimed doctrine that it immediately rescinded its concordat of 1855 (p. 36) and threatened to restore the old State-controlled Church. In France, because of the press's ridicule of *Pastor Aeternus*, the government now felt confident to repress Catholic ultramontanists at will. And in the new German empire, Chancellor Bismarck, confident that no educated German citizen would now consider supporting the Vatican, did not hesitate (as we shall see shortly) in pursuing a policy of persecution against German Catholicism.

In 1871 the newly formed Kingdom of Italy offered Pius IX extensive privileges if he would recognize the Italian government. The Pope refused, sulking in the Vatican during the rest of his pontificate, promising his advisers that God's miraculous intervention would reverse the "disasters" of recent times. (Some Catholic observers felt that Pius's pontificate had been the chief disaster of recent times.) In 1878 Pius died, unaware that an entirely new world had irrevocably supplanted his hoped for neo-medieval, supreme Church, with its infallible monarch sitting at the top of a never-to-be-changed hierarchical pyramid.

On the surface Pius left behind a Church impenetrable to change, but in reality his atavistic policies had shaken the Church to its roots and sown the seed for an inevitable renewal. Yet the Church would suffer from the Pope's misjudgments for almost another century, until the mentality of the First Vatican Council was superseded by that of the Second.

UNIFICATION OF ITALY, 1859-1870

FRANCE

SWITZERLAND

SAVOY
(France 1860)

PIEDMONT
• Turin

LOMBARDY
• Milan

VENETIA

Venice

AUSTRIAN EMPIRE

KINGDOM

Genoa •

PARMA

MODENA

NICE
(France 1860)

• Florence

TUSCANY

PAPAL

STATES

Adriatic Sea

OF

Corsica
(France)

• Rome

• Capua

• Naples
Salerno •

SARDINIA

Tyrrhenian Sea

Mediterranean Sea

KINGDOM OF THE TWO SICILIES

• Reggio

Palermo •
Marsala •

Sicily

AFRICA

| | Kingdom of Sardinia, 1859 | | Acquired in 1866 |
| | Acquired in 1859-1860 | | Acquired in 1870 |

50

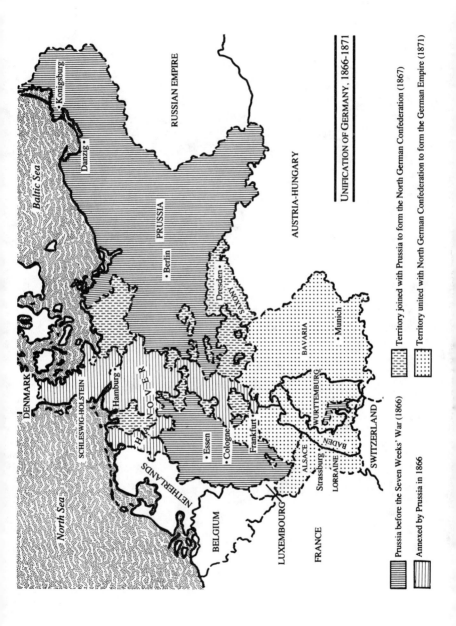

UNIFICATION OF GERMANY, 1866–1871

Prussia before the Seven Weeks' War (1866)

Annexed by Prussia in 1866

Territory joined with Prussia to form the North German Confederation (1867)

Territory united with North German Confederation to form the German Empire (1871)

51

CHAPTER FIVE

RESTORING THE CHURCH ON THE EVE OF ITS 20TH CENTURY

The Era of Leo XIII (1878-1903)

$\mathbf{P}$ope Pius IX's introverted reaction to modernity served notice on the world that Roman Catholicism had become little more than a museum for a bygone age. Pius's successor, Pope Leo XIII, attempted to reverse Pius's reactionary policies in certain respects and to bring the Church out of its shell and into the real world. That is not to say that Leo was a liberal. On the contrary, Leo was every bit as opposed to liberalism as Pius had been. But whereas Pius refused to make the slightest compromise with the post-Revolutionary age, Leo pragmatically resigned himself to making the best of a bad situation.

A PROFILE OF LEO XIII

Gioacchino Pecci, elected as Pope Leo XIII in the 68th year of his life, was both more intelligent and better educated than Pius IX. As bishop of Perugia, Pecci had been outgoing and exuberant. His skill as a pastor was not limited by the kind of personality and health defects that had burdened Pius IX.

Although a promoter of the infamous *Syllabus* (see p. 46), Bishop Pecci had nonetheless written several pastoral letters praising the salutary elements of modern culture, such as the many new developments in technology. (We get a sense of how backward and fearful Pius IX's pontificate had been when we find that Bishop Pecci's letters had raised suspicions among curial bureaucrats for daring to praise the lightning rod, the telephone and the steam engine.)

When Bishop Pecci had extolled modern ingenuity as "a spark from the Creator himself,"[1] and otherwise spoke favorably of the positive aspects of contemporary culture, eyebrows raised in Rome. Pius IX's secretary of state placed Pecci's name on a secret list of "suspect" bishops. Yet Pius IX himself apparently had no doubts about Pecci's loyalty and orthodoxy, for he named Pecci as his *camerlengo*—the cardinal who would serve as chief executive of the Vatican in the pope's absence or incapacity.

As pope, Leo XIII's guiding purpose was to restore Catholicism to a position of respect and credibility—and from there, Leo hoped, to a position of dominance in world affairs. Leo believed that Pius IX's policies had impeded the Church's spiritual mission; he also believed that the only way for the Church to become the world's spiritual leader was for it to make certain pragmatic compromises with modern times. One observer wrote of Leo that "he chained the modern world again to the tiara," an accurate metaphor to describe Leo's thoughts on the Church's relationship with the world.

One of Leo's greatest gifts was a keen sense of history. As Leo looked at the past, he saw the Catholic Church and the papacy as the chief forces of historical evolution—as the combined progenitor and preserver of Western civilization. For him, a world in which the papacy did not assert a leading role was historically unthinkable. Leo loved to hearken back to the days of the medieval popes, and particularly to the pontificate of Innocent III (d. 1216), whom Leo regarded as the paragon of all popes. He often quoted St. Ambrose's words, "Where Peter is, there the Church is," and he spoke of Rome as the center of Christianity and the source and hub of all spiritual life. And just as Innocent III epitomized for Leo the best of the popes, Thomas Aquinas (d. 1274) stood in Leo's view as the greatest and most authentic spokesman for philosophical truth.

Leo's horizon was infinitely broader than the Curia, the Papal States or even Catholicism; he saw his mission to be at "the service of the sacred cause of Christian civilization."[2] For Leo, the papacy and the Catholic Church were the means by which the modern world could be Christianized.

Undoubtedly Leo's vision was tinted by an overly optimistic idealism, perhaps even naivete, just as his reading of history was influenced by an overly nostalgic evaluation of the Church's effect on Western civilization. Yet Leo unquestionably looked upon the world with a more expanded vision than had Pius IX. For Leo the salvation of the modern world could be accomplished only if the Catholic Church were restored to its previous greatness, and such a restoration meant for Leo the active participation by the Church in the world's affairs.

Let's follow Leo's career briefly as he tried to impose his grand design for Catholic restoration upon the last years of the 19th century and the first three years of the 20th century.

LEO'S VISION OF A RESTORED CATHOLICISM

Although Leo spoke enthusiastically of a "world plan" for Catholic restoration, in actuality the Catholic Church during Leo's pontificate remained essentially a European institution. Even in democracies such as the United States, the native hierarchy modeled itself and thus the American Church on the European model. In the republics of South America, the Church still maintained its Spanish temperament. And in the African and Asiatic missions, attempts to implement a Christianity adapted to indigenous cultures had long ago been squelched by Rome.* It was not until the era of Vatican II that local Churches were permitted by the Vatican to profess their Catholic faith in the demeanor of indigenous culture.

Before we reach Vatican II, therefore, we unfortunately are limited to speaking of a Church with a purely European consciousness. And since that is the case, we must understand a little about European history on the eve of the 20th century.

Leo's 'World'

Insofar as Pope Leo XIII was concerned, the "Catholic world" was comprised principally of Italy, Germany and France. Thus with Italian and German unification (see map V, p. 50 and map VI, p. 51)—that is, as previously disparate provinces and principalities in Italy and Germany were joined together into unified nations—the papacy and the Church faced new challenges.

As we saw earlier, Pius IX refused to acknowledge the new Italian government. Leo XIII followed suit, but attempted in subtle ways to effect a Church-State reconciliation in Italy. In Germany, Chancellor Otto von Bismarck looked upon German Catholicism as an obstacle to his efforts to unify the states of the new German empire. Bismarck thus initiated the *Kulturkampf* ("cultural struggle") against Catholicism. In France, when the Franco-Prussian War of 1870-1871 brought an end to Napoleon III's "Empire" and ushered in the Third

---

* For one of the best books on this subject, read V. Cronin's *A Pearl to India*, the life of the Jesuit Robert de Nobili (1577-1656), which recounts Rome's efforts to thwart de Nobili's innovative evangelization efforts in India.

Republic, new forces threatened to break the Church's ancient alliance with the State.

Let's briefly look at the developments in these countries so that we can understand how Leo XIII attempted to deal with the challenge posed by the refabrication of European society.

Italy

The majority of Catholics in Italy stood by Leo in his rejection of the new Italian government. The latter, in addition to annexing the Papal States, promulgated several laws which completely eradicated the papacy's previous hold on Italian politics. For example, the government refused to validate Church marriages, confiscated the property of religious orders, abolished religious education in public schools and took over previously Church-run charitable organizations.

Pius IX had responded to the threat of secularization in Italy by issuing the decree *Non Expedit* ("It is not expedient"), which forbade Catholics from voting in Italian elections. In actuality the new Italian government had extended suffrage to only two percent of the population anyway, and thus most Catholics were already prohibited from voting. Pius IX had nonetheless clearly drawn the line between acceptable and unacceptable Catholic collaboration with the new government.

Although Leo XIII did not abolish *Non Expedit*, he spoke of it in conciliatory language. He interpreted it—in the words of the official Vatican newspaper, *L'Osservatore Romano*—as a means of "preparing" Italian Catholics for participation in the new government. In 1887, Leo even offered the new government the hand of reconciliation, writing diplomatically that "...the path to harmony is subject to the condition that the pope not be subjugated to any authority and enjoy absolute freedom, as is his right."[3] The anticlerical Italian government, however, rejected Leo's subtle overture, and thus Italian Catholics organized themselves into various parties by which they sought to engage in politics in a way that was acceptable to the Pope.

The *Opera Dei Congressi* ("Opera" for short), the chief organ of the Catholic labor movement, soon became the principal agent in Italy for achieving political reform according to Catholic doctrine. Leo himself played an active role in the activities of the *Opera* by helping to organize it and streamline its administration. Leo, of course, wanted the *Opera* to address the problems of Italian society from a strictly religious perspective—that is, he saw the *Opera* chiefly as a means by which the Church could minister to the *spiritual* needs of Italy's ever-growing working class. This policy appealed to many Italians but alienated others, who looked to the new Italian Socialist Party as a more effective means of addressing the day-to-day, practical needs of the working class.

Partially in response to the socialist challenge, the Catholic labor movement in Italy began to expand its mission: It began to take on a more political demeanor and to promote purely social reforms under the banner of "Christian democracy." This phrase grated on the nerves of many churchmen. For them "Christian democracy" was a contradiction in terms. For most prelates words like *democracy* smacked of Protestantism, revolution, anarchy and defiance of authority.

Yet Leo himself did not want to dampen the enthusiasm of the Catholic labor movement if it could be made to submit its agenda to the Church. As a result, in 1891 Leo issued his most famous encyclical, *Rerum Novarum* ("Of New Things"), in which he specifically addressed himself to the conditions of the working class. The appearance of this encyclical shocked conservative Catholics in Italy, but encouraged many younger Catholics to press on for social reform through concerted "Catholic Action."

'Rerum Novarum'

In actuality, *Rerum Novarum* was a rather conservative document. It reaffirmed traditional Catholic teaching that the family was the basic unit of society. For the protection and preservation of the family, Leo said, individuals (individual men, not women) had the right to own private property and to be paid a just wage, defined by Leo as "enough to support the wage-earner in reasonable and frugal comfort." Socialism was condemned as destructive of the family, and the woman's place was said to be in the home.

Perhaps the encyclical's most daring innovation was its support for the idea of workers' associations and collective bargaining agreements as a means to arrive at just wages. The State was urged to protect the rights of workers, and the Church was said to have a moral obligation to uphold the human dignity of the laborer and to promote his interests.

In spite of its cautious tone, *Rerum Novarum* stunned conservative Catholics. Yet we should not read the encyclical as an endorsement of liberalism and a repudiation of Pius IX's conservatism. *Rerum Novarum* was simply one element in Leo's overall program for establishing the Church's leadership in world affairs. Aside from his genuine interest in social justice, Leo realized that the working class was a powerful new force in society and that the Church could not ignore it. In fact, a large segment of the working class in Italy and elsewhere had already irrevocably committed itself to socialism or to other reform movements; thus *Rerum Novarum* had little practical effect on the policies of European governments.

Germany

When Leo became pope, German Chancellor Bismarck's *Kulturkampf* had already been in progress for seven years. In violation of the Prussian Constitution of 1850, Bismarck had trampled on the Catholic Church's right to exist independent of State control. In 1872 a law was passed which dissolved the Jesuits and expelled them from Germany. A year later the State assumed the right to supervise all clerical education, thereby intruding directly into the operation of Catholic seminaries. The German government then gave itself the right to veto all clerical appointments and required all persons seeking marriage to be wed in a civil ceremony.

Catholic bishops were ordered to swear allegiance to the new laws. When they refused, they were imprisoned or dismissed from their offices. In the "Breadbasket Law" of 1875, the government ceased all State subsidies to recalcitrant clergy, thereby depriving most dioceses and parishes of the necessary funds to maintain themselves. (In Germany, tax revenues were tithed by the State directly to the Church.) Finally, the government prohibited most of the remaining religious orders in Germany from exercising their ministries.

Two years before Leo became pope, and only because Bismarck realized that his *Kulturkampf* had virtually eliminated one of his best allies in the struggle against the rising tide of social democracy, the Chancellor began to retreat from the *Kulturkampf*. Nonetheless, when Leo assumed the papacy, nearly half of the German bishops had been "fired" by the State. Other bishops and hundreds of priests were still in prison. In spite of the fact that most German Catholics regarded Bismarck as the devil incarnate, Leo nonetheless entered into negotiations with the Chancellor to repeal the onerous anti-Catholic legislation.

As pragmatic as Leo was, however, he refused to budge when Bismarck demanded the right to screen all papal episcopal appointments. Finally, as Bismarck's other domestic policies became increasingly conservative, his war against the Church became counterproductive. Thus Leo won from the German government virtually a total repeal of its hostile legislation.

By 1885 diplomats traveling between Rome and Berlin had achieved the reconciliation which both Leo and Bismarck wanted. Bismarck then decided to terminate all traces of the *Kulturkampf* by declaring himself publicly in favor of papal sovereignty. He took the momentous step of asking Leo to arbitrate a dispute between Germany and Spain over their respective claims in the Caroline Islands. Since Bismarck's proposal would allow Leo to regain for the papacy much of its lost credibility in the international community, the Pope gratefully accepted Bismarck's offer. Shortly thereafter, as the world watched in amazement, Leo awarded the former archpersecutor a papal honor known as the Order of Christ. Consistent with his deepest desires, Leo's pragmatism had rewon for the papacy a portion of its medieval prestige.

France

The establishment of the Third Republic in France brought with it increased anticlerical opposition to the Church's ancient policy of collaboration with the State. In the French legislative assembly, many representatives voiced opposition to continuing the old Napoleonic Concordat of 1801 (see p. 10), which had guaranteed the Church some autonomy within the State. In 1879 the assembly passed a law restricting the Church's monopoly on primary education. To implement this policy, the government expelled the Jesuits from France in 1880 and shortly thereafter expelled other religious orders deemed threatening to the Republic. Yet a series of surveys undertaken by the government revealed strong support for the Church in many areas of France. This fact, coupled with republican fears of the growing socialist movement, motivated the government to stop short of abrogating the Napoleonic concordat.

Catholics in France now faced a dilemma. Many of them regarded the increasing democratization of French society as a compromise with the evil French Revolution. Partially in response to their distaste for republican ideals, many French Catholics had become ultramontanists, throwing all of their support behind the pope in hopes of restoring the "good old days." Yet now the very republicans who wanted to secularize France and end the Church's influence on society sought, for pragmatic reasons, to preserve the Napoleonic concordat which had kept Church and State united. Conservative Catholics were now put in the position of either repudiating their past opposition to republican ideals, or sticking to their old principles while the even more dangerous socialists replaced republicans as the leading voices in French politics.

Leo XIII analyzed this situation and concluded that the interests of the Church in France would be best served if French ultramontanists receded to the background of French politics. The toning down of ultramontanist rhetoric, Leo reasoned, would motivate moderate republicans to pursue a policy friendly to the Church. Accordingly, Leo instructed his French nuncios to dampen the ardor of the same ultramontanist press which Pius IX had done everything to encourage.

The 'Ralliement'

Leo's *rapprochement* with the Third Republic—shocking to many conservative churchmen in both France and Italy—reached its climax in 1890 with a policy known as the *ralliement* ("rally"). On November 12, 1890, Cardinal Charles de Lavigerie, primate of French Algiers, made a toast at a banquet for French naval officers in which he urged French Catholics to "rally" behind the Third Republic. Leo seized upon the ensuing *ralliement* sentiment as an opportunity to win influence for the Church in France. In 1892 he wrote an encyclical endorsing Cardinal Lavigerie's declaration of support for the Republic and its democratic ideals.

Ralliement represented an about-face which no one could possibly have foreseen in the heyday of Pius IX. The papacy, in the eyes of many Catholic conservatives, now embraced the devil by recognizing a form of government which just a decade before it had categorically denounced. In actuality Leo's aim was not to enthrone liberal, democratic ideals, but to unite all Catholics in France for the "conversion" of the Third Republic to Christianity. Further, through *Rerum Novarum*, Leo hoped to drain away working-class Catholic support for the socialist labor movement.

Leo's policy initially resulted in gains for the Church in France; the years 1896-1898 came to be called "the golden age of clericalism." Leo's endorsement of the *ralliement* eventually failed, however, for two reasons. First, Catholic opinion concerning the *ralliement* splintered; some Catholics favored the *ralliement* but many others opposed it. Second, the "Dreyfus Affair" rocked French society in 1894 and destroyed much of the Church's prestige.

The Dreyfus Affair

Alfred Dreyfus was a Jewish captain in the French Army. He was falsely accused of espionage, found guilty of treason and sent to the notorious Devil's Island in French Guiana.

Through a long and complicated process he was eventually exonerated and released, but not before France had become bitterly divided over the issue. The "anti-Dreyfusards"—those who wanted Dreyfus kept in prison—were made up of a large number of Catholics (including many priests) who were both anti-Semitic and supportive of a restored monarchy. When Dreyfus was cleared, the Church's alliance with the Third Republic collapsed.

Catholics were now lumped together as opponents of justice and as clandestine conspirators against the Republic. On July 1, 1901, the "Associations Law" took effect: The foundation of new religious congregations was forbidden without prior State approval, and the continued existence of old congregations was placed at the mercy of the government. In 1902 the anticlerical Emile Combes was elected premier. He promptly closed some 3,000 Catholic-run schools and abolished 54 male religious congregations. Pope Leo's hoped-for Christianization of the Third Republic had foundered on the rocks of political reality.

In 1905 (during the pontificate of Leo's successor, Pius X), the Napoleonic Concordat of 1801 was officially abolished. Freedom of conscience became the law of the land; no longer was Catholicism to be the favored State religion. All ties between Church and State in France were broken. The State would no longer appoint clerics to State posts and would no longer pay their salaries. Finally, all Church property was to be taken over by private corporations which had no ties to the State.

THE QUESTION OF SOCIAL JUSTICE

The Church's life on the eve of the 20th century was interconnected with issues raised by the growth of an industrialized society and the large new class of workers to which that society had given birth. Here was a problem which the Church was unprepared to confront. From the time of Constantine the Great (see *The People of the Creed,* Chapter One) until the coming of the French Revolution, the Church had imposed on European society a model in which royalty, clergy and peasantry each played its preordained role in human affairs. Beginning in the late Middle Ages, however, a new class of people had intruded into the Church's dream of a conveniently organized feudal hierarchy. That class of people was the *bourgeoisie,* or middle class, for whom Catholic social theorists had little to offer.

The Era of the 'Bourgeoisie'

Many members of the bourgeoisie—lawyers, merchants, financiers, artisans, entrepreneurs—were attracted to Protestantism. They found the Protestant emphasis on individual discernment of Scripture and on an autonomous spiritual life free of an absolute teaching authority more in tune to their "upwardly mobile," independent life-style than Catholicism. Consequently, most of them, particularly in England and northern Europe, became Protestant.

When the French Revolution broke out, many of the bourgeoisie were in the forefront, demanding a radical change in the organization of society. The old feudal model comprised of royalty, clergy and peasantry was shattered and a new model established in which talent, hard work and education (rather than birth and privilege) became the bases on which political power rested.

The Catholic hierarchy had fought tooth and nail against the rising power of the bourgeoisie all during the 19th century until the time of Leo XIII when, in an effort to co-opt the inevitable, Leo attempted to make pragmatic compromises with the bourgeoisie's republican governments.

The Evolution of Socialism

As the bourgeoisie increased its hold on Western society, another new class entered the picture, the working-class poor of industrialized cities. Now the bourgeoisie, themselves former revolutionaries, became targets of *socialist* radicals. The very advocates of radicalism in 1789—then outside the organized structure of society—now became conservative champions of the status quo. Largely because it was their investments which had financed the Industrial Revolution, it was the bourgeoisie who most feared the workers' demands for fairness and justice.

The bourgeoisie had placed its hopes on republican democracies in which earned wealth controlled the political process. (Universal suffrage, or "one man, one vote," did not exist in the 19th century.) The political philosophy developed to support bourgeois goals was *republicanism*. Likewise, many members of the new working class developed a political philosophy which came to be known as *socialism*.

Modern socialism appeared in the 1830's. Count Henri de Saint-Simon (1760-1825), a French nobleman, of all people, argued for a completely egalitarian society in which the industrial workers would have a voice in the political process. In England, Robert Owen (1771-1858), experiencing guilt over the wealth he had earned at the expense of workers in his Scottish textile mills, began to preach the cooperative control of industry by both employers and employees. Although Owen became an enlightened employer, many other industrialists of his era egregiously exploited their employees, enslaving them to low-paying jobs and lifelong poverty (as brilliantly illustrated in Charles Dickens's novels *Bleak House* and *Our Mutual Friend*).

More radical socialist thinkers, such as Pierre-Joseph Prudhon (1809-1865), attacked private property itself as the source of bourgeois injustice. By far the most prominent socialist was the revolutionary Karl Marx (1818-1883).

Karl Marx

For Marx, history was the movement of a class struggle between the privileged and the oppressed. Just as the struggle between the bourgeoisie and the royalist-clerical class had resulted in the former's victory, so too the proletariat's struggle against the bourgeoisie would now bring about the working class's triumph.

The result, Marx said, would be a classless society in which the producers of goods and services would control their own destinies by combining into workers' collectives. Along the way, Marx taught, God and religion—"the opiate of the masses"—would be discarded. In place of heaven, enlightened workers would substitute an earthly utopia, a "workers' paradise."

The Church's Response to Socialism

Marxism, with its disbelief in God, was obviously antithetical to Christianity. Yet Catholic thinkers—even members of the hierarchy—felt less discomfort in addressing themselves to the needs of the working class than in relating to the liberal bourgeoisie. As we saw in Chapter Three (see pp. 36-37), even archconservatives like Cardinal Manning displayed a sincere concern for the workers' plight. And, of course, *Rerum Novarum* epitomized the hierarchy's concern to protect industrial workers from unscrupulous employers.

Consequently, although Leo XIII explicitly condemned socialism in his famous encyclical, many Catholics were much more sympathetic to socialism's demand for justice for oppressed workers than they were to bourgeois republicanism. Indeed, one could perhaps characterize the Catholic response to the social issues raised by industrialization as follows: "How can a good Catholic be antiliberal and at the same time a Christian socialist?"

The answer to this question took many forms. As we saw in Italy (see pp. 56-57), the *Opera* party took a conservative stance in reaction to the new Italian government while at the same time professing support for urban workers. *Rerum Novarum* itself made a plea both for workers' rights *and* for the old order; in fact, Leo saw the protection of the workers precisely *in* the preservation of the old order. In *Rerum Novarum* Leo did not call for the radical usurpation of power by workers but for the fatherly, even paternalistic, support of workers as vulnerable children who needed to be protected from the vices of the liberal industrial State.

Other Catholic social theorists displayed this same dichotomy between antiliberal and pro-working-class thought. The Belgian economist Charles Perin (1815-1905), for example, condemned liberalism and argued that industrialists should practice Christian asceticism on behalf of industrial workers by restricting the amount of profit they allow themselves to earn. In France Frédéric Le Play (1802-1882), like Pope Leo, preached paternalistic Christian charity on behalf of defenseless workers. In Austria Christian socialism was advanced by a famous professor of moral theology, Franz Schindler (1847-1922), who advocated profit-sharing programs for workers as well as the harnessing of unbridled economic competition. The common thread in all of these Catholic writings was the rejection of liberal ideals coupled with zeal for protection of the workers.

No Catholic social theorist (including Leo XIII) could admit that industrial workers deserved the right of self-determination—as opposed to the Church's fatherly supervision of their lives. Thus Catholicism's answer to socialism never really gained respectability with non-Catholic social theorists. Nor did it ever appear as anything other than a minority position in the legislative assemblies of Western society.

Consequently, the Church lost a historic opportunity to win the new industrial class to Catholicism. By default it allowed secular social theorists to dominate the labor movement because they treated workers as adults who deserved equal standing in society, rather than as children needing the protection of an all-knowing father. Nonetheless, in its own paternalistic way, the Church had gone on record as being in favor of justice for the laboring poor and against their exploitation by the rich.

CHAPTER SIX

THE BATTLE TO DEFINE MODERN CATHOLICISM

Reform and Controversy Under Pius X (1903-1914)

Giuseppe Sarto, cardinal-patriarch of Venice, was chosen Leo's successor by 38 Italian and 24 non-Italian cardinals (including the first American to vote in a papal election). Sarto placed himself squarely behind the policies of Pius IX by choosing the name Pius X. He described himself as following in the footsteps of popes, "who, in past centuries, had courgeously fought against sects and rampant errors."[1] Thus Pius X began his pontificate in a state of mind adamantly opposed to compromising with modernity.

STRUGGLING AGAINST MODERNITY, REFORMING THE CHURCH

Pius X was miles apart from the pragmatic politican-pope he had succeeded. Pius X disliked politics and the intrigues of diplomacy. In contrast to Leo's familiarity with worldly-wise politicians, Pius X preferred to associate with ordinary Catholics for whom he felt personal responsibility as a spiritual father and pastor.

Pius X was known for his high moral character and deep spirituality. One French abbot recorded his impression of an audience with the Pope in this way: "I have seen an honest, strong, and beautiful holiness."[2]

Along with his unquestioned personal sanctity, however, went Pius X's aversion to the liberal trends of modern times. Like Pius IX before him, Pius X was a thoroughgoing reactionary. One French historian, quoting a high-placed adviser to a French cardinal, wrote that Pius X "prepared the dictatorship that would save the Church."[3] Pius indeed ruled the Church with a strong hand, because he—like his predecessors in the 19th century—felt that only firm and clear leadership could keep the Church free from secular incursions.

The 'No-Compromise' Pope

Unlike Leo XIII, Pius X refused to make pragmatic "deals" with the states of Europe. While the Napoleonic concordat was going up in flames in France (see p. 61), Pius refused to enter into any negotiations which might deter the Combes government from segregating the French Church from the State. On another occasion Pius threatened to sever diplomatic relations with Catholic Austria unless government officials suspended a professor of canon law who had advanced modern viewpoints in the classroom.

In 1910 Pius wrote an encyclical commemorating the 300th anniversary of the Catholic Reformation's greatest bishop, Charles Borromeo, by harshly criticizing Luther and Protestantism. The Pope's anti-Protestant sentiments were also revealed when he refused to grant an audience to Theodore Roosevelt unless the former American president canceled his announced visit to a Methodist church in Rome. (Roosevelt refused.)

Such incidents as these illustrate how Pius X returned the Church to the "fortress mentality" of Pius IX's pontificate—that is, to the mentality of "us versus them." The Church was considered the last defender against the modern world's attacks. Pius X saw himself as the commander of a fortress under bombardment, a situation which he saw as "demanding for God's sake omnipotent power [for the pope] over man and beast."[4]

Pius X's Reforms

Pius used his "omnipotent power" both to fend off the external attacks of modern culture and to reform the internal structure of the Church's bureaucracy. This internal reform proved to be one of the most lasting achievements of his pontificate. Pius abolished many useless offices within the Curia and supervised the revision of canon law. By 1917 (three years after Pius's death), Pius's revisers would publish a greatly simplified *Codex Iuris Canonici*, divided into five books, which remained the complete Code of Canon Law until the pontificate of Pope John Paul II.

Pius also reformed the liturgy. Since the Jansenist heyday of the 17th century, Catholics had looked upon the Eucharist as sacred food reserved to the saintly few who could approach the altar worthily (see pp. 43-44). Pius attempted to abolish such thinking, first by approving daily Communion for adults and then by allowing all children who had reached the "age of discretion" to receive Holy Communion on the same terms as adults. According to the Pope, "Jesus meant to be the daily remedy and the daily food for our daily shortcomings,"[5] and not a reward for virtuous conduct. This was in keeping with the Pope's belief that the Church's liturgy was "the first and irreplaceable source of Christian strength."[6]

In a certain sense Pius X was first and foremost a pastor with a high degree of practical intelligence. He realized that the faith of the Church rises from below rather than descends from above. He therefore gave a great deal of attention to reforming the "lower ranks" of Catholicism. He instituted a major overhaul of the seminary system and the methods by which bishops and priests were selected. He kept files on all candidates for the episcopate, and carefully scrutinized his notes before making an appointment.

He also personally directed a reform of catechetics. "It is much easier," he said, "to find a brilliant speaker than a catechist who is an excellent teacher."[7] Returning to the policy of the early Church (see *The People of the Creed*, Chapter One), Pius encouraged laypersons to serve as catechists. Once, when asked what was the most urgent need of modern times, Pius answered, "Today, it is most important that every parish have at its disposal a group of enlightened, virtuous, decisive, and truly apostolic laymen."[8]

THE MODERNIST CONTROVERSY

Pius X was a complex person with both reforming zeal and reactionary temperament. The great crisis of his pontificate involved the so-called Modernist controversy—"so-called" because it proved to be very difficult to define precisely what Modernism was. The name was coined in 1905 by certain Italian bishops who issued a pastoral letter condemning "Modernism." In order to understand what this controversy was about, let's return for a moment to the pontificate of Leo XIII.

Prelude Under Leo XIII

On August 4, 1879, Leo had issued the encyclical *Aeterni Patris* in which he endorsed Thomas Aquinas's philosophy ("Thomism") as—"aside from the supernatural assistance of God"[9]—the greatest means of finding philosophical truth. Leo's encyclical had been an integral part of his overall effort to win society back to the medieval reverence for Christian philosophy. For example, Leo had established the Roman Academy of Saint Thomas and appointed his Jesuit brother, Giuseppe Pecci, as president.

Leo's Thomistic restoration ran contrary to the direction in which Protestant theology and some currents of Catholic theology were headed—namely, in the direction of historical research and analysis rather than in the old direction of commenting on moral theology and engaging in metaphysical speculation (recall the discussion on pp. 45-46). By becoming more interested in the historical development of dogma, Catholic theologians showed that the Church over the centuries had in fact often changed the manner in which it presented its teaching. But to admit that was to admit that change is possible *now*. Such a thought was threatening to Leo XIII, who absolutized Thomism as the one and only "package" in which Catholicism could be wrapped.

Consequently, in most Catholic universities and seminaries, historical research was virtually off limits. As a leading Dominican professor had expressed it in 1889, "For us exegesis and the description of the traditional doctrines of faith and morals are the essential elements in theology. History can only be granted the rank of an ancillary science."[10]

When a learned French Catholic historian, the priest Louis Duchesne (1843-1922), published studies gleaned from his research in archaeology and ancient Church documents, he unleashed a furor of protests from some churchmen. Because of the interest in the new historical method, Leo issued *Providentissimus Deus* in 1893. In this encyclical Leo acknowledged the usefulness of historical research for the field of biblical scholarship, but he condemned excessive reliance on this method. Any errors or textual ambiguities in the Bible, Leo said, are simply the result of mistakes made in copying the original lost manuscripts. (This encyclical was indirectly aimed at the work of certain Catholic scholars whom we shall shortly discuss.)

'Americanism'

Already disturbed by new trends within Catholic academia, Leo reacted harshly in 1899 to a controversy over Walter Elliot's biography of the American priest and founder of the Paulists, Isaac Hecker (1819-1888). Although Hecker, a convert, had devoted himself to proselytizing Protestants, he had raised suspicions in Rome because he resented the imposition of European ways on the American Church. When the archbishop of St. Paul, Minnesota, John Ireland, spoke of Hecker in the introduction to Elliot's book as "the priest of the future," and when the French edition of the biography recommended "the American Way" to the French clergy, many French prelates condemned the book.

Archconservatives among the French clergy fulminated over the dread terror of "Americanism," although none of them seemed to know what it was. The Americanist scourge nevertheless, became the fear of the moment, and prominent cardinals persuaded Leo XIII to condemn it. Accordingly, Leo wrote a denunciatory open letter on the subject and sent it to the cardinal-archbishop of Baltimore, James Gibbons (1834-1921)—a man whom President Theodore Roosevelt had once called "the most respected and venerated citizen of the United States."[11]

In his letter Leo equated Americanism with the following propositions: (1) that the clergy are not to guide the individual believer's discernment in matters of faith; (2) that it is easier to arrive at truth naturally than it is to do so supernaturally; (3) that the contemplative orders should enter into active pursuits; (4) that religious vows are outmoded; and (5) that a more conciliatory approach to non-Catholics should be encouraged.

How Leo deduced these propositions from Elliot's biography is uncertain. Cardinal Gibbons wrote to the Pope concerning the condemned propositions as follows: "I do not believe that there is a bishop, a priest, or even a layman in this country who knows his religion and utters such enormities. No, this is not, has never been, and will never be our 'Americanism.'"[12]

When the Paulists withdrew Elliot's biography from the market, conservatives sighed with relief over the erasure of "Americanism" from the Church. Little did they know that an even more turbulent controversy was about to follow.

Loisy and the Bible

Leo XIII's encyclical on the Bible, *Providentissimus Deus*, was at least partially a reaction to the studies of a prominent Catholic biblical scholar, Alfred Loisy (1857-1940). Loisy was a country priest who had been motivated by Duchesne to apply new methods of historical research to the Bible. In 1890 Loisy became professor of Sacred Scripture at the Catholic Institute in Paris. His published treatises on the Bible stirred such suspicions in Rome that he was forced to resign his professorship.

In 1902 Loisy published his famous work, *The Gospel and the Church*. In it he argued that the Gospels are not a factual record of Jesus' ministry but rather the collective impressions of the early Church's *faith* in Jesus. Loisy wrote this as a loyal Catholic, and his book was, in part, a response to a theory proposed by the Protestant scholar Adolf Harnack (more on him in a later chapter). Harnack had argued that the Gospels do not reveal Jesus as having established either an institutional Church or sacraments; thus, he said, historical Catholicism was not true to the Scriptures.

Loisy admitted Harnack's premise but denied his conclusion. In Loisy's words, "Jesus announced the coming of the Kingdom, and what transpired was the Church."[13] In other words, while neither the institutional Church nor the sacraments are spelled out in detail in the Bible, Jesus' rudimentary teaching evolved, under the inspiration of the Holy Spirit, into the empirical second-century Church, and from there to the Church we know today. For the first time a Catholic scholar of the highest academic credentials had argued for Catholicism's superiority to Protestantism strictly on the basis of scientific-historical studies.

Loisy's intentions were lost on hierarchical critics. Two months after *The Gospel and the Church* was published, Cardinal-Archbishop Adolphe Perraud of Paris condemned the book. Leo XIII declined to enter the controversy openly, but soon after Pius X was elected (nine months after the book's publication), the debate became both public and heated.

Loisy's next book argued that Jesus' virginal birth, his resurrection and his divinity are not facts which can be scientifically validated; rather, he said, all of these doctrines are simply evidence of what the early Church came to *believe* about Jesus. Shortly thereafter Rome condemned Loisy's writings.

The Controversy Spreads

Despite the condemnation of Loisy's works, the question still remained whether his historical-critical method could properly be used by Catholic scholars. The debate over this issue fueled the fire on the Modernist controversy.

Many younger priests in France rallied behind the cause of unhindered scientific scholarship in the areas of biblical studies and Church history. The French Jesuit, Henri Bremond (1865-1933), wrote a biography of St. Jane Frances de Chantal (d. 1641) in which he departed from the usual glowing hagiography and depicted Chantal as an actual woman of flesh and blood, thereby earning Bremond the reputation in Rome as a Modernist.

An Oratorian priest, Lucien Laberthonniere (1860-1932), wrote several essays which were eventually put on the Index of forbidden writings. Laberthonniere espoused a theology inspired by the Catholic philosopher, Maurice Blondel (1861-1949). Blondel taught that knowledge of God comes principally from the choices of one's will as surrendered to God rather than through rational speculation, an idea which ran counter to the Thomist view that one can approach authentic knowledge of God through the intellect.

As Blondel's philosophy, and that of two other prominent philosophers, became popular among intellectuals of the day, the hierarchy condemned any churchman's writings which appeared based on their works. The first of these philosophers was the American William James (1842-1910) who argued that knowledge of God is a purely pragmatic decision—that is, we believe in God simply because we are, as James put it, "better off" for having done so. The second was the French philosopher Henri Bergson (1859-1941) who subordinated the human intellect to intuition. For him, morality was not a question of speculative determination of divine truth—as for Thomists—but rather the product of an inner impulse which he called the *élan vital* ("life force") and which he equated with God, thereby making human growth a necessary result of God's action within the soul.

Such thinking was opposed to traditional Catholic teaching on grace. Catholics who flirted with such ideas were labeled as Modernist and their collective theories as Modernism, though it still remained very difficult to define precisely what Modernism was and who was a Modernist. Those accused of being Modernists attempted to define their own beliefs.

The English Modernist George Tyrrell (1861-1909), for example, wrote, "I understand a Modernist to be a Christian of any denomination who is convinced that the essential truths of his religion and the essential truths of modern society can enter into a synthesis."[14] Another English Modernist, Baron Friedrich von Hügel (1852-1925), wrote in a similar vein: "I try to do everything I can to make my old Church intellectually as acceptable as possible, not because reason is the most important thing in religion, but rather because my old Church already possesses all the knowledge necessary to guide spiritual life; while for reasons that would fill a volume, it is less equipped to deal with the needs, the rights, and the duties of rational life."[15]

The Italian Modernist Romolo Murri (1870-1944) spoke more critically of returning the Church to the gospel and liberating it "from the warmed-over semiheathen customs, from the juridic concepts derived from Roman law, from the decadent monastic institutions that are incapable of rejuvenation, and from the abstract categories that kill like the letter of the law."[16]

Those accused of being Modernists differed widely in their views, but they all tended to support the following ideas: (1) adherence

71

to a historical-critical method in biblical research which did not attempt to deny contradictions and inconsistencies; (2) a preference for a theology of action and involvement as opposed to a speculative, "ivory-tower" theology which never entered into contact with the real world; and (3) a belief in the evolution of doctrine toward an ever fuller appreciation of the Church's mission, as opposed to the traditionalists' attempt to fix normative doctrine in a past era of greatness, such as the 13th century.

Traditional theologians, on the other hand, accused the Modernists of opposing the inspiration of Scripture, the divinity of Christ, the superiority of Thomism as the means of philosophical truth and the supremacy of episcopal authority over theologians' opinions.

The Vatican Takes Action

On July 17, 1907, the Holy Office (the Vatican congregation in charge of suppressing heresy) issued the decree *Lamentabili* which condemned 65 propositions said to be Modernist. On September 8, 1907, the encyclical *Pascendi Gregis* followed. In essence it condemned the various Modernist tendencies discussed above and decreed several disciplinary measures aimed at keeping Modernism out of seminaries and schools. The hierarchy's suppression of Modernism was perhaps needed in order to clarify those aspects of modern thought which were inconsistent with Church teaching; but the result of the two decrees was virtually to destroy creative Catholic scholarship.

In 1910 Pius X hammered the final nail in the coffin. He declared the Church to be "in a state of siege" to Modernism, and he ordered that all clergy take an anti-Modernist oath, swearing allegiance to *Lamentabili* and *Pascendi*. Yet even after this step, the Pope was still concerned. In 1911 he wrote, "the error spreading these days is much more murderous than that of Luther."[17]

A Fearful Entry Into the 20th Century

The Pope's continued fears inspired the Integralist Reaction, a concerted effort on the part of many prelates to suppress even the slightest trace of scholarly activity not adhering to strict Thomism. Such persons called themselves "integral Catholics" because, as one advocate wrote, "...we prefer over everything and everybody not only the traditional doctrine of the Church in regard to absolute truths, but also the directives of the pope in the area of pragmatic contingencies. The pope and the Church are one."[18]

The hierarchy no doubt had valid reasons for questioning certain aspects of Modernism. Yet instead of throwing out the baby with the bath water, the hierarchy could have probed deeper and more patiently into Modernist works to determine if some of them could help the Church proclaim the gospel in contemporary language.

But the times were still not ripe for a peaceful dialogue between Catholicism and modern culture. Instead of seeking dialogue, the hierarchy continued to lash out fearfully at anything which detracted from the medieval model of the Church. Thus the Church entered its 20th century on a note of suspicion and fear. It had not yet fully heeded Scripture's teaching that "...love is not yet perfect in one who is afraid" (1 John 4:18).

CHAPTER SEVEN

THE CHURCH IN AN AGE OF WORLD WAR

Benedict XV, Pius XI and Pius XII (1914-1958)

Each in its own way, the papacies of Pius IX, Leo XIII and Pius X were preoccupied with the Catholic Church's struggle against modernity. A gradual thaw in the Church's cold war against the modern world can be detected, however, during the pontificates of Benedict XV (1914-1922), Pius XI (1922-1939) and Pius XII (1939-1958). Let's take a brief look at each of these "transition popes," so named because they prepared the way for the Second Vatican Council and its monumental restatement of Catholic tradition.

BENEDICT XV AND WORLD WAR I

Giacomo della Chiesa, cardinal-archbishop of Bologna, was elected pope by the Conclave of Cardinals on the 10th ballot. He came to the papacy with a reputation for being a dedicated pastor and spiritual father. Elected pope only a month after the outbreak of World War I, Benedict dedicated his entire papacy to promoting peace among warring nations and attending to the needs of the war's victims.

Since a large number of Catholics served as combatants on both sides of the conflict, Benedict adopted a policy of strict neutrality; he did not want to appear as a partisan for either the "Central Powers" (Germany and Austria-Hungary) or the "Entente" (Britain, France and Russia) (see map VII, p. 76). Consequently, the Pope limited his statements on the war to vague appeals for peace and a continuing condemnation of what he called "the butchery." Papal neutrality,

North Sea

NORWAY

SWEDEN

Baltic Sea

DENMARK

GREAT
BRITAIN

NETHERLANDS

GERMANY

RUSSIA

BELGIUM
LUXEMBOURG

FRANCE

SWITZERLAND

AUSTRIA-HUNGARY

RUMANIA

SPAIN

ITALY

MONTENEGRO

SERBIA

ALBANIA

BULGARIA

Black Sea

GREECE

Aegean Sea

TURKEY

Mediterranean Sea

AFRICA

EUROPE IN 1915

The Allies (the Entente)   The Central Powers   Neutral nations

Benedict believed, was based on Christ's own compassion for all people.

Belligerents on both sides criticized Benedict's neutral posture. Each side, of course, believed its position to be the only moral course to follow. Thus, on several occasions, the warring nations characterized Benedict's repeated calls for peace as an obstruction to a just victory for God's anointed champions.

Benedict was wise enough to understand that God was on the side of neither set of combatants. For the first time in centuries, a pope refused to involve the papacy—whether militarily, politically or rhetorically—in a major European war. Perhaps centuries of meaningless bloodshed had finally convinced a pope that the Church's only response to war was to preach and to practice peace. Benedict's example was to be followed by all of his successors; from Benedict's pontificate onward, no pope ever spoke favorably of war or allied the papacy to the cause of a warring nation.

Ministering to the Victims

Instead of offering assistance to the belligerents—as popes of old had done only too often—Benedict XV put the resources of the Catholic Church to work for the *victims* of the war. World War I produced turmoil and suffering on an unprecedented scale. Never had so many noncombatants been uprooted and dispossessed of their homelands. As just one example, nearly one million Armenians (who lived in the northeastern corner of today's Turkey) were either massacred or deported from their homes. All over the war-torn world, hundreds of thousands of people were victimized by hunger, many to the point of starvation.

Benedict put the Vatican's bureaucracy in the service of those victimized by the strife. Vatican officials acted as intermediaries in prisoner exchanges, financed housing facilities for the sick and wounded, and opened orphanages for children whose parents had either been killed or simply lost in the confusion of deportations and exiles. Perhaps the greatest service performed by Vatican officials, as well as by bishops in war-torn areas, was to establish missing-persons bureaus. In Germany alone, Catholic bishops processed close to a million inquiries into the status of missing persons and actually located a large number of the missing who were still alive.

The Loss of Political Credibility

When World War I ended the victors excluded the papacy from the postwar peace conference. This was a departure from the practice at the conclusion of nearly every other war involving European nations.

The popes of the 19th century, by their intransigence in the face of liberalism, had by now convinced the great powers that the papacy did not comprehend modern political realities. Further, since Catholic nations had not heeded the Benedict's repeated calls to stop the bloodshed and seek a peaceful solution to the conflict, European politicans correctly concluded that the Pope's influence in affairs of State was at an end.

Benedict XV had unwittingly contributed to this development by urging peace only in the vaguest and most "spiritual" of terms. Never during the war did he propose specific guidelines for the settlement of the conflict. Toward the end of the war when the Pope's talented nuncio to Germany, Eugenio Pacelli (the future Pope Pius XII), began to propose concrete solutions, it was too late to make a difference. By 1917 the Vatican was no longer considered a credible political entity.

The Aftermath of World War I

Perhaps because World War I occupied so much of Benedict's energy, he lacked the capacity to continue Catholicism's war with the modern world. Yet, in a certain sense, World War I seemed in retrospect something of a vindication for the "hands-off" policy toward modern times adopted by Benedict's predecessors.

World War I, in a sense, represented "enlightened" liberalism's admission of defeat. If, as the liberals promised, humanity left to its own devices could march unimpeded into a new world of unlimited progress, then why had humanity succumbed to a war more brutal and destructive than any ever fought by partisans of the Old Regime? Why had enlightened self-interest, why had a humanity supremely confident in its own abilities been unable to prevent a new and more terrible episode of slaughter? In short, why had the Enlightenment philosophes' "new humanity," which worshiped itself rather than God, not produced its promised brave new world?

Humanity's faith in progress was badly shaken after World War I. Although no one was ready to reestablish the ancient alliance between throne and altar, many wondered if the papacy and the Catholic Church—the two most stable absolutes in a world of confusing relativism—did not possess at least some degree of wisdom after all. By mobilizing the Church's resources on behalf of the war's poor and lowly, the Pope restored the Catholic Church as a focal point for absolute values in a postwar world which had largely come to doubt liberalism's belief in human self-perfectibility and the inevitability of social progress. This was the principal achievement of Benedict XV.

The Rise of Totalitarianism

The failure of European liberalism, as evidenced by World War I's new age of barbarism, gave birth to a new type of political entity—the totalitarian state. The agents of this new entity were Marxism-Leninism in Russia, Fascism in Italy and National Socialism in Germany. Whatever the label and however these states claimed to be guided, the results in Russia, Germany and, to a lesser degree, Italy were the same—the control by tyrants of the *totality* of human existence.

For the first time in history, despots possessed the technology to manipulate every aspect of human existence—thought, feeling, belief, behavior—so as to model human nature into a preconceived ideological pattern. The French Revolution's ambitious proclamation of "liberty, equality, fraternity" was as laughable to dictators like Stalin, Hitler and Mussolini as the Apostles' Creed. By the end of World War I Europeans had lost confidence in Liberalism and Christianity in equal measure. Many could now put their trust only in totalitarian creeds which, when imposed at the end of bayonets by demagogic egomaniacs, inspired a renewed if uncertain feeling of hope.

Communism, Fascism and Nazism sounded the death knell for optimistic liberalism at the same time they tolled Christianity's failure to respond to humankind's deepest aspirations. Had the Church of the 19th century been able to preach the gospel in terms that appealed to modern men and women, there would have been no need for those men and women to convert to the new State religions proclaimed by Marx, Lenin, Stalin, Hitler and Mussolini.

Europe following World War I was dominated by utopian ideologies which debased the human person while exalting the State as a quasi-religious entity. It was in this new Europe that Popes Pius XI and XII assumed their pontificates.

PIUS XI—BETWEEN WORLD WARS

Achille Ratti, cardinal-archbishop of Milan, was 65 years old when 42 out of the 53 cardinals meeting in conclave elected him as Pope Pius XI on February 6, 1922. In his first encyclical Pius XI showed a keen grasp of the problems confronting the postwar world. Far from shunning the modern world, Pius asserted that the Church must play a leading role in society if Christianity was to survive in the face of totalitarian ideologies. Pius combined the intellectual acumen of a scholar (he had once served as prefect of the Vatican Library) with the common sense of a pastor. His motto was "The peace of Christ in the kingship of Christ," and he dedicated his papacy to winning back for the Church the prestige which a kingly savior deserved.

A New Kind of Pope

Pius liked to stroll unannounced through curial offices shouting, "Life is action!" or, "Don't put off until tomorrow what you can do today!" Unlike his predecessors who had set up commissions of cardinals to study nearly every conceivable matter, Pius disliked delegating authority and ran the Vatican ship with his own hand at the helm. As a scholar, he did not feel as threatened by the Modernists as had Pius X, and thus he retreated from Pius X's campaign against them. He even reinstated several eminent professors who had been purged by Pius X, and he encouraged the study of modern science in Catholic schools. To ward off even the appearance of impropriety in his personal life (and as if to announce that papal nepotism had finally come to an end), he visited with his relatives in rooms reserved for official public audiences. To the end of his life he fasted and prayed like a monk.

When Pius XI announced in 1936 the formation of the Vatican Academy of Science and invited important scientists (Protestant and Catholic) from around the world to present lectures, he in effect declared an end to the papacy's war against modern culture. The Pope updated seminarian instruction by calling for the introduction of modern educational methods. In his many encyclicals he admonished world leaders to treat defeated and uprooted national minorities with compassion and respect.

Pius XI tried in every conceivable way to bring the richness of the Catholic past into constructive union with the present age. He urged peaceful dialogue between Protestants and Catholics. He praised Thomas Aquinas as the paragon of Christian scholars, urged the Franciscans to revivify the spirit of their founder, and celebrated the 1500th anniversary of St. Augustine's death by giving a lecture on the harmonious union of faith and reason which this greatest of Western bishops had epitomized.

Social and Spiritual Concerns

Pius XI was no sycophant, however. He confronted Communism head-on, putting the Catholic Church on record as irrevocably opposed to the world-changing events taking place in Russia. In Italy, Spain, Portugal and Austria he personally promoted "Catholic Action"—unions or associations of Catholic politicians, students, intellectuals or laborers all working for the promotion of social change in harmony with the Gospels. With his encyclical *Quadragesimo Anno* (1931), "on the 40th year" after Leo XIII's *Rerum Novarum*, Pius XI reaffirmed Leo's concern for the laboring poor, emphasizing the harm resulting to workers from unrestricted competition and centralized administrative control of their lives.

Stressing that socialism was incompatible with Christianity because it substituted the State for the family as the fundamental unit of society, Pius recommended the formation of laborers' guilds by which industrial workers could control their own destiny. The greatest hardship caused by modern industrialism, Pius said, was the separation of workers from the products of their labor. If his solution to this problem—the guild system—strikes us as anachronistic, we should nonetheless give Pius credit. Today's corporations are adopting a similar idea through such mechanisms as "quality circles," where workers are encouraged to participate in the entire gamut of the production process.

Aside from his interest in such practical concerns as workers' life-styles, Pius XI was also devoted to the improvement of the Church's spiritual condition. He sponsored several Jubilee Years and Eucharistic Congresses. To tie the modern Church to the greatest moments of Catholicism's past, he advocated numerous canonizations. During his pontificate Robert Bellarmine, Peter Canisius, Albert the Great, John Vianney, John Bosco, Bernadette Soubirous, John Fisher and Thomas More all entered the ranks of canonized saints.

Pius's overarching concern was to bring Catholicism into the modern world as a respected and credible witness to the gospel; he wanted to reestablish a truly universal Church which, like the apostle Paul, would become all things to all people in order to save at least some of them. In many respects Pope Pius XI has not received the praise he deserves for rerouting the Church toward reconciliation with modern times. His historical anonymity is tied to the fact that his pontificate was eclipsed by that of one of the most talented men ever to occupy St. Peter's throne, Pope Pius XII, whom we shall discuss shortly.

Pius XI and the Dictators

The greatest challenge of Pius XI's pontificate involved the Church's relationship with the postwar dictatorships. Just as he had sought to end the Church's battle with modern culture, so too Pius XI realized that nothing could be gained either by simply ignoring the postwar dictatorships or by condemning them out of hand. Pius took his first step toward normalization of relations with the new regimes by agreeing to negotiate a concordat with the Italian Fascist leader, Benito Mussolini.

In secret negotiations between 1926 and 1929, the Italian government and the Vatican eventually concluded the Lateran Treaty of June 7, 1929. For the first time the Vatican recognized the legitimacy of the Italian government. Italy, for its part, recognized Vatican City as a sovereign state and compensated the Vatican in the amount of 1.75 billion lire for the seizure of the former Papal States. Mussolini also guaranteed autonomy for Italian Catholic Action—that is, for independent groups of students who pursued their own social agenda free of Fascist control.

As Catholic Action gradually began to pose a threat to Fascist monopoly of the political process, Mussolini reneged on his guarantee of autonomy. In 1931 all associations not submitted to Fascist control were dissolved. In an encyclical of June 29, 1931, Pius XI struck back, condemning Fascism as a "deification of the State." Fascism, Pius concluded, "is not compatible with Catholic teaching."

Mussolini yielded and entered into a compromise agreement in which Catholic Action was allowed to exist, but only in 250 separate geographical units corresponding to the boundaries of Italy's dioceses, thus, for all practical purposes, destroying Catholic Action's effectiveness. Pius XI accepted this compromise begrudgingly, and only because it was the best that could be made of a bad situation.

By 1938 when Italy allied itself to Nazi Germany, relations between the Vatican and "Il Duce" were strained to the breaking point. Pius XI condemned Hitler's racist theories in no uncertain terms. The tenuous concord between Church and State in Italy evaporated for good when Mussolini's government ruled that Church-sanctioned marriages between Jews and Catholics were invalid according to civil law. From that moment until Mussolini's fall from power in 1943, the Vatican cooperated with the Italian government only insofar as necessary to maintain the Church's independent existence.

Pius's relationship with the dictatorships could perhaps be characterized as "spiritual pragmatism." His own words on the occasion of undertaking negotiations with the Soviet Union can best explain his approach: "If there would be a question of saving a single soul," Pius said, "...then we would have the courage to treat with the Devil in person."[1] (In actuality, the Pope's negotiations with the Soviet Union came to nothing. Vatican Secretary of State Eugenio Pacelli could not induce Stalin to make even the slightest concessions to the Church's quest for autonomy.)

With Hitler's Germany the Vatican concluded the Concordat of 1933 by which Hitler promised (as had Mussolini) to guarantee the autonomy of various Catholic associations. Since the concordat permitted the government to decide which associations would enjoy this guarantee, the Vatican's ratification of the treaty was a great blunder. Hitler flaunted the concordat as a sign of the Pope's support for Nazi policies, and thus achieved a major propaganda victory. Many German Catholics interpreted the concordat as a green light for compromise with Nazism, whereas Pius had ratified the treaty simply to buy a modicum of independence for the German Church and had otherwise persistently condemned the Nazi program.

Gradually, as Hitler's heinous policies became more apparent, Vatican Secretary of State Pacelli tried to distance the Church from the Nazi regime. Pacelli, for example, condemned Nazism's "divinity of race" and its "absolutizing of the nation."

When the Nazis flagrantly violated the Concordat of 1933 by abolishing all associations which were not subordinated to the Nazi party, Pius XI sent the bishops of Germany his encyclical *Mit Brennender Sorge* ("With burning anxiety"). On Palm Sunday 1937 the encyclical was read in every Catholic parish in Germany. In the most strident terms Pius virtually declared war on Nazism, which he chacterized as "idolatrous worship" completely incompatible with Christian faith. Pius decried the Nazi belief in the State as an entity superior to the individual. In contradistinction to Nazism, the Pope said, the individual person has "God-given rights" which cannot be abrogated by the State.

Pius XI wanted the Catholics of Germany to understand that the Third Reich was engaged in a campaign to destroy Christianity, and that their pope had unequivocally identified himself as the foe of Nazism. Hitler responded to *Mit Brennender Sorge* with a propaganda campaign intended to drive a wedge between German Catholics and their bishops and pope.

The leaders of the Third Reich eventually abolished all parochial schools in Germany proper as well as in the newly-annexed Sudetenland (sections of northern Bohemia and Moravia). By the time of Pius's death on February 10, 1939—just eight months before Hitler's invasion of Poland precipitated World War II—the Third Reich and the Vatican had become implacable foes.

Pius XII and World War II

The odds-on favorite to succeed Pius XI was his talented secretary of state, Eugenio Pacelli. Pacelli's outstanding intellectual and spiritual qualities were so prominent that the electoral conclave lasted only one day. On March 2, 1939, Pacelli became Pope Pius XII. Like his predecessor Benedict XV, Pius XII served the Church in an age of world war. As Hitler's invasion of Poland drew nearer, Pius urgently pleaded for peace. Yet, as with Benedict XV, world leaders ignored the Pope's appeal. The cynical Communist leader Joseph Stalin, when told of the Pope's admonitions, asked, "How many divisions does the Pope have?"

A Policy of Impartiality

Pius stayed in his residence in Rome all during the war, thereby winning for himself the affection of Italy's Catholics. He turned Vatican offices into a missing-persons bureau, furnishing information to the families of nearly two million soldiers on both sides of the conflict. Like Benedict XV, Pius adopted a posture of strict neutrality, although he preferred to call his policy "impartiality."

The Pope explained his choice of words by saying that neutrality connoted "passive indifference," while impartiality meant "judgment of things in accord with the truth."[2] In a famous Christmas radio broadcast he declared that the Church as a mother should not be asked "to favor or to oppose the part of one or the other of her children."[3]

Pius's policy of impartiality gained him detractors on both sides. While Rome lay under the control of the Axis powers, Pius sheltered in the Vatican Allied diplomats and couriers, thereby guaranteeing their diplomatic immunity. Franklin Roosevelt's aide Myron C. Taylor, for example, made seven trips to Rome during the height of the war, something that would have been impossible had not the Vatican served as a safe haven for Allied diplomats. By the same token, when the Allies drove the Germans out of Rome, Pius offered the same immunity to Axis diplomats, earning for himself the opprobrium of several Allied newspapers.

Pius's impartiality was based on his belief that the Church's independence and unity had to be preserved at all costs, even to the extent of alienating countries who fought to destroy the monstrous Nazi State. As a skilled diplomat, however, Pius XII did not hesitate to lecture the world on the conditions necessary for securing a lasting peace. He thus called for the establishment of an international institution that would have legal authority to assure the political independence and economic stability of all nations and peoples.

The condition of postwar Europe if Pius XII's call for an international tribunal went unheeded was bluntly prophesied by Pius's secretary of state, Cardinal Domenico Tardini: "Two dangers threaten European and Christian civilization, Nazism and Communism. Both are materialistic, antireligious, totalitarian, cruel, and militaristic." Only

84

if both dangers were eliminated, he continued, could "a peaceful and ordered coexistence of European nations"[4] be possible.

Pius XII and the Jews

Beginning sometime in 1943,* information began to reach the Vatican of Hitler's extermination of Jews, subjugated national minority groups and Catholic religious leaders who had not succumbed to Nazism. Pius secretly began to provide information about these atrocities to Allied headquarters in London and to assist elements of the German underground to coordinate their activities with Allied intelligence. Publicly, however, Pius remained "impartial." When American Jews urged the Pope to take a firm stance condemning Hitler's "Aryan" policies, the Vatican replied perfunctorily that it was already doing all it could do.

Behind the scenes, however, Pius XII supervised several diplomatic lifesaving missions to countries where Hitler's murderous policies were taking effect. One prominent historian[5] estimates that these missions were directly responsible for saving well over half a million Jews from extermination.

Why did Pius XII not make his condemnation of Hitler's atrocities more public and vocal? Pius feared an even worse holocaust if the Catholic Church were to launch an aggressive anti-Nazi campaign. Pius XI, with his publication of *Mit Brennender Sorge*, had learned the hard way that public resistance to Nazism was brutally counterproductive. In order to prevent even worse reprisals against the Jews and other victims of Nazi murders, Pius therefore continued secret diplomacy to save the Jews while maintaining in public only a vague posture of disapproval. According to Vatican Secretary of State Tardini, a vigorous public condemnation by the Pope would have simply stirred the Nazis "to carry out even more vigorously the anti-Jewish measures."[6]

After the war Jewish leaders came forward to praise Pius XII for his efforts on behalf of their persecuted brothers and sisters. Because of Pius's efforts on behalf of the Jews and other war victims, one postwar observer wrote, "at no time since 1848 has the papacy had so good an international press as today."[7]

Until Pius's death his reputation as an advocate of Jewish freedom remained unsmeared. Not until the publication in 1963 of a

---

* For several years the Nazis had managed to hide from the world the horrible truth of what was actually going on inside their "deportation camps." Allied armies themselves were shocked to discover, as late as 1945, the magnitude of the slaughter that had taken place in the concentration camps which they liberated.

play entitled *The Deputy* were questions raised about Pius's "silence" on the Jewish issue. The play defamed Pius by portraying him as an underhanded cohort of the Nazis. The furor surrounding *The Deputy*, which by all scholarly opinion was completely inaccurate in its depiction of the Pope's activities, proved the old adage that people simply believe whatever they choose to believe.

Openness to Change

Aside from his wartime activities, Pope Pius XII continued Pius XI's policy of updating Catholicism by seeking to find common ground with the modern world. As an indication of this process of reconciliation, Pius elevated a large number of non-Italian bishops to the cardinalate. By 1953 only one-third of the College of Cardinals was Italian. In this respect, at least, the Catholic Church was now steering toward true universality.

In his encyclicals Pius XII continued to show openness to change. In *Mediator Dei* (1947), for example, he anticipated Vatican II's liturgical renewal by emphasizing the laity's role as true participants in the Mass. And in *Humani Generis* (1950) Pius spoke favorably of adjusting theology to the insights of modern scientific methods, but at the same time he condemned certain modern belief systems. (He singled out Existentialism, a philosophy which, in certain respects, tends to define salvation strictly in terms of one's own choices for authentic existence.)

In *Divino Afflante Spiritu* (1943), issued on the 50th anniversary of Leo XIII's *Providentissimus Deus* (see p. 68), Pius encouraged modern biblical scholarship by allowing Catholic exegetes to undertake textual criticism of the Bible. Pius thus enabled Catholic biblical scholars to analyze the text of the ancient Latin *Vulgate* and point out any errors which were unrelated to faith and morals.

This new freedom prepared the ground for updated Catholic translations of the Bible two decades later, such as the *New American Bible* and *The Jerusalem Bible*. Pius encouraged biblical scholars to probe into the authorship of the Bible's books so as to situate those books in their historical and cultural milieu. He also encouraged the use of history, archaeology and literary criticism as scholarly tools.

Divino Afflante Spiritu, more than any other development since the time of the Modernist crisis, signaled the demise of the Church's war with modern thought. Pius's pontificate, in the words of one of the most respected works on modern biblical scholarship, "marked a complete about-face and inaugurated the greatest renewal of interest in the Bible that the Roman Catholic Church has ever seen."[8]

The Assumption of Mary

Without doubt, Pius's most famous encyclical was *Munificentissimus Deus* (1950). In it he taught, as a matter of infallible dogma, that Mary, the mother of Jesus, "having completed her earthly course, was in body and soul assumed into heavenly glory."

The Church's belief in Mary's Assumption was an ancient one (see *People of the Creed*, p. 144). By declaring this belief to be divinely revealed dogma, Pius was merely restating what the Church had long believed. The encyclical was no doubt motivated at least in part by the growing effect on the Catholic world of the Marian apparitions at Lourdes and Fatima. Pius himself was said to have experienced several visions of Mary during the weeks prior to the proclamation of the Assumption doctrine.

The doctrine of the Assumption, along with Pope Pius IX's encyclical on the Immaculate Conception (see p. 44), constitute two of the greatest obstacles to reunion among Christians. Pius XII, an astute observer of the modern world, unquestionably realized that his encyclical on the Assumption would send shock waves throughout the Protestant and Orthodox Churches (as it did). Further Mariological reflection by both Protestants and Catholics is no doubt needed before all Christians can state their position on Mary in commonly accepted language.

TOWARD CATHOLIC RENEWAL

The pontificates of Benedict XV, Pius XI and Pius XII, taken as a whole, represent a gradual erosion—a disavowal even—of the fearful and obscurantist policies of their predecessors. Because of the change in attitudes of these three popes, the Catholic world was gradually prepared for the most all-encompassing updating of the Catholic faith ever achieved. Beginning in the next chapter, then, we take up the story of the remarkable process of renewal which culminated in the Second Vatican Council.

CHAPTER EIGHT

AGGIORNAMENTO

John XXIII, Paul VI and the Second Vatican Council (1958-1978)

The Conclave of Cardinals which met in 1958 to elect Pius XII's successor chose the patriarch of Venice, Angelo Giuseppe Roncalli. Roncalli named himself John XXIII, in order to settle a controversy which had erupted during the course of a papal schism in the 15th century (see *The People of the Faith*, p. 142). By selecting the same name as that chosen by one of the protagonists in the schism, John said, in effect, let's allow that episode in our history to die a peaceful death.

John XXIII was competent to make such a historical judgment; he had served in his early days as a professor of Church history. But while his name selection may have concluded one tumultuous era in Church history, he was about to inaugurate an even more tumultuous one. In fact, the world was about to witness the most revolutionary renewal of the Catholic Church ever undertaken.

A MAN NAMED JOHN

Who was this simple man from peasant stock whom the cardinals had elected at age 76 to be (they thought) a "transition pope"? John's portrait next to that of Pius XII provides a striking contrast. Pius, the thin, refined, seldom-smiling patrician from one of Rome's best families looks almost uncomfortable in the presence of the chubby, squat peasant with the air of a mischievous schoolboy. A military chaplain during World War I, avid student of Church history and patrology, apostolic delegate to Turkey and Greece and later nuncio to France, John surprised everyone by the depth of knowledge and diplomatic common sense which coexisted with his affable, lighthearted manner.

John was a deeply spiritual man (as indeed were all the popes from Pius IX onward). His devotional life was influenced largely by Thomas à Kempis, Ignatius Loyola, Charles Borromeo and, above all, the Virgin Mary, in whose honor John recited the Rosary daily. Because of his sponsorship of Vatican II, it is tempting to think of John as a radical who wanted to break with Catholic tradition. Nothing could be farther from the truth. John was at heart a traditional country pastor with a high degree of common sense born with an instinctive ability to read the signs of the times.

Precisely because of this unique combination of a highly developed historical consciousness and a practical, commonsense way of looking at life, John concluded that his Catholic tradition needed a good measure of updating. Perhaps in the same way that John's farming kinfolk would have thought it senseless to continue using agricultural methods that new technology had long since improved upon, pastor John spontaneously decided to plow up the Church's soil in order to improve the harvest.

Shortly after he became pope, John began to make remarks about the need for modernizing the Church which caused curial officials and cardinals from "better stock" to wonder if John's election had not been a mistake. The aristocratic Cardinal Spellman of New York, for example, publicly expressed his disdain for John by saying, "He's no pope—he should be selling bananas."[1] Spellman, for his part, played the cardinal role to the hilt. He was fond of wearing satin gowns with trains so long that two priests had to carry them—an absurdly anachronistic symbol of the degree to which some bishops lived in the medieval past.

John was well aware that such hierarchical power brokers as Spellman looked upon him as a laughable peasant who, as pope, could not do the Church any harm until a younger and more urbane pope came along to succeed him. On his way to the conclave which elected him, John had remarked, "Rome will be a bed of thorns."[2] Aside from the fact that John had no affection for curial politics, his feelings about traveling to the conclave stemmed from an underlying premonition, which he shared with his most trusted friends, that he might be elected pope. Once actually elected, he knew what he must do: convene an ecumenical council that would inaugurate what he called "a new Pentecost."

INAUGURATING THE COUNCIL

Before he left for Rome, Archbishop Roncalli had made an enigmatic statement to the seminarians of Venice: "The Church is young," he said. "It remains, as constantly in its history, amenable to change."[3] Few could have guessed what John had in mind by this statement—nothing less than the convocation of a council dedicated, as John put it in his opening speech at Vatican II (October 11, 1962), to making the Church "greater in spiritual riches, gain new strength and energies, and look to the future without fear."[4]

In this inaugural address, Pope John issued a ringing declaration on behalf of renewal which shocked many old-guard bishops in attendance:

> In the everyday exercise of our pastoral ministry, greatly to our sorrow, we sometimes have to listen to those who, although consumed with zeal, do not have very much judgment or balance. To them the modern world is nothing but betrayal and ruination. They claim that this age is far worse than previous ages, and they go on as though they had learned nothing at all from history—and yet history is the great teacher of life. They behave as though the first five centuries saw a complete vindication of the Christian idea and the Christian cause, and as though religious liberty was never put in jeopardy in the past.
>
> We feel bound to disagree with these prophets of misfortune who are forever forecasting calamity—as though the end of the world were imminent.[5]

Going on to explain his purpose for convening the Council, John said:

> Our task is not merely to hoard this precious treasure [Church doctrine], as though obsessed with the past, but to give ourselves eagerly and without fear to the task that the present age demands of us—and in so doing we will be faithful to what the Church has done in the past 20 centuries.
>
> So the main point of this Council will not be to debate this or that article of basic Church doctrine that has been repeatedly taught by the Fathers and theologians old and new and which we can take as read. We do not need a Council to do that. But starting from a renewed, serene and calm acceptance of the whole teaching of the Church...Christians and Catholics...all over the world expect a leap forward in doctrinal fidelity to authentic teaching. But this authentic doctrine has to be studied and expounded in the light of the research methods and the language of modern thought. For the substance of the ancient deposit of faith is one thing, and the way in which it is presented is another.[6]

VATICAN II: AGENDA, FORMAT, DOCUMENTS

Pope John envisaged a threefold program for reform: (1) unity among Catholics, (2) unity among Christians and (3) unity of humankind. Taken together, these three points constituted Pope John's plan for conciliar *aggiornamento* ("renewal").

As soon as John had announced his decision to convene the Council (January 25, 1959), it became obvious that Vatican II would not be simply a 20th-century version of Vatican I. For one thing, many more bishops, abbots and other religious leaders would attend Vatican II than had attended Vatican I (see p. 47). Some 2,540 voting delegates at the first session would make this the most well-attended council in history. It was not just the *quantity* of delegates that made Vatican II different, however, but the *quality* of delegates as well. Whereas Vatican I had been virtually an Italian bishops' synod, at Vatican II the Italian delegation numbered only 379, less than one-fifth of the total.

Further, Vatican II invited Protestant and Orthodox nonvoting "observers," as well as nonvoting lay Catholic men and eventually even a handful of women as "hearers" of the theological debates. And unlike Vatican I, where Pius IX's handpicked theologians and canon lawyers submitted the agenda to the delegates, at Vatican II delegates themselves were among those who prepared the items to be debated by the full Council.

By August 6, 1962, the various preparatory commissions had completed some 69 proposals to be debated. These proposals were, in turn, refined by the "Central Commission," the committee which drew up the rules by which the council would function. The actual debate on the floor of the Council was supervised by a "Presidency" of 10 cardinals (later expanded to 12) appointed by Pope John. The Pope reserved the right to intervene in the debate, as well as the right to veto any conciliar decree.

Unlike previous councils, Vatican II did not issue "anathemas" ("let it be cursed")—that is, statements condemning erroneous doctrines. In keeping with Pope John's intent, Vatican II was to be *for* renewal rather than *against* errors. The achievement of the Council was put into the written form of four "Constitutions," nine "Decrees" and three "Declarations." These writings, arranged in order of descending authority, are listed in the box on the facing page.

We could perhaps summarize this threefold hierarchy of Council decisions in this way: (1) The four Constitutions restated unalterable Catholic *doctrine*. (2) The Decrees proposed nine categories of *renewal* requiring further implementation. (3) The Declarations gave apostolic *instruction* on three important subjects. Much of the confusion about Vatican II has resulted from people's *leveling* this hierarchy of truths and assigning all of the Council documents equal weight. In actuality, the nine Decrees and three Declarations are very flexible, "breathing" documents, intended to be given ongoing life by the world's bishops in consonance with the teaching of the four Constitutions.

DOCUMENTS OF VATICAN II*

Constitutions

On the Sacred Liturgy (December 4, 1963)

On the Church (November 21, 1964)

On Divine Revelation (November 18, 1965)

On the Church in the Modern World (December 7, 1965)

Decrees

On the Means of Social Communication (December 4, 1963)

On the Catholic Eastern Churches (November 21, 1964)

On Ecumenism (November 21, 1964)

On the Pastoral Office of Bishops in the Church (October 28, 1965)

On the Up-to-Date Renewal of Religious Life (October 28, 1965)

On the Training of Priests (October 28, 1965)

On the Apostolate of Laypeople (November 18, 1965)

On the Church's Missionary Activity (December 7, 1965)

On the Ministry and Life of Priests (December 7, 1965)

Declarations

On Christian Education (October 28, 1965)

On the Relation of the Church to Non-Christian Religions (October 28, 1965)

On Religious Liberty (December 7, 1965)

---

* Arranged in order of descending authority, with the dates on which they were approved.

The bishops at Vatican II did not write a new Bible, as it were. Rather, they reincorporated the ancient truths of the faith, dressed them in modern garb and then gave them to their brother bishops saying, in effect, "Here is our definitive statement of modern Catholicism. Now you, along with the priests, religious and laity in your dioceses, figure out how to put these documents into effect in the real world in which you live."

A NEW POPE CONTINUES JOHN'S WORK

On June 6, 1963, Pope John XXIII died as a man deeply loved by nearly all who knew him. His successor was the cardinal-archbishop of Milan and a leading progressive spokesman at the temporarily interrupted Council—Giovanni Battista Montini, Pope Paul VI (1963-1978).

Pope Paul defined his own agenda for the reconvened council at the start of Session II on September 29, 1963, as follows: (1) a doctrinal statement on the *identity and mission of the Church*, which would (2) clarify the relationship between pope and bishops, so that the *collegiality* of the Bishop of Rome with his brother bishops would be emphasized, while at the same time, (3) the *laity as participants* with the hierarchy would seek (4) to bring *separated Christians* into a renewed and reincorporated Body of Christ.

Under Pope Paul's leadership the Council moved forward with Pope John's "new Pentecost." Pope John died before the Council issued a single formal decision. It was Pope Paul, through Conciliar Sessions II (September 29—December 4, 1963), III (September 14—November 21, 1964) and IV (September 14—December 8, 1965), who concretized John's vision by overseeing the promulgation of the documents listed on p. 93. On December 6, 1965, the Council delegates greeted the Pope and his 24 concelebrants at the closing Mass with thunderous applause. The Second Vatican Council would soon be history, but the Church would continue feeling the aftershocks from the upheaval.

In their understandable state of euphoria at the Council's conclusion, the bishops may not have appreciated how prophetic were the words spoken by Pope Paul during his homily: "...[N]ot a few questions which were taken up during the Council await a satisfactory conclusion."[7]

CHAPTER NINE

THE PROTESTANT PATH

An Overview of Protestant Theology
From the French Revolution to Vatican II (1800-1962)

Before saying more about Vatican II, we will examine in more detail some of the theological currents flowing in and around the corridors of the Church from the time of the French Revolution to the era of Vatican II. In so doing we will see that Vatican II is the culmination of a long process of evolution rather than a sudden revolution.

We will begin our study in this chapter with a summary of pre-Vatican II Protestant theology as it influenced Catholic thought. In the next two chapters we will take a look at the principal Catholic theological influences on the Council.

NEW DIRECTIONS IN THEOLOGY

Protestant theology from the time of the French Revolution until the 1960's was unquestionably more creative and innovative than Catholic theology. With no hierarchical censors looking over their shoulders, Protestant theologians could express themselves freely and openly. This is not to say that Protestant innovators were free from criticism or censure. In Protestant Prussia, for example, the State often exerted a power of censorship over dissenting voices every bit as harsh and effective as its curial counterpart in Rome. But even where there was State censorship or simply rejection by one's peers, Protestant theologians were nonetheless able to get their works published. On the other hand, innovative Catholic theologians who wanted to remain Catholic were often denied the *imprimatur*—and therefore publication—when they deviated from strict Thomism.

We concluded our discussion of Reformation-era Protestant theology in *The People of Anguish: The Story Behind the Reformation* by observing that Lutheran and Calvinist theologians had erected their own dogmatic systems, rivaling the ponderous systems of their Catholic predecessors. In Protestant universities theologians constructed doctrinal theologies every bit as intricate, elaborate and "philosophical" as anything the medieval Scholastics (who had been condemned by Luther and Calvin) had constructed. So closely had Reformation theologians patterned themselves after the methods of Catholic theology that by the 18th century it had even become fashionable to speak of "Protestant Scholasticism."

Thus by the early 19th century, there had unquestionably grown up a Protestant *tradition*, a word which Luther had blanched even to mutter, so antagonistic was he to any theology not based strictly on the Bible. This Protestant tradition, as with any intellectual system over a period of time, had become ossified and inflexible, absolutely certain of its premises and fearful of change and innovation. Like their Catholic counterparts, many orthodox Protestant theologians regarded the liberal philosophies of the Enlightenment as incompatible with the gospel. They too became conservative in their outlook, turning in upon themselves to fortify the structures of their own creeds and dogmas.

Friedrich Schleiermacher

Within this somewhat stifling climate there appeared "the progenitor of the spirit of modern religious understanding,"[1] and the father of modern Protestant theology, Friedrich Schleiermacher (1768-1834). Schleiermacher had been raised in a Pietist environment (see *The People of Anguish*, pp. 160-161) and thus was disposed from early age toward a religious outlook inspired by feeling. As a preacher in Berlin's State-supported Trinity Church (whose congregation was comprised of both Lutheran and Reformed members) and as a professor of theology at the University of Berlin, Schleiermacher worked to integrate Romanticism into Protestant theology.

Like the Enlightenment philosophes, Schleiermacher believed that religious sentiment is an innate human attribute. In *The Soliloquies* (1800) he spoke of the individual's personal religious feeling as the basis of all organized belief systems. In another publication he characterized Christianity as a religion in which one is transformed by the sudden onrush of joy—"a universal pulsing of joy," as he put it—which comes from the work of Christ in the soul. In his masterpiece *The Christian Faith*, published first in 1821 and again in 1830, he spoke

96

of thinking and feeling as two essential components of theology. As he wrote to a friend, "Understanding and feeling in me...remain distinct, but they touch each other and form a galvanic pile. To me it seems that the innermost life of the spirit consists in the galvanic action thus produced in the feeling of the understanding and the understanding of the feeling...."[2]

Schleiermacher's theology focused on the question, "What is human nature as it is affected both by God and the world?" Notice that unlike Luther and Calvin, who had started from the point of God and his revelation, Schleiermacher began with human beings, thus adopting the perspective of the 18th-century philosophes, who had based their own religious inquiry on the human person. This tendency by Schleiermacher troubled traditional Protestant theologians, some of whom spoke disparagingly of Schleiermacher's theology as "liberal theology."

Unlike his peers who spoke only of Christ, the Bible and Christian dogma, Schleiermacher's theology was concerned with *religion*. He wanted first to examine the universal human impulse toward the divine before examining its particular manifestation in Christianity. For him, religion is the self-awareness that one is absolutely dependent on God, "a sense and taste for the infinite," as he put it. Thus instead of starting theological inquiry with an analysis of dogma and morality, one should first investigate the universal religious feeling which everyone possesses and then reason back to Christianity as fulfillment of this feeling.

"Feeling," for Schleiermacher, is "the immediate presence of the whole, undivided personal existence, both sensible as well as spiritual, the unity of the person and its sensible and spiritual world."[3] Thus Schleiermacher's principal innovation—like the secular philosophes of the Enlightenment—was to study Christianity within the context of the universal human desire for transcendence.

Christianity, for Schleiermacher, is but one manifestation of religious sentiment, unique only in that the particular religious feeling which Christianity inspires has its origin in Jesus Christ. It is not its dogma which makes Christianity unique, Schleiermacher said—dogma, in fact, detracts from the genius of Christianity. Rather it is the person of Jesus Christ and the communication of his Spirit to human beings which stamps Christianity as unique.

Schleiermacher thus segregated theology from philosophy and rationalism. He grounded it in a personal faith based on inner transformation as experienced in the individual's sense of God's own Spirit stirring within the human soul. He returned Protestant theology

97

to Luther's emphasis on personal faith as the transforming power of Christ, downplaying Protestantism's reliance on dogma and speculation and emphasizing its starting point in personal experience. Yet by focusing on the individual and humanity's innate religious drive, he opened the awareness of Protestant theologians to the methods of psychology and science.

Henceforth liberal Protestant theology would concern itself with humankind as a thinking, feeling organism which gropes its way toward God in real-world situations that do not always fit into the neat categories defined in theology textbooks. Whereas theology previously had started with certain axiomatic "givens" from which it attempted to construct its vision of God, world and humanity, now humanity itself in all of its real-life complexities would be the basis of Protestant theological speculation.

Søren Kierkegaard

Schleiermacher's theology influenced one of the most significant religious thinkers of all time, Søren Kierkegaard (1813-1855). Kierkegaard was born into a wealthy Copenhagen family and, because of a physical handicap and a melancholy spirit, became a brooding, introverted man who could find little in life to enjoy. As he listened to his father's companions discuss nothing but business and money-making for hours on end, he wondered how it was that these men could call themselves Christian.

As Søren surveyed Denmark's middle-class Lutheran society with an ever-more-jaundiced eye, he became convinced that the so-called Christians of his day knew and lived nothing of the gospel. Being a good Danish Christian, Kierkegaard concluded, "meant being a respectable, prosperous and satisfied citizen, content like a goose being overfed for Michaelmas and with no desire to use its wings and fly."⁴ He thus began to write treatises (often pseudonymously) in which he condemned this false Christianity of civic virtue.

In a work entitled *Either/Or* Kierkegaard described people living three levels of existence: (1) *the aesthetic*, in which one simply pursues comfort and sensory gratification; (2) *the ethical*, in which one ascribes to certain universally applicable norms of conduct; and (3) *the specifically Christian*, in which one's existence is transformed from ethics and civic virtue to a state of love and absolute dependence on God. Kierkegaard characterized middle-class civic piety (the chamber-of-commerce ethos of his day) as living on "level A." What is needed, he argued, is to get people to move from "A" to "B," or to a specifically Christian life-style.

In *The Attack Upon Christendom* he described the clergy as "shopkeepers' souls in velvet" and as "cannibals," who perpetuated a false religiosity by telling people what they wanted to hear—namely, that their wealth, prestige, power and fame were God's reward for hard work. In contrast to this spurious Christianity, Kierkegaard preached a Christianity based on suffering, repentance, humility and the total surrender of one's self into the hands of God. "Infinite humiliation and grace," he said, "and then a striving grounded in gratitude, this is Christianity."[5]

Kierkegaard is commonly regarded as the founder of Existentialism. For him, life is not a logical system capable of being integrated into the doctrinal categories of theologians. Rather, life is made up of irrational paradoxes and complexities. The starting point of growth toward the Christian life is human existence, by which Kierkegaard meant "men's peculiar predicament as the creature of God, dependent absolutely for his being upon that God's creative fiat."[6] Yet human existence at the same time comprises the freedom to shape its own destiny, so that responsible human existence involves a constant choosing of alternatives which lead either to an authentic or inauthentic life-style.

For Kierkegaard, "truth is subjectivity"—that is, truth exists only as the individual experiences it in his or her response to God's love. There is no objective truth expressed as absolute dogma which is universally applicable to everyone. "God," Kierkegaard wrote, "is a subject and therefore exists only for subjectivity in inwardness"; in other words, God and his demands on the human person can only be known by that person from within, not by ascribing to certain tenets of dogma. Hence the term *Existentialism*, the belief that one is ultimately responsible for one's *existence* through the life choices which one makes.

Existentialism came to mean other things in the form preached by atheistic 20th-century philosophers like Jean-Paul Sartre (1905-1980). For them existentialism stood for the proposition, as Sartre put it, that "existence precedes essence"—that is, the fact *that* one is prior to *what* one is. And since there is no God, Sartre said, human beings are responsible to no one and have absolute freedom to become whatever they choose.

Kierkegaard certainly did not teach this form of Existentialism. He insisted that one's existential, moment-to-moment choices must always be submitted to the authority of God and guided by the love of Jesus Christ in whom God has spoken the ultimate word about the meaning of human existence.

Rudolf Otto

Both Schleiermacher and Kierkegaard attempted to move Protestant theology away from speculative dogma and overly rationalistic analysis toward the subjective and intuitive awareness of God as mystery. This tendency reached its climax in the person of Rudolf Otto (1869-1937), a professor of theology at the University of Marburg in central west Germany.

In *Naturalism and Religion* (1904) Otto spoke of "the fresh revelation of the depth of things and of appearance, the increasing recognition that our knowledge is only leading us toward mystery."[7] For Otto, creation is permeated by what he called "the numinous," a spiritual foundation to all things and the creative source of the physical world. This numinous realm is all-holy, and "wholly other," the ultimate mystery "which cannot be fully determined conceptually: It is nonrational, as is the beauty of a musical composition which also eludes complete conceptual analysis."[8]

Thus theology—the study of the all-holy—was for Otto "an attempted statement, in conceptual terms and by analogy, of something that at bottom is incapable of explication by concepts.[9] With Otto, Protestantism discovered the rich tradition of Byzantine mystagogy discussed in *The People of the Faith: The Story Behind the Church of the Middle Ages* (page 21).

Like Kierkegaard, Otto felt that the institutional Church of his day was in a state of decay. The reason for this, Otto thought, was that traditional theology had stripped Christianity of its numinous, mystical dimension. The core of the gospel, Otto believed, is the inbreaking Kingdom of God which, in the person of Jesus, brings the all-holy and the world into synthetic harmony. This Kingdom is a mystery which can be comprehended only by those whose consciousness has been attuned *by the holy* to the holy. Humanity by itself, Otto said, cannot recognize or appreciate the Kingdom of God by speaking only in empty theological concepts which do not transform the human heart. That is why, he said, the Church exists in a moribund, vacuous condition. People cannot be expected to *believe* that which they do not *experience*.

Otto felt that every person has a faculty which he called "divination," defined as the capability "of genuinely cognizing and recognizing the holy in its appearances."[10] The function of the Church, Otto believed, should be not the inculcation of doctrine but the training in divination. Otto devoted his career to assisting the Church in this task. Thus he studied Hindu mysticism, seeking to make available to Christianity the insights of one of the richest traditions of the East.

Otto's studies led Protestant theologians to consider Christianity as but one expression of a universal mystical impulse. His desire to restore the Christian's awareness of the all-holy led many Protestants to return to a more Catholic view of the Church in which the liturgy and the sacraments were looked upon as meeting-points between God and humanity—that is, as very tangible sources of holiness rather than simply as opportunities to hear the Bible or doctrine preached. Otto's all-encompassing respect for the world's non-Christian religions and his openness to the resources of Catholic mysticism were unquestionably important contributions to Vatican II's ecumenical spirit.

THE REVOLUTION IN BIBLICAL SCHOLARSHIP

Adolf von Harnack

Along with new directions in theology went an entirely new way of looking at the Bible. As we left Protestant biblical studies in the 18th century (see *The People of Anguish*, pp. 140-142, 145), we found everywhere a dependence on static literalism. In the 19th century all that changed. One of the leading forces for change was Adolf von Harnack (1851-1930), professor of Church history at the University of Berlin.

Harnack's historical studies led him to conclude that what has come down to us as Christianity—received traditions, dogmas and creeds, both Protestant and Catholic—is actually a distortion of original Christianity. The latter, he said, is not "the sum of doctrines handed down from generation to generation...but that disposition which the Father of Jesus Christ awakens in men's hearts through the gospel."[11] Thus the mission of the Church, Harnack said, is not to dispense doctrine but to proclaim the gospel in such a way that people are moved to reject or accept it.

Unlike Schleiermacher, Harnack was unconcerned with Christianity as an expression of the universal religious impulse. For Harnack, Christianity is *the* religion because, as he put it, "Jesus Christ is not one among other masters but *the* master, and because his gospel corresponds to the innate capacity of man as history discloses it."[12]

Harnack pursued the uniqueness of the Christian revelation to such a degree that he eventually concluded that the Church should not regard the Old Testament as inspired Scripture. Despite this shortcoming, Harnack's historical studies of the New Testament introduced an entirely new approach to biblical scholarship, characterized by an attempt to situate the various books in their historical and cultural settings.

Albert Schweitzer

Albert Schweitzer (1875-1965) employed the historical methodology in *The Quest of the Historical Jesus* (1906) in which he developed an interpretation known as "thoroughgoing eschatology." Jesus, Schweitzer said, had been motivated principally by the belief that his sacrificial death would usher in the end times. When this expectation failed to materialize, Schweitzer said, the early Christians began to "de-eschatologize" Jesus' teaching by forming doctrines that would make sense of continued human existence and give a rationale to ethical behavior.

Schweitzer's teaching that the Church must discover the authentic, "historical" Jesus, who was not necessarily the same person as the Jesus of the Gospels, was typical of an entire school of 19th-century Protestant biblical theology. By the first quarter of the 20th century, however, Protestant scholars had produced a bewildering variety of pictures of Jesus and the search for the historical Jesus led to a dead end of confusion. As a result two other Protestant Scripture scholars, the Englishman C. H. Dodd (1884-1973) and the German Rudolf Bultmann (1884-1976), developed interpretative methods of biblical exegesis which differed from Schweitzer's.

C. H. Dodd

Dodd's method led to the concept of "realized eschatology." This meant that in the person of Jesus the Kingdom of God is a fully present reality, so much so that Dodd viewed references in the New Testament to Jesus' Second Coming as "mere accommodation of language."[13] Each time the gospel brings a person to a crisis of belief in which he or she is transformed by the power of God, Dodd said, the Kingdom of God is present (for that person) in its fullness.

What we find in the New Testament, according to Dodd, is the record of Jesus' own interpretation of himself as the one who proclaims and brings into existence the messianic Kingdom prophesied in the Old Testament. Further, Dodd wrote, the New Testament is a portrait of how the early Church reacted to Jesus' proclamation of the Kingdom. Thus, while the Gospels are not biography, they are an accurate portrait nonetheless of the believing community as it mediates its understanding of Jesus to future generations through the written text of Scripture.

Rudolf Bultmann

Rudolf Bultmann was more skeptical than Dodd. From studying the New Testament, he said, "we can know almost nothing concerning the life and personality of Jesus."[14] Bultmann developed a discipline known as "form criticism," a scholarly tool for subdividing the various elements in the Gospel narratives into "forms"—such as parables, teachings, miracle stories, and so on. The Gospels, Bultmann said, are not true accounts of Jesus' ministry but the early Church's selective piecing together of preexisting forms for the purpose of evangelizing nonbelievers. What we have in the New Testament, therefore, is not history but a cleverly conceived myth about the God-man, a story which, while not factual, conveys a deeper, hidden truth—namely, God's plan for saving humanity through the person of Jesus.

Karl Barth

In contrast to the new wave of Protestant biblical scholarship represented by such exegetes as Schweitzer, Dodd and Bultmann, stands the work of the greatest Protestant theologian of the 20th century, Karl Barth (1886-1968). Barth rejected the liberal Protestant effort to "demythologize" the Bible—as Bultmann had written—and sought instead to read the Bible principally as God's call to conversion.

A professor of theology at the University of Basel in Switzerland, Barth had been raised in the liberal tradition and studied for a while under Harnack in Berlin. Ordained as a minister in 1909, Barth gradually became so disenchanted and confused by the findings of the new biblical scholarship that he considered leaving the ministry. He stated that when he stood before his flock in the pulpit he could think of nothing significant to tell them.

Like Luther before him, Barth sought refuge in the Epistle to the Romans. Here he suddenly discovered, as he would say later, "the strange new world within the Bible."[15] Barth concluded that the Bible focused on God as the center of the universe, whereas liberal theology had replaced God with humanity as the focal point of inquiry. From that moment on Barth became a persistent critic of Protestant liberalism and its new theories of biblical criticism.

Barth was an amazingly prolific systematizer whose voluminous treatises could justify our characterizing him as the Protestant Thomas Aquinas. His *Church Dogmatics*, unfinished at his death, comprised 12 volumes of nearly 1,000 pages each. Barth steered Protestantism away from Existentialism, mysticism and feeling and returned it to Luther's emphasis on the sovereignty of God and the supremacy of the Bible. Yet almost despite himself, Barth could not escape completely from the revolutionary findings of such men as Harnack, Schweitzer, Dodd and Bultmann; he was, therefore, no fundamentalist/literalist.

With Karl Barth Protestant biblical studies came of age. He

managed perhaps better than anyone in the 20th century—Catholic or Protestant—to unite the scholar's critical analysis of the Bible with the believer's humble submission to the Word of God. In him both the childish literalism of the 16th and 17th centuries and the adolescent experimentation of the 19th century were purged of their excesses, harmonized and put into the service of the Church.

It was Barth who coined the phrase *pilgrim Church*, which was later used by the bishops at Vatican II in their own *Dogmatic Constitution on the Church*. Yet Barth's understanding of this nomenclature was at odds with Catholic belief. For him the pilgrim Church could not survive in an earthly institution. Like the more radical reformers of the 16th century, Barth would have done away with institution and dogma altogether. "Religion," he said, "is the enemy of faith."[16] Despite this anti-ecclesiastical tendency, however, Barth was nonetheless a champion of ecumenism, and he is highly admired today by biblical scholars of every denomination.

PROTESTANTISM'S RELATION WITH THE WORLD

In addition to Barth's influence in other areas, he also encouraged the Church to enter into the marketplace and minister to modern men and women in their real-life situations. For Barth, a theologian was a person in the world, coexisting with fellow human beings in their suffering and striving, not someone counseling them from the ivory tower of academia. Three other well-known Protestant theologians likewise focused their attention on the Christian's place in the world: Reinhold Niebuhr (1892-1971), Dietrich Bonhoeffer (1906-1945) and Paul Tillich (1886-1965).

Reinhold Niebuhr

Niebuhr was an American of German extraction who studied in the Yale Divinity School before accepting a post as pastor of Bethel Evangelical Church in Detroit. In the 1920's Detroit was the center of the American Industrial Revolution and Niebuhr, as a pastor to automobile workers, experienced firsthand the dehumanizing and depersonalizing effect of industrial labor on the individual and the family. In 1928 he left his pastorate and became professor of applied Christianity at Union Theological Seminary in New York City. There he dedicated himself to his life task, "exploring the meaning and significance of the gospel in the context of modern industrial society...[and] investigating the various forces which come into play when the gospel confronts the world."[17]

Niebuhr concluded that while religion could be the force to reverse the depersonalizing influence of industrial, technological society, this was not the role religion actually was playing. He judged contemporary religions to "have no vital influence upon the life of modern man, and their continued existence only proves that history, like nature, is slow to destroy what it has found useless, and even slower to inter what it has destroyed."[18]

Like Kierkegaard, Niebuhr saw human beings as in need of self-transcendence—that is, in need of dependence on God rather than on themselves. But human beings cannot recognize their need for dependence on God in the context of an institutional structure—whether industrial or ecclesiastical—because an institution by definition depersonalizes and dehumanizes. What humanity needs is to forsake its "will-to-power" (epitomized in the institution) and to surrender in faith to God. Only then will humanity find the freedom for which it strives, and only then will it replace its faith in the institution as savior with faith in God, the only truly transcendent and liberating power.

The role of the Christian is to mediate between God and society. The Christian does this not by inviting society into the Church, but by taking the Church out into society. First, however, Christians themselves must overcome their own will-to-power, their own desire to transcend their human limitations by subjugating and controlling others. In short, Christians must first be free themselves before they can mediate freedom to others. "Man is most free," Niebuhr wrote, "in the discovery that he is not free"[19]—that is, in the discovery that humanity is most human in its absolute dependence on God. The Christian is to be a sign and a witness of this freedom—not in church on Sunday morning, but in the world, as leaven for the masses.

Dietrich Bonhoeffer

One Protestant theologian who vividly demonstrated his freedom in Christ as well as his love for others was Dietrich Bonhoeffer. Bonhoeffer received the best theological education which Protestantism offered. A student of Harnack and a disciple of Barth, he came under Niebuhr's influence on a trip from Berlin to New York in 1931. Returning to his teaching position at the University of Berlin, Bonhoeffer soon became a vigorous critic of the new Nazi movement.

Shortly before the outbreak of World War II, Bonhoeffer was in America on a second visit, exploring Niebuhr's offer to find him a faculty position at an American university. Yet Bonhoeffer declined the safe haven which such a position would have afforded him and returned to Germany to be with his fellow Christians suffering Nazi oppression.

After supervising an underground seminary and collaborating with Germans attempting to overthrow Hitler, Bonhoeffer was arrested by the Gestapo, imprisoned in Flossenberg concentration camp and, less than a week before the Allied victory, executed.

Bonhoeffer was a spokesman for "costly grace" in opposition to the "cheap grace" preached by the Church. God's grace is costly, Bonhoeffer said, "because it costs a man his life, and it is grace because it gives a man the only true life."[20] Bonhoeffer obviously knew that of which he spoke. His entire life was a witness to the true discipleship of Christ which he wrote about in *The Cost of Discipleship* (1937).

In the letters and notes published after his death, Bonhoeffer advocated "Christian worldliness"—that is, a Christianity "not on the borders of life but at the center."[21] For Bonhoeffer this meant a Christianity which terminates its ceaseless doctrinal analysis and squabbling and puts the love of Christ into effect in the world:

> ...[O]ur traditional language must become powerlessness and remain silent, and our Christianity today will be confined to praying for and doing right by our fellow men....Man is challenged to participate in the sufferings of God at the hands of a godless world. The Bible directs [men] to the powerlessness and suffering of God; only a suffering God can help.[22]

Paul Tillich

Like Niebuhr and Bonhoeffer, Paul Tillich believed that the gospel must influence the entirety of human life and not just the religious sphere. Tillich saw it as his task "to witness to the holiness of all being and to proclaim that everything that is, *is* only through the power and grace of God, and that therefore the profane and the sacred cannot be artificially separated."[23]

Like Niebuhr, Tillich saw men and women divided within themselves, suffering from "existential negativity, meaninglessness and guilt which not only the sick person, but man universally, carries."[24] The way out of this condition, said Tillich, is for humanity to forsake its quest for that which is not "ultimate"—power, possessions, wealth—and to seek instead only what is of "ultimate concern."

The problem with modern culture, he continued, is that it has no ultimate concern; rather, it is fixated narcissistically on human sensory gratification. Unless it refocuses its cultural aspirations on the ultimate concern, Tillich warned, Western civilization is doomed to self-destruction.

The task of religion is to point modern culture toward the ultimate concern. In the last analysis, "only the ultimate itself deserves ultimate concern,"[25] so that until the human heart is captured by the divine it will never know peace. Humanity must be saved from outside of itself by a "New Being," which Tillich equated with the eternal Word present in Christ. (Tillich did not say that the Word *is* Christ, but that it is *in* Christ.)

Wherever contemporary culture manages to reorient people toward the ultimate concern, Tillich said, it is exercising one of the fundamental activities of religion. For that reason, far from segregating itself from modern culture, religion should instead seek to inspire modern culture with the desire for the ultimate and to cooperate with culture when it speaks for humanity's deepest aspirations.

A SUMMARY OF PROTESTANT TRENDS

Our brief overview of Protestant theology leads to the unquestionable conclusion that Protestant theology before Vatican II far outstripped Catholic theology in creativity, originality, depth and variety. Whether we agree or disagree with the theologians discussed above, we must conclude that they radically updated and modernized the language in which the gospel was presented—all during a time when many Catholic theologians were afraid of taking their heads out of the sand lest they be labeled Modernists.

While these Protestant theologians did not always agree among themselves, it is still possible to identify several trends in Protestant theology which had an undeniable effect on Vatican II: (1) the trend represented by Schleiermacher and Kierkegaard to focus on the human person in his or her existential, real-life situation as the starting point for one's life in Christ; (2) the trend represented by Otto, Barth and Niebuhr to define the Church as something other than an institution—as the mystery of God's Kingdom present in the living, breathing organism known as the People of God; (3) the trend represented by Harnack, Schweitzer, Dodd and Bultmann to analyze the Bible in terms of the effect which the attitudes and beliefs of the first Christians had on the Bible's composition; and, finally, (4) the trend represented by Niebuhr, Bonhoeffer and Tillich to eliminate the artificial separation in Christian thinking between the Church and the world and to call Christians to bring the gospel to bear on modern culture precisely by immersing themselves in the world.

CHAPTER TEN

CATHOLICISM AND MODERNITY: A DIALOGUE BEGINS

The Evolution of Catholic Theology Before the Council (1800-1962)

Just as Pope John XXIII was no revolutionary wanting to overthrow centuries of Catholic tradition, Vatican II itself was not a radical departure from the Catholic faith but a profoundly new expression of that faith. And just as Pope John in his person epitomized the culmination of a process of growth in Catholic thinking, so too did the Second Vatican Council represent the capstone of a process of evolution in theology. Catholic theology, learning a great deal from Protestant theology, had begun to express the gospel in modern language. The Council was not, therefore, an aberration. It was the result of a ground swell of growth toward modernity which had been percolating within the Church for several decades.

While 19th-century Protestant theology was venturing into new territory, Catholic theology was limited virtually to a restatement of Thomas Aquinas. And rather than a creative reinterpretation of Thomas, most Catholic seminaries and colleges simply taught a dry-as-dust recitation of archaic principles enumerated so as not to deviate from the official party line. By the turn of the 20th century, however, and especially as popes after Pius X ended the Modernist panic, creative Catholic theologians began to emerge all over Europe.

THE NEO-THOMIST REVIVAL

To say that Catholic theologians generally taught the philosophy and theology of Thomas Aquinas in a "dry-as-dust" fashion is not to say that Thomas's thought itself was vapid and unoriginal. As we showed in *The People of the Faith: The Story Behind the Church of the Middle Ages* (pp. 110-113), Thomas's creative synthesis of faith and philosophy was one of the greatest achievements of the Middle Ages and, indeed, of all Western civilization. Yet by confining Thomas's thought strictly to the 13th-century structure in which Thomas had conceived it, the Church did Thomas an injustice and prevented Thomism from adapting itself to the needs of modern times.

Cardinal Désiré Joseph Mercier

In the early decades of the 20th century creative Thomists began to use Thomas's thought in new ways. They initiated a gradual process of adapting the Catholic Church's official mode of expressing itself—philosophically and theologically—to modern times. This "Neo-Thomist revival" started with Cardinal Désiré Joseph Mercier (1851-1926), primate of Belgium during World War I and after.

Although Mercier was an avid opponent of Modernists like Tyrrell (p. 71), he was willing to bring Thomism to bear on the modern sciences. He wanted to show how Thomism was the "science of sciences," or the only system of thought which brought the various scientific disciplines into an integrated whole through the power of synthetic thought.

Maurice de Wulf

Along with Mercier, Maurice de Wulf (1867-1947), professor of the history of philosophy at the University of Louvain in Belgium, likewise did much to reconcile Thomism with modern culture. Much more so than Mercier, de Wulf candidly called for Catholic thought to adapt itself to "modern intellectual needs and conditions." He actually urged the outright abandonment of many outmoded concepts of traditional Thomism.

"Let us freely accept the conclusion," de Wulf wrote, "that a Catholic may, in good faith, give his allegiance to systems other than the new Scholasticism. This being so, it is clear that there can be no such thing as a *Catholic philosophy* any more than there can be a *Catholic science*."[1] Non-Thomist de Wulf's call for independent thinking in Catholic circles stimulated authentic Neo-Thomists to update 13th-century Thomism and thus reconcile it with modern thought.

Jacques Maritain and Étienne Gilson

Two of the brightest lights in the Neo-Thomist revival were the Frenchmen Jacques Maritain (1882-1973) and Étienne Gilson

(1884-1978). Both of these theologians brilliantly attempted to make Aquinas relevant to modern times by taking the essence of Thomism and reconstituting it in contemporary language.

Maritain was a convert to Catholicism. During his student days at the Sorbonne he had believed that the natural sciences could give satisfactory answers to the great questions of life. Gradually, however, he realized that modern science had became distorted into "scientism"—an exaggerated confidence in natural science applied to philosophy, theology, social science and the humanities. Impressed by the philosophy of Henri Bergson (see p. 71), Maritain devoted himself to exploring the nature of "the Absolute" which underlay relative creation. Thomism soon became the vehicle by which he undertook this task.

Maritain characterized Thomism as "Existentialist Intellectualism." Like Kierkegaard (although in a somewhat different sense) he said that to exist is to act—that is, to make conscious choices in favor of increasingly authentic existence.

For help in making such choices, one should make use of the intellectual insights gleaned from science, philosophy, poetry and mysticism, but one must keep ever in mind that the human person is the fundamental principle of society. By "human person" Maritain did not mean simply "the individual," a cog in the wheel of the State. He meant the totality of the human organism created by God, in dependence on God and infused with divine dignity. He believed that only such a view of the human person could prevent the submission of the individual to the deified totalitarian State.

During his career Maritain taught at various times at the Catholic Institute in Paris as well as at Princeton, Columbia and Notre Dame in the United States.

Étienne Gilson was born into a Catholic family and, like Maritain, attended the Sorbonne. His doctoral dissertation discussed the relationship between the thought of René Descarte (d. 1650) and the medieval Scholastics. Recuperating from a wound received during a battle in World War I, he spent hours studying the writings of Bonaventure (see *The People of the Faith*, p. 108). Gilson eventually came to be regarded by many as the leading authority in Europe on medieval philosophy. He was an advocate of Aquinas's teaching that philosophy and theology mutually influence each other, and he argued that the Christian revelation could benefit from reason while at the same time fulfilling the deeper aspirations of reason.

Maritain and Gilson contributed to the Neo-Thomist revival by bringing Aquinas's thinking on essence and existence to bear on modern philosophy. Modern non-Thomist philosophy was largely "positivist"; it had largely adopted the methodology of science, in which truth is said to be knowable only through the senses or through the realm of created essences. If there is a realm of existence beyond the sensory realm, positivist philosophers said, it is unknowable through traditional scientific methods and thus not really meaningful. Since Aquinas himself had reasoned from essence to pure existence, or from the created world to God, Maritain and Gilson were both able to make good use of Aquinas's method in entering into dialogue with positivist philosophers.

Maritain, for example, spoke of three degrees of knowledge—scientific, metaphysical and mystical—and tried to show how modern philosophy truncated human knowledge by focusing exclusively on the scientific approach to truth. Beyond and above scientific knowledge, Maritain said, is metaphysical knowledge—a means of knowing God through analogizing him to his creation. And although we can never know God as he is, we can nonetheless say that God does exist. Completing metaphysics is suprarational knowledge, or mysticism. Here the soul knows God face-to-face in a mysterious fashion that is incapable of being reproduced on the verbal-scientific plane.

Like Maritain, Gilson spoke of the aim of all knowledge as Being itself, or God. Thus for Gilson, the pursuit of philosophy is fruitless unless it recognizes that the goal of its efforts lies beyond created essences and in God as pure Being, the source of all truth.

All of this, of course, was an attempt to reconcile modern scientific philosophy with traditional Catholic theology. At the same time, however, it was a respectful *dialogue* with modern thought. It was this attempt to speak with modern thinkers respectfully and in their own terminology that allowed Maritain, Gilson and other representatives of the Neo-Thomist revival to make Catholic philosophy respectable again. Gone was the insecure, defensive apologetics of the 19th century in which the Catholic writer first paid lip service to the official Thomist position before excoriating modern thinkers as fiends. Maritain and Gilson were original philosophers in their own right rather than apologists, and they brought the true spirit of Thomas Aquinas to bear on the modern search for truth.

20th-Century 'Apologists'

This attempt to restore to modern thought a concern for the spiritual dimension of reality—best represented by Maritain's and Gilson's updating of Thomist metaphysics—was something of a common theme uniting 20th-century Catholic thinkers. The German Catholic theologian Karl Adam (1876-1966), for example, addressed this very issue in *The Spirit of Catholicism*. He criticized those aspects of modern thought that behave "as though Christianity is and must be a mere object of knowledge, a mere subject for scientific investigation, as though the living Christian faith could be resolved into a series of ideas and notions which might be examined, considered, and classified according to their provenance and according to their relation to a supposed primitive Christianity."[2] Karl Rahner, S.J., another German theologian of whom we shall say more in a later chapter, defined faith as "the assent of the whole man to the message of God,"[3] and not simply as the mind's assent to a set of doctrinal propositions worked out in accordance with contemporary scientific reasoning.

The Neo-Thomists were not afraid to hold up Christian revelation to the modern world as the fulfillment of that world's search for truth. But they were also unafraid to enter a dialogue with modern thought. Unlike their 19th-century predecessors, 20th-century Neo-Thomists saw no necessary contradiction between segments of modern thought and the Christian gospel. Therefore they dared to put Thomist thought into the idiom of modern philosophy.

Catholics like Maritain, Gilson, Adam and Rahner used Thomism to point modern thought to a higher degree of truth. At the same time they demonstrated to the Church that modern thought in itself was not to be feared, but improved upon. So too had the apologists of the second century adapted Platonism to the gospel in order to evangelize philosophers who thought exclusively in the Platonic idiom.

THE POPES AS THEOLOGIANS

Perhaps the most innovative pre-Vatican II Catholic theologians were the 20th-century popes. After World War I the Vatican increasingly addressed itself to the problems raised by a technological society in which the new religion of totalitarianism competed aggressively with Christianity. Pope Pius XI issued encyclicals against Fascism, Communism and Nazism respectively. Pope Pius XII addressed himself repeatedly to the integrity of the human person and the right of that person to an autonomous existence in the face of ideologies which would subjugate the individual to the State. Pope John XXIII wrote of the Church's social teaching as "an integrating component of the Christian doctrine of mankind."[4] Let's look briefly at the various themes developed by these theologian-popes.

The Church's Role as Teacher

In a world where the Church had lost much of its credibility, the popes first had to defend the Church's right to educate the world in Christian doctrine. In *Quadragesimo Anno* Pius XI spoke of Catholic doctrine as "the deposit of truth entrusted to Us [the pope] by God," and he declared it his "holy duty" to instruct the world on its social and economic responsibilities. Pius XII concurred with his predecessor, calling the Church "the vital principle of human society,"[5] which owed a duty to humanity to impart Christian doctrine. John XXIII followed suit, characterizing the Church in one of his encyclicals as *Mater et Magistra*, "mother and teacher."

John XXIII in particular broke new ground in his encyclicals by speaking of truth as embodied in human relationships. In his encyclical *Pacem in Terris* ("Peace on Earth"), John spoke of a "happening of truth" which takes place when "people mutually exchange their perceptions in the bright light of truth."

This was a radically new way for a pope to speak. Here truth is not defined as the immutable law of the Church passed from on high to those below, but as a process which occurs when persons submitted to the gospel interact with each other in love. Further, John said, the right of people to express themselves freely arises "from nature" and is a liberty which the Church encourages. Gone was the fearful climate of suspicion engendered by Pius IX in which virtually any knowledge outside of Thomas Aquinas or papal decrees was thought to be heretical.

The new attitude toward the search for truth was eloquently summarized by Vatican II in its *Pastoral Constitution on the Church in the Modern World* (*Gaudium et Spes*, December 7, 1965): "The experience of the historical past, the progress of scholarship, the riches which lie in the various forms of human culture, through which human nature comes ever more clearly to manifestation and new ways to the truth are opened, redound also to the Church's good."[6]

The Church's Social Teaching

The 20th-century popes' social teaching was perhaps the greatest innovation in pre-Vatican II Catholic theology, and one of the most significant influences on the council's documents. Pius IX's dread of modern society and his condemnation of democratic governments had virtually eliminated the Catholic Church as a credible authority in the social sphere. But with Leo XIII's *Rerum Novarum* as the first example, the Church gradually opened a crack here or there in its fortified walls and began to teach vigorously on the Christian's life in modern society.

114

By the time of Pope John XXIII, the crack had become a chasm through which the popes regularly passed in order to dialogue with the world on the subject of living the gospel in modern society.

In this dialogue the popes developed five principles on which society should be based, all five of which are subsumed under Pope John's teaching in *Pacem in Terris* as follows: "At the basis of any human coexistence that should be well ordered and fruitful must lie the principle that every human being is by essence a person."[7]

The first of the popes' five principles, then, is *personalism*, the doctrine that the human person is an autonomous organism endowed by God with the right of self-determination. Society and the State exist to serve the person and his or her legitimate needs, and not the other way around. Personalism is not the same thing as individualism or the belief in "me first." Personalism stands for the proposition that society must preserve the basic rights of each autonomous person as a human being with God-given dignity and inalienable rights. Society's rights as a collective body can never outweigh the individual's right to exist as a free and autonomous person. Said Pope Pius XII, "This is the Catholic worldview!"[8]

The second of the popes' five principles is that of *subsidiarity*. This principle is related to personalism in that it stands for the proposition that no higher or more complex form of social organization can usurp the function of a lower, less complex form of social organization. Pius XI stated this principle in the following way: "Just as whatever the individual man can accomplish on his own initiative and with his own abilities must not be taken from him and allotted to the activity of society, so it is contrary to justice to claim for the wider and higher community whatever the smaller and subordinate communities can achieve and lead to a good end."[9] Thus, for example, it is unjust for the State, as in Communist countries, to substitute its judgment on child-rearing for that of competent parents. Or, as another example, it is unjust for a diocese to decide for a parish something that a parish is competent to decide for itself.

The third social principle advanced by the popes is *solidarism*, the doctrine that all human beings are united to each other as brothers and sisters and have mutually binding responsibilities to safeguard the personal worth of each individual person. Thus, by the principle of solidarism, Christians in the United States would be morally obligated to protect the personal dignity of blacks in South Africa, Christians in Poland or Jews in the Soviet Union.

Fourth, society should be organized to enhance *the common good*. This was defined by John XXIII as "the aggregate of those social presuppositions which make possible or easier to people the full development of their values,"[10] always in keeping with the principle that society exists to serve the individual person rather than the reverse.

This principle was expanded by Pope John to encompass the fifth social principle, the *"universal common good"*—the doctrine that no one society has the right to deny to the citizens of any other society the same degree of personal integrity which it grants to its own citizens. Thus, for example, American society may not morally exploit the labor and resources of Third World countries so that citizens of such countries are subjugated thereby to a life of poverty.

TOWARD A NEW SYNTHESIS

During all the theological activity so far discussed, one man worked almost unnoticed to construct an entirely new synthesis between Christianity and modernity. His name was Pierre Teilhard de Chardin (1881-1955). In the view of many, no Catholic thinker since Thomas Aquinas has better expressed the inherent harmony between matter and spirit, nature and grace, faith and reason, science and religion. Many would argue that his synthesis contributed more to the achievement of Vatican II than the thinking of any Christian in modern times. For that reason, we must discuss Teilhard's writings in some detail.

CHAPTER ELEVEN

PROPHET OF HOPE

Teilhard de Chardin: Harmonizer of Religion and Science, Church and World

Pierre Teilhard de Chardin (*Tay*-yard-duh-Shar-*dan*) was a Jesuit priest, paleontologist and mystic. He was, as he put it, a child of the earth and a child of heaven. His lifelong desire was to help others reconcile what for him had been intuitively reconcilable from his earliest years: the supposed distinction between science and religion, phenomenology and metaphysics, living in this world and being a servant of the transcendent God. Toward the end of his life this unfulfilled desire became more and more painful for him. He wondered why the harmony between spirit and matter, so obvious to him, seemed to escape the vision of so many of his contemporaries.

His writings reveal a man of peace and great inner joy; yet, on one level, his life was a series of frustrations and disappointments. Even though he was a respected Jesuit scientist and member of the intellectual elite of the Catholic clergy, his writings were repressed by the Church throughout most of his life. Scientists and intellectuals in America constantly urged him to give up his vocation and his religion so that he might teach and write without hindrance. Despite this advice, however, he remained staunchly loyal both to his Jesuit vow of obedience and to the Church in general, maintaining to the end of his life that the Catholic Church was "the central axis of evolution."

Since his death in 1955 he has been recognized by scientific and religious thinkers alike as a man of profound creative genius and unparalleled vision. At the same time, some Catholic theologians have continued to be critical of Teilhard's writings. Before we summarize

Teilhard's achievement, let's first acknowledge the substance of that criticism.

Many have said that Teilhard so harmonized and integrated the heavenly and the earthly in his vision of evolution that he virtually did away with the concepts of grace and sin. Such critics read Teilhard as saying, like Henri Bergson (see p. 71), that the world is *necessarily* evolving by its own inner life force toward a new stage of spiritualized existence—thereby making God's grace unnecessary and doing away with the notion of sin. In other words, Teilhard's critics accuse him of saying that creation will *inevitably* evolve toward perfection in Christ, regardless of the moral choices which human beings make. Let's keep this criticism in mind as we proceed and determine for ourselves whether it seems justified.

A BRIEF BIOGRAPHY

Teilhard's father was a French gentleman farmer. At age 18 Teilhard joined the Jesuits, and at 24 began teaching at the order's college in Cairo. He became a priest in 1911. During World War I, in which he served as a stretcher bearer rather than as a chaplain, he earned the French Legion of Honor for bravery. After the war he devoted himself to his first loves, paleonotology and geology. In China he established himself as a paleontologist of the first rank by participating in the excavation of Peking Man.

Fascinated by the correlation between the earth's physical evolution, which he studied at close hand, and the evolution of the spirit of the Church, which he found in Church history, Teilhard began to write on the uncompleted process of human evolution in both its intrinsic and extrinsic forms. His writings were so novel and startling, however, that he quickly fell into disrepute with curial officials in Rome. Shortly after his publication of *The Phenomenon of Man* in 1940, he was ordered not to publish anything but strictly scientific works. Even most of his fellow Jesuits deserted him. It was only after his death in 1955 that Teilhard's works began to surface and to exert a powerful influence on the development of Catholic thought.

TEILHARD'S VISION

Teilhard's method in his first major work, *The Phenomenon of Man*, was to trace the earth's evolution throughout time until it reaches the pinnacle of evolution in human beings. In doing this he was concerned not only with the more traditional observation of evolution

118

as it manifests itself externally (the "without of things"), but also with the evolution of consciousness within creation (the "within of things").

With the coming of the human species, Teilhard said, life has achieved the end of its biological impetus, because with humanity the evolution of consciousness is no longer from one association of cells to another more complexified form. Instead, in humanity the evolution of consciousness has achieved its goal—reflection upon itself, involution. Humanity knows that it knows.

In terms of the further evolution of *homo sapiens*, this means that humanity will evolve into a new organism—what Teilhard called a fully developed "mankind." The new species mankind will be an organism distinct from all the men and women who go into its formation—just as the plant and animal combinations of cells are new and distinct forms of life, something other than all the individual cells which make up the combinations.

The fact that human consciousness is self-reflective, however, means that humanity is in charge of its own evolution. Thus since the coming of *homo sapiens*, Teilhard said, evolution has meant "auto-evolution."

So this prerogative of human nature carries with it an awesome responsibility: the obligation to choose between love or hate as the means by which auto-evolution will continue. Humanity, Teilhard said, is faced literally with a life-or-death question: Will humanity choose love and life, thereby impelling evolution ever upward toward higher degrees of complexification, or will humanity reject love and life and choose death for the species? One is reminded of a similar choice which Moses once placed before the Israelites in the desert three millenia ago (see Deuteronomy 30:19-20).

Love, for Teilhard, is the energizing force of evolution; it should be thought of as coming not only from behind evolution, but from ahead of it as well. A magnetizing force of love calls all persons into union at a point ahead. This synthesizing point Teilhard called the Omega Point, and its attributes are autonomy, actuality, irreversibility and transcendence.

The Omega Point is personal—a "Who" and not an "It." Diagramatically, Teilhard conceived the Omega Point as the apex of a "cone of consciousness." Throughout time, Teilhard said, the law of "complexity-consciousness" has been in operation, drawing the discordant, multifarious elements of creation into ever greater synthesis and harmony, into union with the Omega Point as the goal of all evolution.

The Omega Point, for Teilhard, is the Cosmic Christ. With the incarnation of the eternal Word, evolution has progressed to its final state—"Christogenesis." Evolution, then, is fabricating the mystical Body of Christ. This is the goal of all evolution and the end product of time. The risen, mystical Christ draws all people toward him in an embrace of love, urging them to join with him in the work of building the earth. Auto-evolution in the last analysis, then, means accepting the harmonizing influence of Christ's love.

Having thus described his new Christian metaphysics, Teilhard proceeded in other writings to describe how—on a practical level—individuals can participate in the process of auto-evolution.

TEILHARD'S SPIRITUALITY

Teilhard's greatest frustration was his inability to convey to his fellow Christians the implications of his new science-gospel synthesis for their spiritual lives. Toward the end of his life he tried repeatedly, in essay after essay, to communicate to the modern Christian his understanding of God's creation, the gospel and the new religion he saw rising on the horizon.

In his most famous spiritual work, *The Divine Milieu*,[1] he addressed himself specifically to Christians' failure to catch the vision of the awesome glory of God's creation as revealed simultaneously in Scripture and by science. While the world hungers for a religion which calls forth its best human efforts, its best attempts at creativity and cooperation with a power greater than itself, Christianity often appears to offer only a gloomy picture of passivity, withdrawal and detachment, Teilhard wrote. He characterized this false understanding of Christianity as the belief that "perfection consists in detachment; the world around us is vanity and ashes."*

The Christian ordinarily deals with the conflict between this passive understanding of Christianity and the call to involvement in the world, Teilhard said, in one of three ways: (1) by withdrawing from the world and focusing entirely on the spiritual realities of the Second Coming and the afterlife (what he called the choice of "distortion"); (2) by dismissing the gospel altogether and following what appears to be "a complete and human life" (the choice of "disgust"); and (3) by confusedly leading a double life, a life in which one's spiritual life and one's earthly vocation are never reconciled (the choice of "division"). Yet there is in actuality a fourth way, Teilhard said, a way which promotes "striving toward detachment and a striving toward the

---

* All quotes, unless othewise noted, are from *The Divine Milieu*.

enrichment of our human lives" at one and the same time.

The Value of Human Effort

Teilhard thought it utterly false to regard human action as important only with regard to its moral intention—as if God really does not care what we do in life so long as we are not immoral in doing it. In actuality, Teilhard argued, the *results* of our actions are every bit as important as the intentions which motivate them. The Christian life should not be seen as an endless ritual of digging holes and filling them in, so we can accumulate merit points in heaven. God, according to Teilhard, has no need of filled-in holes.

Instead, God calls us to do work which contributes toward the practical advancement of humanity and the universe. Such work could be as world-changing as discovering a cure for cancer or as humble as drying the dinner dishes, so long as "we unite ourselves in the shared love of the end for which we are working"—that is, so long as we contribute to the earthly progress of the human family toward its fulfillment in Christ. As Teilhard put it: "God does not deflect our gaze prematurely from the work he himself has given us, since he presents himself to us as attainable through that very work....The closeness of our union with him is in fact determined by the exact fulfillment of the least of our tasks."

It was this "sanctification of human endeavor," as he called it, which Teilhard so deeply desired the Church of Christ to espouse. In his opinion, only such an attitude toward life would overcome the great objection to Christianity in our time—"the suspicion that our religion makes its followers inhuman." Elsewhere he wrote: "'Christian' and 'Human' are tending no longer to coincide. In that lies the great schism that threatens the Church....We must preach and practice what I shall call 'the Gospel of Human Effort.'"[2]

The first practical application we can make of Teilhard's vision, therefore, is to live believing that our human efforts really do matter. Getting up in the morning and going to the same routine job day after day can be seen in reality as participation in the most fascinating and meaningful of tasks—the unfolding and fulfillment of the universe and its transformation into the New Jerusalem. Let us explore this thought more fully.

For Christians who accept the call of "The Gospel of Human Effort," a new dimension of life begins gradually to appear. We start to realize that what we are participating in forming is, at the same time, drawing us onward to completion. Like Jacob wrestling with the angel of God, Teilhard wrote, we soon find ourselves "in the grip of what we thought we could grasp." We find, in other words, that there are certain "passivities" involved in our actions, whereby "that which is not done by us is undergone." These passivities are of two types: the passivities of growth and the passivities of diminishment.

Passivities of Growth

By the action of these passivities we come to realize that "we undergo life as much as we undergo death..." and, further, that "my self is *given* to me far more than it is formed by me." In other words, the more we become engaged in action and work that contributes to human progress, the more we realize that our abilities, talents and skills are all gifts. There is a sense in which work undertaken to build the Kingdom of God becomes for each individual less of a strain and effort and more of a spontaneous participation in a common endeavor.

Thus we become gradually more detached from our labor—not because, as a false sense of detachment would have it, this labor does not matter, but because we become totally engrossed in our labor as a key element in the fulfillment of creative evolution. Teilhard sees this fulfillment as the *pleroma*, or "fullness" (see Colossians 1:19), which St. Paul described—namely, the fabrication of the Body of Christ, the completion of evolution and the transformation of creation into the cosmic Christ.

Passivities of Diminishment

The second set of passivities, those of diminishment, are "the hostile powers which laboriously obstruct our tendencies, and hamper or deflect our progress toward heightened being." They are of two types: those whose origins lie outside of us, and those whose origins lie within us. The former includes "the barrier which blocks our way, the wall that hems us in, the stone which throws us from our path, the obstacle that breaks us, the invisible microbe that kills us." Intrinsic passivities of diminishment include "natural failings, physical defects, intellectual or moral weaknesses, as a result of which the field of our activities, of our enjoyment, of our vision has been pitilessly limited since birth." Here Teilhard was referring to what has traditionally been called "original sin."

How do these passivities of diminishment—"the waste matter of our experiences"—contribute to our individual spiritual growth?

Suffering Versus Sacrifice

Teilhard's answer is perhaps a surprise: Instead of calmly accepting the evils engendered by these passivities of diminishment, the Christian's initial response should be to resist them and to strike out against them. Teilhard thus rejects the oftentimes typical Christian response—that we find God through the passive toleration of our sufferings. Teilhard says the opposite is true: "We cannot hope to find God except by loathing what is coming upon us and doing our best to avoid it. The more we repel suffering at that moment, with our whole heart and our whole strength, the more closely we cleave to the heart and action of God."

The Christian, then, regards suffering itself as an evil to be conquered in the name of him who conquered death. There is thus a great distinction to be made, Teilhard believed, between *suffering* and *sacrifice*. The Christian life should be one of sacrifice, diminishment of self for others, but not a life of suffering for suffering's sake. Such great suffering exists in our world, Teilhard said, because of the refusal by so many, Christians included, to lead a life of sacrifice.

What, then, of those moments in our lives when, even after much struggle, effort and sacrifice to diminish evil, we have to admit that our actions have failed and we find that suffering overwhelms us? It is then that God, like the master sculptor who finds a fault in his block of marble, moves to transfigure our lives into something higher, "provided," Teilhard said, "we lovingly trust him."

The Cross and Transformation

These considerations bring us to the shadow of the Cross. For Teilhard, the Cross is "the dynamic and complete symbol of a universe in a state of personalizing evolution."[3] To illustrate what he meant by this, Teilhard turned to the characteristics of evolution in nature. The first characteristic of evolution is that it calls for hard work. Second, it leaves behind a long trail of disorder, suffering and error. Third, it involves death. Finally, it requires at its peak a magnetic principle "amorizing" (or transforming through love) the entire functioning of the universe.

We find in the life and death of Jesus similar characteristics. By his death and resurrection, Jesus became the agent by which all creation begins its transformation into a higher species—a spiritualized, "divinized" species ("mankind," as Teilhard put it earlier; see p. 119). This species is as different from humanity as we now know it as humanity is from lower animal species.

And, like Jesus, Teilhard says, each of us is an agent of transformation in this process of the spiritualization of the cosmos. We are cooperators with Christ in the evolution, the building up, of the cosmos into its completed form. And the tool which we use to do this is the Cross. Without this tool we would be forever lost, relegated to a "lower-species" existence in which we would never truly progress past the level of biological and spiritual achievement at which we presently find ourselves. The Cross should therefore symbolize for us the means by which we not only leave behind all that restricts us but by which we also fabricate a new environment and level of existence.

The Dignity of Matter

To explain his vision of the practical Christian life, Teilhard used the analogy of a mountain climber going from lower zones to higher zones. The climber must make use of everything available to get to the higher zone. As for the climber, so for us, "Matter is simply the slope on which we can go up as well as go down.... The task assigned to us is to climb toward the light, passing through, so as to attain God, a given series of created things which are not exactly obstacles but rather footholds, intermediaries to be made use of, nourishment to be taken, sap to be purified, and elements to be associated with us and borne along with us."

Thus we may regard matter—the elements of the created world—in two different senses. One sense is the carnal sense, represented by the zone of the mountain we have left behind and into which we should not fall back. The second sense is the spiritual sense, represented by the zone toward which we are climbing. Although "the frontier between these two is essentially relative and shifting," matter itself is our ally in the climb. "By virtue of the incarnation," Teilhard writes, "*nothing* here below is profane for those who know how to see."

Like the Cross, then, the elements of the created world are sacred for Christians. Christians must work in the world so that its discordant and multifarious elements may be transformed more effectively into a higher realm of existence. Christians must not abandon the world to those who see human fulfillment only in terms of maximizing sensual pleasure and comfort. Christians must lead their confreres to a higher awareness of life.

At the same time, Christians must not sit back waiting sadistically for the day when "sinners" will receive their deserved wrathful punishment from God. The Christian's place, Teilhard said, is not on the fringes of society but at the very center of society. Today's Christian must not become a sort of 20th-century court jester, showing up every now and then to entertain those who do the real work of society with pious anecdotes and irrelevant rituals. Rather, the Christian must *do* the real work of society.

Faith, Hope and Charity Revisited

To prepare for doing this work, Christians must gird themselves with the three theological virtues. But, as with everything else upon which Teilhard focused, these virtues take on a new dimension once Teilhard has defined them. *Faith*, according to Teilhard, is "an operative power." "In our hands...the world and life...are placed like a Host, ready to be charged with the divine influence, that is to say, with a real presence of the incarnate Word."

Teilhard's definition shows that faith is far more than numb assent to a list of dogmas. Faith, for Teilhard, is not something which sums up our beliefs; rather, faith is something we *do*: "To read the gospel with an open mind is to see beyond all possibility of doubt that Christ came to do more than bring us new truths concerning our destiny; he brought us not only a new concept of it, more exalted than that which we already had in our minds, but also, in a very real way, a new physical *power* of acting upon our temporal world."[4]

Teilhard approved of, but elevated out of its often selfish context, the popular expression: "God helps those who help themselves."[5] Christian faith, he said, "jettisons neither the rational method of conquering the world, nor man's confidence in himself; on the contrary, it stimulates and inspires them....If, in the name of Christ we believe vigorously in our own power, we shall see the aimless meanderings of chance obediently accept our control."[6] And again, "Through the operation of faith, Christ appears, Christ is born, without any violation of nature's laws, in the heart of the world."[7]

Christian *charity*, as Teilhard defined it, is "nothing else than the conscious cohesion of souls engendered by their communal convergence in *Christo Jesu.*" By loving one another as Christ commanded us, we generate the energy which builds up and holds together the universal Body of Christ. Teilhard said that, "in a real sense, only one man will be saved: Christ, the head and living summary of humanity." By excluding anyone, then, by denying love to anyone, we deny our collective fulfillment as a species.

This is because we are biologically related to each other in such a way that our individual "centers of consciousness" must align themselves with all other individual centers, with the totality focused on the divine center—Christ—before we can truly develop fully as human beings. Thus one's own evolution cannot proceed at a rate faster than that of the entire body. Teilhard wrote, "The world must be converted in its whole mass, or it will, by physiological necessity, fall into decay."[8]

Christian *hope*, for Teilhard, applies ultimately to the final consummation of the world and the coming of the Reign of God in its fullness. Teilhard said of hope that it is "perhaps the supreme Christian function and the most distinctive characteristic of our religion." But at the same time he lamented, "In reality we should have to admit, if we were sincere, that we no longer expect anything."

The reason for this lack of hope, Teilhard said, is that Christians no longer share with the rest of humanity "those aspirations, in essence religious, which make the men of today feel so strongly the immensity of the world, the greatness of the mind, and the sacred value of every new truth." Only by sharing these aspirations with all those who push back the frontiers of knowledge about ourselves and about our world will Christians learn again to hope. For Teilhard, the golden age of human history lies ahead, not in the Middle Ages; and Christians must develop a hunger for it, as have their many non-Christian brothers and sisters, before they can once again be stirred to excitement over the promise of Christianity. "We must," Teilhard writes, "try everything for Christ; we must *hope* everything for Christ."

For Teilhard, then, the Christian stands astride two worlds—the earthly and the heavenly, the material and the spiritual. Our task is to take the "stuff of the universe," assimilate it into our souls, and transform it into spirit. Thus we must stand at the center of the world, because it is there that we most readily find matter to transform into spirit. The collective action of every person doing this is what builds up the Body of Christ. "One day," Teilhard said, "the whole divinizable substance of matter will have passed into the souls of all men; all the chosen dynamisms will have been recovered; and then the world will be ready for the Parousia."

Science and Religion

Though Teilhard was very much a man of modern science, he was motivated primarily by an impulse more consonant with the Old Testament worldview which saw sympathy between the spiritual and the material in every sphere of activity. "When will theologians understand," he once wrote in a letter to a friend, "that Matter and Spirit are not two opposite or simply juxtaposed things, but positively and even genetically joined?"[9]

The artificial separation between science and religion, which grew out of the theological and philosophical speculation of the late Middle Ages and Renaissance, weighed heavily on Teilhard. He had experienced from his earliest childhood "a sort of profound feeling for the organic reality of the world,...[an] awareness of the synthesis of all

126

things in *Jesu Christo*."

For Teilhard, all creation manifests a marvelous unity. In observing and studying this creation he found not an antipathy between science and religion, but a harmonious complementarity. The meaning of the Latin roots for our words *science*—"to scan, to analyze"—and *religion*—"to bind together"—perhaps better suggest Teilhard's intuition of science and religion as inseparable elements of the same human endeavor.

That endeavor is humanity's search for greater harmony, both within itself and with others, and eventually with the summit of all created life, whom Teilhard called the "Ultra-Christ." It would be a mistake, however, to think that, when Teilhard referred to the "synthesis of all things in Christ," he was sermonizing about some sort of mystical union between the individual aspects of creation and a God who resides "out there." When Teilhard referred to "synthesis in Christ," he was referring to what he saw as a scientifically verifiable process that has taken place within creation from the beginning of time and is, even now, impelling all creation, by means of Christ's love, into a higher form of life.

TEILHARD'S CHRISTOLOGY

The implications of Teilhard's vision for theology were far-reaching. What is called for, he said in his letters, is no less than a "new Christology, with Christ drawn to the size and to the organicity of the present universe....Oh, how much we need to reform—a reform not just of manners, but in our very conception of God himself!"[10]

In another letter he wrote, "It is disquieting to see both here and in Rome the multiplication of emotional 'Marial' rallies at which they cry 'Death to Materialism!' never dreaming that for us there's no such thing as 'pure matter' or 'pure spirit,' that the only way of conquering Communism is to present Christ as he is, not as an opiate, but as the essential Mover of Hominization"[11] (Teilhard's word for the process by which "mankind" evolves into greater consciousness and complexity).

In place of a world in which spirit and matter, science and religion, God and humanity are antipodes, Teilhard posited an organically whole universe coextensive with the body of the risen Christ. In this universe God depends on humanity as much as humanity depends on God. Teilhard agreed completely with the writer of Colossians: "...I fill up what is lacking in the sufferings of Christ for the sake of his body, the church" (1:24).

As humanity's consciousness grows, its freedom and power to

create and evolve keep pace. Likewise, the consequences of humanity's actions and choices become more profound and effective. In the end the shape of the world is really left up to humanity. It has been given the power to mold its future as it chooses.

Teilhard denied neither sin nor grace, yet he preferred to focus on the divine-human partnership effectuated by Jesus Christ and to point Christians' vision ahead toward the amazing implications of the gospel—that in and through Jesus Christ humanity has been placed in charge of its continuing evolution. In and through Jesus Christ humanity has been given the awesome task of co-creating the future of the human race. Teilhard acknowledged frequently in his writings that humanity can say no to the divine-human partnership (that is, sin) and thus choose death for the species. He also acknowledged constantly that the divine-human partnership was entirely the work of Christ's love, and thus Teilhard never for a moment denied the supremacy of grace in the Christian life.

TEILHARD'S VINDICATION

Because of the climate of suspicion which surrounded Teilhard all during his life, he died a forsaken, nearly friendless man. On April 10, 1955, he was buried in a funeral ceremony attended by only 12 persons. He did not live to see the Church council which would do so much to legitimate his vision of the world as the focal point of Christian life, or to watch the bishops of Vatican II tear down the artificial walls erected by the popes of the 19th century segregating the Church from contemporary culture and the Christian from the world.

In letters written toward the end of his life, Teilhard seemed to have a prophetic glimpse of the tremendous changes about to take place within Roman Catholicism. "Too many people," he wrote, "wear their Christianity like a pair of blinkers to shut out the grandeur and the value of the world. To tell the truth, I really think that this is what lies at the heart of the spiritual problem of the modern world. Nothing (Christianity included) can possibly hold together unless it has faith in an earthly human process directed upwards."[12]

For Teilhard, the purpose of the Church was to "inflame the earth." Ten years before Vatican II he wrote, "The crust of fixity and inertia accumulated around the Church through 2,000 years of earthly sovereignty is so thick and paralyzing that one almost catches oneself hoping for some shock which will put the spirit of Christ back in circulation among the newborn waves of the universe...." And again, shortly before his death, "Without any bitterness and with growing optimism, I see the 'new' God rise more and more gloriously on the horizon....[T]he 'ever-greater God' is going to arise irresistibly."

It was perhaps with Teilhard in mind that the bishops of Vatican II wrote, "...Christ is now at work in the hearts of men by the power of his spirit; not only does he arouse in them a desire for the world to come, but he quickens, purifies and strengthens the generous aspirations of mankind to make life more humane and conquer the earth for this purpose" (*Gaudium et Spes* #38).

After Vatican II Teilhard's works became widely disseminated, and there followed a virtual explosion of interest in his thought. Teilhard had become not only acceptable, but the rage. The works of the stoned prophet were suddenly resurrected and given a place of prominence in the most unlikely of settings.

Teilhard's work was explicitly exonerated and his contribution to the Church in the modern world specifically commended. Pope Paul VI wrote, "Father Teilhard is indispensible for our times. His apologetic is necessary." And Pope John Paul II's secretary of state, Cardinal Agostino Casaroli, wrote of Teilhard, "Our time will certainly remember, beyond difficulties of conception and deficiencies of expression in this bold attempt at a synthesis, the witness of the unified life of a man seized by Christ in the depths of his being and concerned to honor faith and reason at the same time, responding in advance, as it were to John Paul II's appeal: 'Do not be afraid; open wide the doors to Christ, the immense fields of culture, civilization and development.'"

Pierre Teilhard de Chardin, the 20th century's prophet of hope, was at last welcomed back to the home he never once desired to leave.

CHAPTER TWELVE

'JOY AND HOPE': THE MESSAGE OF VATICAN II

A Council Overview Through the Eyes of Karol Wojtyla

The documents of Vatican II are lengthy and detailed—one could even say unnecessarily dense. The most popular English translation runs over a thousand pages. And one is struck by the repeated recurrence of common themes—the result of various commissions of bishops and theologians working separately on the various documents. Had one person written the documents, this redundancy would have been eliminated, but then one person could not possibly have composed a treatise involving so many complex issues.

As with any writing composed "in committee," freshness and lucidity are often sacrificed to the spirit of compromise. Thus we detect in the documents the typical ecclesiastical effort to please everyone and offend no one, which often results in a majority proposition being qualified by a minority proposition. In places the documents stack qualification on top of qualification so that one is left wondering if the original point is still valid. This characteristic has no doubt contributed to much of the confusion over Vatican II: As with the Bible, people frequently pick and choose those documents which support their own preconceived notions.

This criticism aside, however, one must acknowledge that, considered in their context and read in their entirety, the documents make a remarkably clear definition of the Church in the modern world and of the Christian's role in that Church. Further, as far as Catholics are concerned, the documents give perhaps the most lucid exposition ever written of the Bible as it pertains to daily Christian living. Indeed, many Catholics circa 1965 began to rediscover the Bible simply by reading the documents.

It would take several books to analyze the documents thoroughly. Here we will simply offer an overview of what the bishops at Vatican II taught by summarizing the more important teachings found in the documents.

The best way to do this would be to ask someone who was closely involved in the conciliar debates to explain the documents to us. We are fortunate to have just such a person—Karol Wojtyla (Voy-*tee*-yah), who since 1978 has been better known as Pope John Paul II.

WOJTYLA AND THE COUNCIL

As archbishop of Krakow in Poland, a doctor of philosophy and former professor of theology, and a multilingual world traveler with a keen insight into contemporary problems, Wojtyla was uniquely qualified to assume a leading role at Vatican II. Both Pope John XXIII and Paul VI appointed him to important conciliar commissions. Along with Pope Paul and other progressive bishops such as Cardinal Josef Leon Suenens of Belgium, Archbishop Wojtyla became one of the leading spokesmen at the Council for Church renewal.

On September 23, 1963, Wojtyla made a momentous speech at the Council proposing that the Church be defined in its entirety as "the People of God" rather than in the traditional sense of a hierarchy dominating the laity. The Council thus was urged to return Catholicism to a biblical definition of the Church and move away from the medieval-clerical definition.

A month later Wojtyla—now regarded as one of the Council's leading lights—urged yet another radical departure from the past. As bishop in a communist state, Wojtyla understood the practical necessity of dialogue—even with Christianity's most dedicated enemies. He thus argued as follows against the draft of a proposed document condemning atheism:

> It is not the role of the Church to lecture unbelievers. We are involved in a search along with our fellow men....Let us avoid moralizing or the suggestion that we have a monopoly on the truth. One of the major defects of the draft before us is that in it the Church appears merely as an authoritarian institution.[1]

'Sources of Renewal'

On the 10th anniversary of the opening of Vatican II, in October 1972, Archbishop Wojtyla published in Poland *U Podstaw Odnowy*, translated into English as *Sources of Renewal: The Implementation of Vatican II*.[2] In this work the future pope gave his analysis of the conciliar documents and his working plan for their implementation. We can find no better guide for our study of the documents than *Sources of Renewal*, written as it was by a man intimately involved in the agenda of the Council and thus uniquely qualified to explain what the bishops of Vatican II intended to teach. (Imagine, for example, how fortunate we would consider ourselves if we possessed the apostle Peter's notes on the deliberations of the Council of Jerusalem described in Acts 15.) So let us follow Archbishop Wojtyla through the documents of Vatican II.

The Enrichment of Faith

Wojtyla considered the central theme of Vatican II to be "the enrichment of faith." In analyzing this theme, he referred to faith in two different senses—*objective* and *subjective*. Vatican II enriched faith objectively by restating in a profoundly new way traditional Catholic *doctrine*. Subjectively faith was enriched as Vatican II enriched the believer's own *practice* of the Christian life and his or her participation in the Church.

Wojtyla summarized this subjective sense of the faith in a question which he imagined the council fathers asking each Catholic: "What does it mean to be a believer, a Catholic and a member of the Church?" (SR* 17). Wojtyla felt that this question, calling for an *existential response* from each believer, was far more important to the council fathers than the question, "What is the real meaning of this or that truth of the faith?" (SR 17). Thus Wojtyla saw the Council first and foremost as pastoral council, calling people to make a decision for Jesus Christ and his Church and to effectuate that decision through life choices in favor of the gospel.

Such life choices, however, cannot be made willy-nilly. They must be based on an accurate understanding of Christ, the gospel and the Church (faith in the objective sense). Unlike previous centuries' teaching on religious truth, Vatican II did not begin with doctrinal

---

* SR refers to Wojtyla's book, *Sources of Renewal*, followed by the page number. Other abbreviations throughout this and following chapters refer to Vatican II documents (see Appendix, page 193, for a complete list of Latin titles, abbreviations and English titles), followed by section numbers.

foundations arrived at through theological speculation—in a vacuum, as it were, and isolated from the actual life of the believers. Vatican II's starting point for the formulation of doctrine was the human person. And in considering how that person arrives at religious truth, first place was given to human freedom.

Vatican II's first contribution to humanity's quest for religious truth, therefore, was to focus on human beings as *subjects* rather than *objects*—that is, as free and noble creatures who choose of their own initiative to respond to God's revelation rather than as automatons upon whom that revelation is forced. Vatican II's first message to the believer was, in effect, "Claim your freedom! You are children no more but adults called to relate to God in a mature and responsible way."

Thus the laity can no longer abdicate to the clergy their responsibility to live as mature adult Christians. Vatican II proposed not a Church of children led by surrogate parents, but a community of adult believers—all of whom are priests in the general sense (1 Peter 2:9) and some of whom are priests in the ministerial sense (1 Timothy 4:14)—all together comprising the People of God.

'CHURCH, WHAT DO YOU SAY OF YOURSELF?'

Vatican II's principal statement on faith in the objective sense is found in the Council's *Dogmatic Constitution on the Church* (*Lumen Gentium*), which Wojtyla called "the key to the whole of the Council's thought" (SR 35). Wojtyla imagined the Council asking the Church in its entirety, "Church, what do you say of yourself?" (SR 36).

The Church as Communion
The Council answered this question by defining the Church not as an "it" but as an "us"; or, as the Pope put it, the Church "is ourselves. The whole movement instituted by the Council must be a reflection of this reality" (SR 38).

The documents themselves answer Wojtyla's imagined question by stating that "the Church is a people brought into unity from the unity of the Father, the Son and the Holy Spirit" (LG 4).[3] And again, "There is a certain parallel between the union existing among the divine persons and the vision of the sons of God in truth and love" (GS 24).

Thus the nature of God and the nature of the Church are analogous. Both reveal themselves in order to bring humanity to salvation, and both are possessed of an essentially communal character. The social nature of the Church is referred to as *communion*, not community. Wojtyla distinguished the former from the latter by saying

134

that the word *communion* better connotes the essential quality of *self-giving* which characterizes the life of the persons thus bound together.

This understanding of the Church as communion touches on the Second Vatican Council's core teaching—namely, the consciousness that we as Church have of ourselves as the People of God. The greatest failing of the pre-Vatican II Church was precisely its inadequate response to the question, "Church, what do you say of yourself?"

Ever since the fourth century (see *The People of the Creed*, pp. 139-142), the Church had defined itself in terms of a hierarchy segregated from the laity. This tendency to think of the Church as a pyramid with clergy at the top and laity at the bottom became even more solidified during the Middle Ages. By the 19th century this pyramidal model of the Church had become firmly entrenched in Catholic consciousness.

But the Council, relying on the principles of subsidiarity and personalism (see p. 115), taught that "the order of *things* must be subordinate to the order of *persons* and not the other way around..." (GS 26).

The Christian's Life in the World

Though he is never named, Teilhard de Chardin's thought permeates the documents; nowhere is this more true than in the Council's teaching on the meaning and purpose of creation. According to the Council, the beginning point for the formation of Christian consciousness is not a supposed "spiritual life" cut off from the world, but material creation.

The Council thus abolished the false dichotomy between Christ and the world which had always surreptitiously competed in Christian history with Scripture's ultimate statement on the value of the earth and human nature:

"The Word became flesh and
made his dwelling among us...." (John 1:14)

Far from seeing the world as an impediment to faith, the Council affirmed that it is precisely through the world and the use of our human faculties that we enrich our faith. Listen to the echoes of Teilhard's "Gospel of Human Effort" in the following document:

Far from considering the conquests of man's genius and courage as opposed to God's power, as if he set himself up as a rival to the creator, Christians ought to be convinced that the achievements of the human race are a sign of God's greatness and the fulfillment of his mysterious design....

This holds good also for our daily work. When men and women provide for themselves and their families in such a way as to be of service to the community as well, they can rightly look upon their work as a prolongation of the work of the Creator. (GS 34)

With such statements as these, the Second Vatican Council implicitly repudiated the Catholic Church's contempt for intellectual and cultural progress expressed in the fearful denunciations of Pius IX and like-minded popes of the "medieval" Church. Once again Catholics could unite with persons of goodwill everywhere in seeking to synthesize the truths of faith and the findings of science. With Teilhard and with other holy men of science such as Albert Einstein—just as with Thomas Aquinas in the 13th century—humanity could once again *believe* in God and *understand* God's creation as two complementary aspects of the same quest for ultimate truth.

Catholics and Non-Catholics

One of Pope John's principal reasons for convening the Council was to reunite Catholics with non-Catholics and to bring harmony to all of God's children, however those children may express their religious beliefs. The Council completely abandoned earlier attempts to define the different categories of believers. Instead of "Catholics and heretics," "saved and damned" or "us versus them," the Council referred to non-Catholics as "separated brethren."

And instead of suggesting that outside the Catholic Church there is no salvation, the Council referred to Roman Catholics as those who are "*fully* incorporated into the Church...[and] who accept...her entire organization" (LG 14; emphasis added), while other Christians are said to be "in some real way joined to us in the Holy Spirit..." (LG 15). The Council also addressed itself (in LG 16) to the Church's relationship with Jews ("a people most dear for the sake of the fathers"), members of Eastern religions ("those who in shadows and images seek the unknown God") and atheists ("those who, without any fault of theirs, have not yet arrived at an explicit knowledge of God").

Clergy and Laity

Contrary to the rigid pyramidal model of the Church espoused in medieval times, Vatican II taught that "different ranks" (LG 13) within the Church are based not on a distinction in worth or value, but on a distinction in vocation to service. Thus pope, bishops and priests are not distinguished by a greater capacity for holiness, as it was often thought in pre-Vatican II days, but by a different form of service. *Lumen Gentium* refers to the diversity in different persons' vocations within the Church as arising "by reason of their duties" (LG 13)—that is, a *functional* difference exists between clergy and laity.

Lumen Gentium, then, perceives of the hierarchy not as *better* than the laity (as the medieval pyramid suggested), but as *different* by reason of their calling. According to *Lumen Gentium*, clergy and laity are not organized as if occupying different strata of a pyramid, but as if joining together in a circle in which all persons are of equal dignity, although called to different forms of service in the Church:

> In the Church not everyone marches along the same path, yet all are called to sanctity and have obtained an equal privilege of faith through the justice of God (cf. 2 Peter 1:1). Although by Christ's will some are established as teachers, dispensers of the mysteries and pastors for the others, there remains, nevertheless, a true equality between all with regard to the dignity and to the activity which is common to all the faithful in the building up of the Body of Christ. (LG 32)

Relationship Between Bishops and Pope

Consistent with the aim of Pope Paul VI, Vatican II addressed itself to the relationship between bishops and pope:

> Just as, in accordance with the Lord's decree, St. Peter and the rest of the apostles constitute a unique apostolic college, so in like fashion the Roman Pontiff, Peter's successor, and the bishops, the successors of the apostles, are related with and united to one another. (LG 22)

And to implement this "principle of collegiality," the Council established a continuing "Synod of Bishops" to advise the pope and work with him in the episcopal college. Notice that this Synod of Bishops theoretically steers the pope away from his centuries-old reliance on the College of Cardinals as his principal consultative body. With the establishment of the bishops' synod, the pope now avails himself of a more universally constituted body of episcopal advisers. The synod becomes a more Catholic institution than the medieval College of Cardinals, which was frequently composed of men who were simply favorites (or relatives) of the popes.

The Role of Mary in the Church

The Council did not write a separate document about Mary. Rather, it placed the teaching on her in the context of *Lumen Gentium*, thus situating Mary where she belongs—living in the heart of God's people rather than separated from them as an impossible model on a pedestal. The Council said in effect, "The Church is a real people living in a real world, and Mary is a real woman, showing her children how to live the life of faith in the world."

The Council took pains to explain the Church's use of the traditional title "Mediatrix" as it applies to Mary by relating this title to Christ's role as the "one mediator":

> In the words of the apostle there is but one mediator, 'for there is but one God and one mediator of God and men, the man Christ Jesus, who gave himself as a redemption for all' (1 Timothy 2:5-6). But Mary's function as mother of men in no way obscures or diminishes this unique mediation of Christ, but rather shows its power. But the Blessed Virgin's salutary influence on men originates not in any inner necessity but in the disposition of God. It flows forth from the superabundance of the merits of Christ, rests on his mediation, depends entirely on it and draws all its power from it. (LG 60)

'WHAT DOES IT MEAN TO BE A CATHOLIC?'

Having first addressed itself to the question, "Church, what do you say of yourself?" the Council next addressed itself to the question, "What does it mean to be a believer, a Catholic and a member of the Church?" In other words, the Council moved from the realm of theory to that of practice, from a concern with doctrine to a concern for the day-to-day implementation of doctrine.

'Giving Witness to Hope'

When this concern for the practical is related to Wojtyla's overall theme of faith enrichment (see p. 133), one arrives at the essential Christian attitude defined by Vatican II: the obligation to bear witness to the gospel:

> The principal duty of both men and women is to bear witness to Christ, and this they are obliged to do by their life and their words, in the family, in their social group, and in the sphere of their profession. (AGD 21)

Wojtyla added that "bearing witness...must be considered as the proper expression of mature faith" (SR 211).

How does one bear witness? The Council answered that each member of the people of God is to bear witness in accordance with his or her vocation in the Church. Thus, "bishops should devote themselves to their apostolic office as witnesses to all men" (CD 11); vowed religious "should spread the good news of Christ throughout the world"

(PC 25); the laity, by "the witness of a whole life issuing from faith, hope and charity...[and] by announcing Christ by word (AA 16, 6)...should learn to give witness to the hope that is in them (1 Peter 3:15) and to promote the Christian concept of the world..." (GE 2).

Participating in Church and World

Although the individual members of the People of God are called through their unique vocations to bear witness to Christ in different ways, the Church as a whole cannot make its witness effective unless each member participates in the life of the Church. "Faith, in all the wealth of its personal and communal characteristics, is essentially and basically a *participation* in the testimony of Christ" (SR 219).

Here we see most clearly the change in the modern Church's inner life from that of the medieval Church epitomized by the First Vatican Council. All the People of God together, each through his or her special vocation, are partners in "running" the Church—in making the Church a viable, effective, vibrant witness to Christ.

Vatican II encouraged the full participation of the laity especially in the area of liturgy, as when it said:

> The Church, therefore, earnestly desires that Christ's faithful, when present at this mystery of faith, should not be there as strangers or silent spectators. On the contrary, through a good understanding of the rites and prayers they should take part in the sacred action, conscious of what they are doing, with devotion and full collaboration.
>
> (SC 48)

This call to participation by the laity in the liturgy led to the first and most noticeable changes in everyday Catholic life after Vatican II. Prior to Vatican II the Mass was the priest's affair. It was he who was involved, with back to the congregation, in the "holy business" at the altar, while the laity knelt silently, saying the rosary or otherwise attending in body only to the priest's activity. After Vatican II all that changed. Altars were situated so that priest and people faced each other as full participants both in the Liturgy of the Word and the Liturgy of the Eucharist. Instead of serving as attendants to the priest, the laity became full and necessary actors in the drama—something which many Catholics at first had difficulty accepting.

Along with increased participation in the liturgy, Vatican II also encouraged Catholics to take their Christianity into the marketplace. The Council thus repudiated the former prejudice which allocated holiness and dignity only to ordained ministers and vowed religious. Now, in keeping with the spirit of Teilhard, *all* human work was said to be holy and worthwhile—not just in a temporal sense, but in the sense that both laity and clergy, precisely through their work, bring about the spiritual fulfillment of the Kingdom:

> Let there, then, be no such pernicious opposition between professional and social activity on the one hand and religious life on the other. The Christian who shirks his temporal duties shirks his duties toward his neighbour, neglects God himself, and endangers his eternal salvation. Let Christians follow the example of Christ who worked as a craftsman; let them be proud of the opportunity to carry out their earthly activity in such a way as to integrate human, domestic, professional, scientific and technical enterprises with religious values, under whose supreme direction all things are ordered to the glory of God. (GS 43)

Vatican II's teaching on bearing witness and participating did not stop at the boundaries of the Church. The Council reaffirmed that the Christian's place is in the world, participating in Christ's ongoing mission to bring humanity to salvation. Wojtyla referred to the Christian's mission to the world as "the attitude of human identity," and he found this attitude represented especially in *Gaudium et Spes* ("Joy and Hope"), a document he characterized as "one of the essential determinants of the implementation of the council" (SR 273).

Gaudium et Spes begins by saying, "nothing that is genuinely human fails to find an echo in [the human] heart" (GS 1). Yet all must admit today that humanity exists in a very precarious condition, hovering "between hope and anxiety" (GS 4). The mission of the Church is to lead humanity out of its anxiety and into the only real hope, salvation by Jesus Christ. To carry out this mission, the Church—contrary to past ages' thinking—does not flee from the world, but "enter[s] in dialogue with it about all these different problems" (GS 3).

In entering into dialogue with the world, the People of God must be guided by what Wojtyla called "the moral of solidarity" (SR 286), which the Council expressed as follows:

> Let everyone consider it his sacred duty to count social obligations among man's chief duties today and observe them as such. For the more closely the world comes together, the more widely do men's obligations transcend particular groups and gradually extend to the whole world....Then, under the necessary help of divine grace, there will arise a generation of new men, the moulders of a new humanity.
>
> (GS 30)

(No doubt Teilhard would have considered the Council's choice of the phrase "new humanity" similar to his own concept of the new species "mankind.")

'Moral Solidarity' in Various Spheres of Responsibility

The Council defined several spheres of responsibility in which Christians were to implement their attitude of moral solidarity. One of these spheres is married life, called by the Council a "supremely sacred value...[and] a special sacrament" (GS 47,8). Gone is the medieval prejudice which looked upon marriage simply as a Church-sanctioned outlet for lust. (See, for example, *The People of the Faith: The Story Behind the Church of the Middle Ages*, p. 122).

Another sphere of responsibility is the cultural life of society, where Christians are encouraged to foster a "new humanism" (GS 55), "...bringing the human race to a higher understanding of truth, goodness, and beauty, to points of view having universal value" (GS 57). Related to this is "the sphere of economics and social life....[M]uch reform in economic and social life is required along with a change of mentality and of attitude by all men" (GS 63).

The Council likewise encouraged involvement in politics. "Catholics [the document does not say *lay* Catholics] versed in politics...should not decline to enter public life" (AA 14). Rather, they should work in the political system to protect such basic rights as "the right of free assembly, the right to express one's opinions and to profess one's religion privately and publicly" (GS 73). Gone forever is the reactionary attitude of Pius IX.

Notice that there is no room in the documents for Catholic politicans who are "personally opposed but..." (e.g., those who try to straddle the fence on such moral issues as abortion): "The layman, at one and the same time a believer and a citizen of the world, has only a single conscience, a Christian conscience; it is by this that he must be guided continually in both [temporal and spiritual] domains" (AA 5).

Finally, the Council spoke of the urgent need to work for peace. The Council's entire program of hope outlined in the documents "will not succeed...unless everyone devotes himself to the cause of true peace with renewed vigor" (GS 77). Wojtyla added in his own commentary: "The arms race must be ended and war should be completely outlawed by international agreement" (SR 306, GS 80-82).

VATICAN II IN OUTLINE

We conclude our brief analysis of the teaching of Vatican II by means of the chart on pp. 142-143. It attempts to depict the basic message of faith enrichment in both the objective and subjective senses which the Council intended to impart.

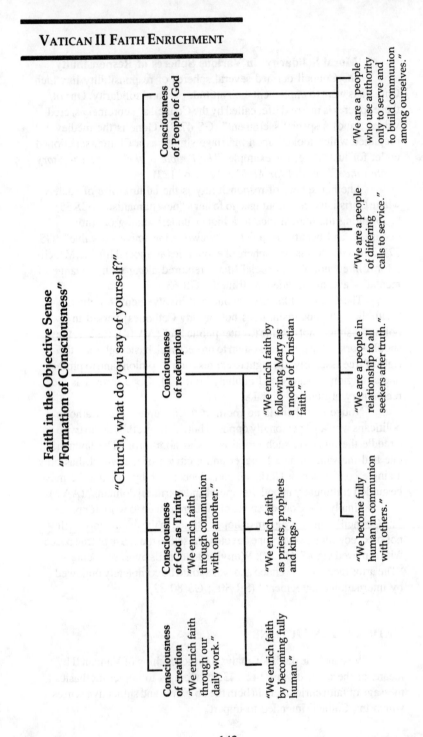

Faith in the Objective Sense
"Formation of Consciousness"

"Church, what do you say of yourself?"

Consciousness of creation
"We enrich faith through our daily work."

"We enrich faith by becoming fully human."

Consciousness of God as Trinity
"We enrich faith through communion with one another."

"We enrich faith as priests, prophets and kings."

Conciousness of redemption

"We enrich faith by following Mary as a model of Christian faith."

"We become fully human in communion with others."

"We are a people in relationship to all seekers after truth."

Consciousness of People of God

"We are a people of differing calls to service."

"We are a people who use authority only to serve and to build communion among ourselves."

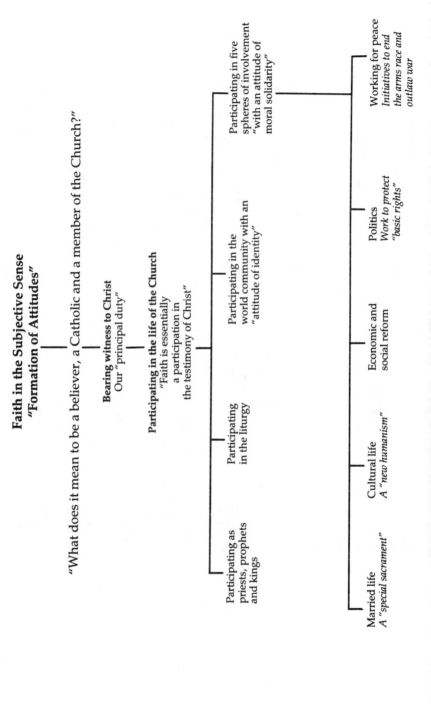

**Faith in the Subjective Sense
"Formation of Attitudes"**

"What does it mean to be a believer, a Catholic and a member of the Church?"

Bearing witness to Christ
Our "principal duty"

Participating in the life of the Church
"Faith is essentially
a participation in
the testimony of Christ"

Participating as
priests, prophets
and kings

Participating
in the liturgy

Participating in the
world community with an
"attitude of identity"

Participating in five
spheres of involvement
"with an attitude of
moral solidarity"

Married life
A *"special sacrament"*

Cultural life
A *"new humanism"*

Economic and
social reform

Politics
*Work to protect
"basic rights"*

Working for peace
*Initiatives to end
the arms race and
outlaw war*

143

CHAPTER THIRTEEN

SHAKING UP CATHOLIC LIFE

What Vatican II Did and Did Not Do

No Church council has been followed by an immediate experience of harmony and concord. Consider, for example, the tumultuous half-century following the Council of Nicaea in 325, which we discussed in Chapter Five of *The People of the Creed: The Story Behind the Early Church.*

And Vatican II was no exception. Since 1965 the Roman Catholic Church has been shaken to its timbers by turmoil, dissension and questioning. For some Catholics this very turmoil is a sign that the Council erred in its decisions. For these Catholics Catholicism should be synonymous with order and stability. Yet such an image of the Church is inaccurate, at least insofar as it is measured against the reality of Church history.

One could make a strong case that it is *only* in times of turmoil and upheaval that the Church is challenged to be most faithful to its Christian calling. Think, for example, of the radical change in mentality and ensuing turmoil which St. Francis of Assisi engendered in the medieval Church (see *The People of the Faith*, pp. 96-100).

In our own day the bishops returning home from Vatican II perhaps had no idea that their recent decisions in Rome were about to produce a bone-jarring shake-up of Catholic life. Perhaps in the minds of some of these bishops the Council's radically new restatement of the ancient Catholic tradition could safely be put to rest on a shelf marked "Ideals" and never actually implemented.

If this was their expectation, they must have been jolted to learn that some Catholics in their dioceses were acting as if they planned to take Vatican II seriously. All over the world Catholics began to respond to the Council's "new Pentecost" as though they had indeed received a fresh burst of the Spirit's energy.

Not all Catholics, however, were receptive to the changes ushered in by Vatican II. And even those who welcomed change within the Church gave a plethora of interpretations to the Council's documents.

Perhaps the principal source of confusion since Vatican II is the ambiguity existing both in the conciliar documents themselves and in hierarchical teaching on the Council. Since the documents were in many cases compromise statements, conservatives, progressives and moderates can all find something in the documents to support their understanding of the Council's achievement. And since bishops and priests likewise come in progressive, conservative and moderate dress, the interpretation given to the Council has often varied from pulpit to pulpit, parish to parish, and diocese to diocese.

A VARIETY OF ANSWERS

One senses within the Catholic community a collective yearning for identity, a search for a definitive answer to the question, "What does 'Catholic' mean in the light of Vatican II?" The problem for the modern Church is not that there has been no answer to that question, but that there has been a bewildering *variety* of answers. Let's try to evaluate these answers by summarizing briefly what the Council said and did not say.

On Papal and Episcopal Authority
The Council did not invalidate papal infallibility or hierarchical authority. What it did was to define hierarchical authority from the point of view of the entire episcopacy rather than from the point of view of papal primacy. Thus all the bishops—the pope included—are seen as sharing in the apostolic authority. Out of this *collegial* authority comes the primacy of the pope as first among brothers. Thus the bishops do not draw their authority from the pope; they are apostolic successors in their own right, in submission only to the pope, who governs the college of bishops with the authority given by Christ to Peter.

On Priests and Laity
In terms of the "privilege of faith" (LG 32) and in terms of "the activity which is common to all the faithful" (LG 32), the laity and hierarchy are said to be "equal." Yet Vatican II did not merge the

ordained ministry and the lay apostolate. The Council spoke of them as functioning in two different spheres—the ordained ministry within the confines of the Church's sacramental life and *magisterium* (teaching office), and the laity within the confines of what is called "temporal" vocations (the five "spheres of responsibility" discussed on p. 141).

The documents speak of priests as "brothers among brothers" (PO 9) who "will not always be so expert as to have a ready answer to every problem that arises" (GS 43). Archbishop Wojtyla commented that this is a warning against "clericalism" (SR 386). According to Vatican II, the function of priests is to "gather the family of God as a brotherhood endowed with the spirit of unity and lead it in Christ through the Spirit to God the Father" (PO 6). This statement would seem to define the priest primarily as one who *enables*—one who affirms the laity and empowers them to exercise their calling to bear witness to the gospel.

Aside from specifically sacramental ministry, which is reserved to the priest, Vatican II envisaged a Church in which priest and laity share a variety of responsibilities. Much of the fallout from Vatican II has settled on the issue of where the line is to be drawn between ordained ministry and lay apostolate. In some parishes laypersons have taken on many functions previously reserved for priests—religious education, for example—while in other parishes the predominant mentality is still "Let Father do it."

On Catholics and Non-Catholics

Vatican II did not disavow the Roman Catholic Church's centuries-old belief that Catholicism alone possesses the entire truth of Christian revelation. Yet the Council acknowledged that other Christian bodies share in varying degrees in the Catholic Church's possession of truth. Instead of simply equating the institutional Church with the Kingdom of God, Vatican II saw the Kingdom as transcending the institutional Church. The institutional Church is said to "subsume" in the entire Church—that is, to be included within the entire body of baptized believers, but not completely congruent with that body.

On Church and World

Vatican II defined the world as "the whole human family along with the sum total of those realities in the midst of which the human family lives" (GS 2). The Council thus disavowed a line of Catholic thinking which saw the Church and world as radically distinct and opposed realities. For Vatican II the Church is not opposed to the world; rather, it is precisely in the world that the Church finds its mission and identifies itself. The world is the background, as it were, against which the Church's portrait is sketched.

Whereas the world's focus is the present, the Church—while always attuned to the "signs of the times"—points humanity ahead to a broader horizon. The Church speaks for "all who are ready to put aside love of self and integrate earthly resources into human life, in order to reach out to that *future* day when mankind itself will become an offering accepted by God" (GS 38).

On Scripture and Tradition

Vatican II may in one sense be thought of as the "Council of the Bible." For the first time—largely from reading the Council's documents—Catholics began to rediscover their biblical heritage.

By emphasizing that Church teaching "is not superior to the Word of God but its servant" (DV 10), the Council did not diminish the importance of tradition: "Sacred tradition and sacred Scripture make up a single sacred deposit of the Word of God, which is entrusted to the Church" (DV 10). What the Council did was not to denigrate tradition but to elevate the place of the Bible in the liturgy and in the daily life of Christians:

> Just as from the constant attendance at the Eucharistic mystery the life of the Church draws increase, so a new impulse of spiritual life may be expected from increased veneration of the Word of God which "stands forever." (DV 26)

These five correlates—papal and episcopal authority, priests and laity, Catholics and non-Catholics, Church and world, Scripture and tradition—may be seen as the principal themes around which the story of the post-Vatican II Church continues to unfold.

THE COUNCIL AS 'GIFT'

The bishops of the world met during December of 1985 at an Extraordinary Synod in Rome specifically to evaluate the achievement of Vatican II. They gave this ringing endorsement to the Council's work:

> All of us, bishops of the Eastern rites and the Latin rite, have shared unanimously, in a spirit of thanksgiving, the conviction that the Second Vatican Council is a gift of God to the Church and to the world. In full adherence to the Council, we see in it a wellspring offered by the Holy Spirit to the Church, for the present and the future....
> From Vatican II the Church received with certitude a new light:

The joy and hope which come from God can help mankind already on this earth to overcome every sadness and anguish, if men lift their gaze to the heavenly city. We hope to be able to communicate to you what we ourselves have received from this synod [namely]:

We are not made for death but for life. We are not condemned to divisions and wars, but called to fraternity and peace. God did not create man for hate and distrust; rather, he is made to love God. He is made for God himself. Man responds to this vocation by renewing his heart. For mankind there is a path—and we already see the signs of it—which leads to a civilization of sharing, solidarity and love; to the only civilization worthy of man.

We propose to work with all of you toward the realization of this civilization of love, which is God's design for humanity as it awaits the coming of the Lord.[1]

CHAPTER FOURTEEN

THE ROAD AHEAD

Developing Trends in the Post-Vatican II Church

Since we are still living in the aftermath of Vatican II, it is difficult to exercise the type of objective historical judgment which a studied hindsight would provide. Yet we are now far enough away from the Council to isolate several clearly observable trends in this post-Vatican II era of the Church's history. In this chapter we will discuss some of these trends in order to isolate what the conciliar documents call the *sensus fidei*, or "the supernatural appreciation of the faith of the whole people" (LG 12).

Because of this *sensus fidei*, the bishops at Vatican II said, "The whole body of the faithful who have an anointing that comes from the holy one cannot err in matters of belief" (LG 12). Notice that this situates infallibility in the whole body of the Church rather than simply in the pope, and does not therefore isolate the pope from the entire body of the faithful, as did Vatican I's decree on papal infallibility (see pp. 48-49).

Thus, in order truly to define the post-Vatican II Church and to discover its ongoing mission, we must look to the aspirations of the "whole body of the faithful"—laity, deacons, pope, bishops, vowed religious, priests, women and men, poor and rich, educated and uneducated, weak and powerful, Christians from a European cultural heritage and Christians from the Third World. So let's focus on some of the aspirations of this diverse body of the Church, as we look at emerging trends in the areas of social justice, vocations, spiritual renewal and hierarchical authority.

THE SOCIAL APOSTOLATE

Both the international synods of bishops and the various national episcopal conferences meeting since Vatican II have endeavored to heed the Council's call to identify the Church with the needs of the poor:

> Let us not be guilty of the scandal of having some nations, most of whose citizens bear the name of Christians, enjoying an abundance of riches, while others lack the necessities of life and are tortured by hunger, disease, and all kinds of misery....Indeed, it is a duty for the whole people of God, under the teaching and example of the bishops, to alleviate the hardships of our times....(GS 88)

In this area of post-Vatican II life, the bishops—at least in their teachings—have borne their responsibility well. For example, the 1971 International Synod declared, "Action on behalf of justice and participation in the transformation of the world appear to us a constitutive dimension of the preaching of the gospel...[and] of the Church's mission for the redemption of the human race and its liberation from every oppressive situation."[1] And the 1974 synod proclaimed the promotion of human rights to be "required by the gospel and central to [the Church's] ministry."[2] The same synod spoke of "the intimate connection between evangelization and liberation."[3]

The bishops' positive reference to "liberation" was typical of an entirely new focus on faith which Vatican II engendered. In that focus, faith and justice are inseparably united. Archbishop Wojtyla's "faith enrichment," then, has been interpreted by the world's bishops principally as a call to promote justice. In addition, an entirely new type of theology—"liberation theology"—has developed from the Church's post-Vatican II emphasis on social justice. (We will discuss specific writings of liberation theologians in the next chapter.)

Liberation Theology

The basic principle of liberation theology—which is largely written by theologians who live in the Third World rather than in Europe or North America—is that practice comes before theory. Before one can truly understand the gospel, liberation theology proclaims, one must first live in solidarity with the poor to whom Jesus himself proclaimed the Good News. Traditional European-centered theology usually put the emphasis the other way around: One studies the Gospels, reflects on them, undergoes a personal conversion and *then* is stirred (it is hoped) to minister to the poor.

Such an approach frequently overlooked the *social* nature of sin, a dimension of sin which has been much more emphasized since Vatican II. In other words, theologians have turned their attention to the sin of institutions, structures and systems which by their very nature dehumanize and debilitate the poor.

The quest for social justice in the post-Vatican II Church received a boost from two conferences of Latin American bishops. At Medellin, Colombia, in 1968, the bishops went on record as locating structural sin in two types of colonialism: the "external colonialism" of rich countries exploiting Latin American resources; and the "internal colonialism" of the rich classes within Latin American countries exploiting the poor. At Puebla, Mexico, in 1974, the bishops reaffirmed their teaching at Medellin by proclaiming the Church to be in favor of "a preferential option for the poor."

John Paul II and Social Justice

Since Karol Wojtyla's election as Pope John Paul II, he has also shown himself to be an unqualified champion of social justice. In his first encyclical, *Redemptor Hominis* ("Redeemer of Man," 1979), the Pope unequivocally united the Church's evangelization efforts to social justice. According to John Paul II, the Church ministers not to humanity in the abstract, but to humanity in particular social settings, one of which is the condition in which the poor find themselves in today's world.

> ...Everyone is familiar with the picture of the consumer civilization, which consists in a certain surplus of goods necessary for man and for entire societies—and we are dealing precisely with the rich, highly developed societies—while the remaining societies—at least broad sectors of them—are suffering from hunger, with many people dying each day of starvation and malnutrition. Hand in hand go a certain abuse of freedom by one group—an abuse linked precisely with a consumer attitude uncontrolled by ethics—and a limitation by it of the freedom of the others, that is to say those suffering marked shortages and being driven to conditions of even worse misery and destitution.[4]

In a second encyclical, *Laborem Exercens* ("On Human Work," 1981), the Pope criticized capitalism for subordinating labor to capital and, at the same time, criticized communism for subordinating labor to the needs of the totalitarian State. Only by subordinating both capital and the totalitarian State to labor, the Pope wrote, can a just society arise. The Church, the Pope said, must support the solidarity of workers who seek control over their own lives, even to the point of advocating the co-ownership of industry by workers and management. In Third World countries, where the poor have not yet become effective producers in society, the Church must encourage the ruling classes to assist the poor to develop meaningful jobs.

A Developing Understanding of 'Vocation'

On the one hand, Vatican II spoke of priests as "brothers among brothers" (PO 9), while in the very same document it exhorted the laity to treat priests as "fathers and pastors" (PO 9). This ambiguity within the documents themselves, coupled with a number of external factors, has precipitated a great deal of discussion since Vatican II as to where one should draw the boundary line between priestly and lay ministry. Out of this discussion there have arisen sometimes sharply opposed views as to what the words *religious vocation* mean.

The Priest Shortage

One factor in this discussion is the ever-increasing shortage of ordained priests, a problem caused both by the exodus of many priests and religious from their vocations after Vatican II and the ever-dwindling numbers of new recruits. In the United States alone, for example, 47,500 men were studying for the priesthood in 1964, compared to roughly 12,000 by 1984. During the same period, 241 American seminaries ceased operation.[5]

By 1985 the average age of priests worldwide had climbed to well above 50, and many parishes throughout the world came to be administered for the first time by persons who were not priests. With such developments, laypersons and unordained religious have been increasingly called upon to assume more and more responsibilities previously reserved to priests.

As laypersons, unordained religious and priests started working together more closely than ever before (at least more closely than at any time since the first three centuries of the Church), the question naturally began to arise as to the suitability of ordaining women and married people as priests. If there is a priest shortage, some people began to ask themselves, why not ordain qualified men and women—married or single—who have already shown themselves in practical situations to be talented priestly ministers?

This question became even more relevant as Catholic schools of theology for the first time admitted both men and women as students who took precisely the same courses taken by young men studying for the priesthood. By the mid-1970's, then, most countries had significant numbers of persons with the same theological training and practical skills as seminarians, but who were denied ordination because they were either married or female (or both).

Priestly Celibacy

As a result, the post-Vatican II Church began to reexamine the traditional Catholic stance on celibacy as a precondition for ordination to the priesthood. (For a discussion of the origins of celibacy as a condition for ordination, see *The People of the Creed*, p. 141, and *The People of the Faith*, pp. 55-56.) Vatican II itself had spoken of priestly celibacy as follows:

> By preserving virginity or celibacy for the sake of the kingdom of heaven priests are consecrated in a new and excellent way to Christ. They more readily cling to him with undivided heart and dedicate themselves more freely in him and through him to the service of God and of men. They are less encumbered in their service of his kingdom and of the task of heavenly regeneration. In this way they become better fitted for a broader acceptance of fatherhood in Christ. (PO 16)

In response to Vatican II's statement, some Catholic theologians questioned why celibacy must be required of *all* priests since, their argument ran, every Christian—celibate or married—is required to give undivided loyalty to the Lord. Did the Council mean to suggest, critics of celibacy asked, that married persons are *not* able to give God their undivided loyalty? If so, then the bishops seemed by implication to be admitting that the Sacrament of Matrimony is inferior to the Sacrament of Holy Orders as a means of grace, a conclusion which the bishops never explicitly stated.

Whatever the proper understanding of priestly celibacy should be, it became increasingly clear in the post-Vatican II Church that many persons sought a reform in the Church's traditional understanding of "religious vocation."

Women's Ordination

And when the arguments against priestly celibacy were considered in the light of Vatican II's declaration against "every type of *discrimination*...whether based on *sex*, race, color, social condition, language, or religion" (GS 29), the debate over qualifications for the priesthood opened up a debate over women's ordination. The debate was intensified when in 1976 the Pontifical Biblical Commission stated that Scripture does not mandate against women participating in the ordained ministry. In response, however, the Vatican in 1977 reaffirmed its traditional opposition to women's ordination.

A contemporary theologian who supports women's ordination expressed the view of many like-minded Catholics when she wrote, "Women's ordination serves as a litmus test for the seriousness and authenticity of the Church's commitment to justice and to the participation of all baptized women and men in its life and mission."[6] Here the issue of women's ordination was placed within the context of the broader issue of reforming the Church's understanding of vocation.

In other words, proponents of both a married and a female presence in the priesthood asked how we as a Church can preach justice to the world if we do not practice justice within the Church. Like charity, they said, justice begins at home, and by reforming our understanding of vocation so that it includes all qualified persons, we adhere to the Church's teaching that justice is a constituent element of the Church's mission. As we shall see in the next chapter when we discuss his theology more fully, John Paul II has steadfastly resisted such arguments.

SPIRITUAL RENEWAL MOVEMENTS

Just as the *devotio moderna* movement of the late Middle Ages (see *The People of the Faith*, p. 161), arose in an era of transition and renewal within the Church, so too the post-Vatican II Church has witnessed a remarkable rebirth of lay spirituality. Many Catholics took seriously Pope John's call for a new Pentecost within the Church. They applied it not simply with respect to the "external" forms of renewal just considered (the social apostolate and the increased participation by the laity in various forms of Church ministry), but also with respect to the interior spiritual renewal that was a necessary correlate of Vatican II's call for an updating of Catholic life in all its forms.

We could not hope to cover all of the post-Vatican II spiritual renewal movements here, and so will mention only the three most prominent: the Charismatic Renewal, the Cursillo movement and Marriage Encounter.

The Charismatic Renewal

It was significant that Pope John XXIII saw the renewal of the Catholic Church in terms of a new Pentecost. By choosing this motto for his council he underscored the necessity of submitting the updating of Catholic life to the work of the Holy Spirit.

Not long after Vatican II finished its agenda, spontaneous outbursts of the Spirit's power of rejuvenation began to manifest themselves all over the Catholic world. In the United States, for example, a group of Catholic laypersons at Duquesne University in Pittsburgh met together in 1967 at a weekend retreat in order to seek the Spirit's guidance on how to best implement the renewal in their day-to-day lives. The result was an outpouring of the Spirit very similar to that recorded in Acts 2, and the group began to experience the gift of tongues and other visible signs of the charismatic gifts discussed by Paul in 1 Corinthians 12—14.

The sight of lifelong Catholics praying in tongues, exercising gifts of healing, worshiping with their hands held aloft and otherwise acting for all the world like Protestant Pentecostals was too much for some traditional Catholics to bear. But the incipient "Charismatic Renewal" soon spread like wildfire, with the campus of the University of Notre Dame becoming a sort of national headquarters for the movement. From South Bend, Indiana, and Ann Arbor, Michigan, where charismatic "covenant communities" were formed (communities where Catholics lived in close proximity to each other under the leadership of lay elders and committed to a mutual code of community discipline), the Charismatic Renewal spread to parishes all over the country.

Within 10 years of its founding at Duquesne, virtually every parish in America had formed charismatic prayer groups. Participants exercised the gifts of the Holy Spirit and rededicated their lives to Christ through a commitment to personal prayer, Scripture reading and communal activities designed to build a unified body of believers. In many parishes "charismatics," as they were now called (often with a tone of derision), became parish leaders for spiritual renewal.

The basis of the Charismatic Renewal is an experience known as "the baptism in the Holy Spirit" (or "the baptism," for short), a phrase which Catholic charismatics appropriated from Pentecostal groups (see Acts 19:1-7). In traditional Catholic thinking, Catholics receive the gift of the Holy Spirit at Baptism, and renew or revivify this gift in the Sacrament of Confirmation.

Catholic charismatics explained the baptism of the Holy Spirit as an experiential appropriation through faith of the gift of the Holy Spirit which had been received in a sacramental way through Baptism and Confirmation. They often used homely but telling examples to explain why ordinary Catholic life needed the rejuvenation of the baptism in the Holy Spirit: They said that while Baptism and Confirmation provide the "electricity" for Christian life, only by "plugging in" to the power source of the Spirit through an adult faith commitment can the power of Christianity actually become available to the believer experientially. The Charismatic Renewal thus stressed the *experience* of the Spirit's power as the foundation to authentic Christian life.

The enormous growth of the Charismatic Renewal eventually required an international headquarters in Europe, with Cardinal Léon-Josef Suenens serving as the pope's official liaison to the movement. The formerly lay movement thus became highly respected by many in the hierarchy. Both Pope Paul VI and John Paul II lavishly praised the movement for its sincerity, dedication and zeal. Many priests joined the movement, and many of them publicly stated that the Charismatic Renewal was responsible for keeping them faithful to their vocations.

It would be impossible to single out all the leaders in the movement, but a few prominent names can be mentioned. The Franciscan priest Richard Rohr headed one of the more successful covenant communities, the New Jerusalem Community in Cincinnati. Two other priests, John Bertolucci and Michael Scanlan, operated from their base at the new Charismatic College of Steubenville, Ohio. And Abbot David Gaerets pioneered the founding of the first charismatic Benedictine monastery in Pecos, New Mexico, which admits both male and female members. All of these have done much to foster the spread of the renewal into the ordinary channels of American Catholic life.

The Charismatic Renewal has not been without its critics. Many have questioned the charismatics' concern for personal spiritual experience as the basis of the Christian life. Others have pointed out that the charismatics have very seldom translated their zeal and energy into apostolic service of the poor and needy. Few if any charismatics, such critics have said, are involved in peace and justice ministries within the Church, and indeed Father Richard Rohr has himself made this very criticism of the Charismatic Renewal. In order to address this concern, Rohr recently started a center in Albuquerque, New Mexico, for the purpose of training laypersons in ministries of peace and justice.

In this regard, we should also mention the work of Richard M. Thomas, S.J., founder and director of Our Lady's Youth Center in El Paso, Texas. The center is a community based on the tenets of the Charismatic Renewal outlined above, but at the same time it has a social justice outreach providing food for the needy, job placement, social case work and advocacy on behalf of Hispanics along the Mexican-American border.

The examples of Rohr and Thomas perhaps represent the next stage in which the Charismatic Renewal will move. If the movement is to remain anything other than a pious, "feel-good" society, many observers have said (including leaders in the Charismatic Renewal), it will have to motivate its members to move beyond a concern for spiritual consolation to doing the works of justice.

Despite any shortcomings, however, one must acknowledge that the Charismatic Renewal, perhaps more than any other movement within the post-Vatican II Church, has put into effect much of the Council's call for renewal. For example, charismatic Catholics have probably done more than any single group within the Church to renew Catholics' appreciation for the Bible. Formal courses of study, such as The Catholic Charismatic Bible Institute at St. Mary's University in San Antonio, Texas, have attracted large numbers of laypersons each summer for training in Scripture, and many diocesan charismatic conferences continually stress the scriptural basis of the Catholic faith.

Further, charismatics, possibly more than any other group within the Church, have contributed to the ecumenical spirit encouraged by Vatican II by collaborating with Protestant Evangelicals and Pentecostals in prayer meetings, Scripture study and community living. Consider, for example, the Episcopal Church of the Redeemer in Houston, Texas. During the 70's it was an interdenominational covenant community where Catholics and Protestants from a wide range of denominations discovered their common heritage in Scripture and prayer, and thus worked on a practical level to overcome many of the differences which separate the various Christian bodies.

The Cursillo Movement

In addition to the Charismatic Renewal, a movement known as *Cursillo* (Spanish for "little course") has done much to renew the spiritual lives of post-Vatican II Catholics. Founded in Spain, Cursillo became enormously popular in the United States among both Catholics and Protestants; like the Charismatic Renewal, therefore, Cursillo has been an effective means of promoting ecumenism.

Cursillo is an intense weekend of prayer and introspection in which former "cursillisto" laypersons share with the retreatants their own experiences of conversion to Christ. The retreatants are then gradually led toward a point of making a personal commitment to Christ—something which before Vatican II would have struck most Catholics as a "Protestant" way of doing things because of its nonsacramental methodology.

Yet there is no doubt that Cursillo has remained a mainstay of Catholic spiritual renewal and, like the Charismatic Renewal, has fostered a ground swell of Catholic interest in Scripture, ecumenism and parish involvement. Both Cursillo and the Charismatic Renewal, then, have been in the forefront of American parish renewal as renewed and energetic cursillistos and charismatics take their newfound devotion to the Lord back into their parishes.

Marriage Encounter

Finally, we must mention the Marriage Encounter movement. Like Cursillo, Marriage Encounter brings people together (this time husbands and wives) for an intense weekend experience of dialogue and sharing in which a couple is led to renew its marriage by basing it on a deep commitment to the Lord. Through a unique method of journal-keeping and dialogue, couples are then encouraged to continue the communication begun on the Marriage Encounter weekend throughout their daily lives. Like the Charismatic Renewal and Cursillo, Marriage Encounter has done much to break down the barriers which have separated Protestants and Catholics for centuries.

A New Attitude Toward Hierarchical Authority

With Vatican II's new definition of the Church as the People of God—that is, with the Church of Vatican II coming to be defined as "we" rather than "it"—and with the increased insights of spiritual renewal movements like those discussed above, more and more Catholics have developed what one could call an adult attitude toward hierarchical officials. That is to say, many Catholics now see priests and bishops less as dominant figures in a parent-child relationship, less as unquestioned experts in every field of human knowledge, less as the sole arbiters of the layperson's conscience, and more as brothers involved with the laity in their mutual commitment to building the Kingdom. This new attitude has led to a situation in which many Catholics are now willing to trust their own consciences over the teachings of pope, bishops and priests.

'Humanae Vitae'

The best example of this growing independence on the part of Catholics in making moral judgments for themselves was the reaction to Pope Paul VI's encyclical on artificial birth control, *Humanae Vitae* ("On the Regulation of Birth," 1968). The question of artificial birth control had long been on the agenda of 20th-century Catholic moral theologians; and before issuing his encyclical Paul VI established a papal commission to advise him on the morality of artificial contraception. The commission perhaps surprised the Pope by concluding that artificial means of birth control were not contrary to

160

Scripture or tradition. (There was a minority position on the commission which disagreed.) In spite of the commission's decision, however, the Pope went on to condemn artificial birth control, basing his decision on the Church's ancient view of marital intercourse as designed by God principally for the procreation of children.

The Pope wrote in *Humanae Vitae*:

> Just as man does not have unlimited dominion over his body in general, so also, with particular reason, he has no such dominion over his generative faculties as such, because of their intrinsic ordination toward raising up life, of which God is the principle....We must once again declare that the direct interruption of the generative process already begun...even if for therapeutic reasons, [is] to be absolutely excluded as licit means of regulating birth. (13, 14)

On this issue large numbers of Catholics refused to follow their pope. Studies showed that, by 1970, 68 percent of American Catholic women were taking contraceptive pills and 90 percent of American Catholics rejected the Pope's encyclical on birth control; and by the late 70's, birth control among American Catholics was as common as for non-Catholics.[7]

The American bishops attempted to soften the Pope's teaching by sponsoring classes in natural family-planning methods, which have been shown scientifically to be more successful in preventing (or inducing) pregnancy than any artificial means. But by the time "Couple to Couple" leagues gained momentum for disseminating information on natural family planning, many Catholic women using artificial birth control chose not to switch to natural family planning.

The reaction to *Humanae Vitae* was but the first prominent example in which Catholics in the post-Vatican II Church used their own discernment on moral issues rather than relying on the hierarchy for guidance. As Pope John Paul II took office, it became even clearer that the laity had developed minds of their own. Wherever the immensely popular and charismatic pope traveled, he was greeted by huge throngs who showered him with love and then continued to ignore his teachings. Despite his popularity as a person, John Paul II has been unable to reverse this trend toward individual autonomy in moral decision-making.

The Growth of National Autonomy

Perhaps this dichotomy between admiration for John Paul's person and simultaneous disregard for his teaching is nowhere more clearly illustrated than in Latin America. There it is an open secret in some places that priests are married with their bishops' tacit approval and women are performing virtually all services officially reserved to men. And, as the Pope's 1984 visit to Sandinista Nicaragua showed, Latin American Catholics make no bones about favoring the policies of their political leaders, even when this places them at odds with the Pope's direct (and, in this case, angry) denunciation of their leaders' interference in Church affairs.

The growing trend toward autonomy, both on the individual level and on the level of national Churches, has had both negative and positive effects. One of the most independent-minded of national Churches, the Dutch Church, exists today as virtually an autonomous Church insofar as Dutch Catholics' loyalty to Rome on questions of morality and doctrine are concerned. When John Paul visited Holland in 1985 he was greeted by large numbers of Catholics (lay and religious) who openly rejected the Church's stand on abortion, the one issue in the Catholic world about which it had been presumed there was a large majority of agreement. Dutch Catholics continue to develop their own agenda, even though John Paul summoned the Dutch bishops to Rome to urge them to restore traditional discipline to their local Churches.

On the more positive side, the growth of autonomy in national Churches has resulted in the true "catholicizing" of evangelization efforts and of the Church's structure in the various countries of the world. Whereas before Vatican II national Churches and their clergy patterned themselves on Roman practices, today one finds much more variety and pluralism.

In Latin America, for example, *communidades de base* (or "base communities") are supplementing and in some cases supplanting traditional parish congregations as the fundamental unit of Catholic communal life. Such communities are frequently led by laypersons rather than by priests. By focusing on smaller numbers of people for their ministries, these communities can produce a more genuine spirit of renewal than is possible in huge parishes where one or two overworked priests can hardly serve as authentic pastors. The base-community movement, then, would seem to be a salutary effect of the trend toward national autonomy in that it is bringing many Latin American Catholics toward a true renewal of their Christian lives.

A similar situation pertains in Africa where native bishops, many of whom are the first African prelates to serve in their particular dioceses, have encouraged the integration of traditional African dance and music into the liturgy. In many other facets of Christian life, too, they have tried to acculturate Rome to Africa, rather than simply imitating European ways as had so often been the case in the days of the former European colonial empires.

In India, pioneering ecumenical figures like Henri le Saux, a Belgian Benedictine, and Bede Griffiths, an English Benedictine, established Christian monasteries based on the structure of Hindu ashrams. They thereby entered into dialogue on the most basic level with Indians, whose religion has for centuries been based on contemplation and inner spiritual growth.

This dialogue with the non-Christain East has flowed back into the West. Spiritual leaders like Jesuits William Johnston and George Maloney and Trappists Thomas Keating and Basil Pennington have shown the essential interconnectedness on the deep level of the spirit of Christianity and all the world's great religious traditions.

CONTEMPLATION IN A WORLD OF ACTION

When we think of post-Vatican II trends within the American Church, we wonder what person, if any, epitomizes the development and progress of Vatican II American Catholicism. Is there anyone to whom we can point as having internalized in his or her Christian walk the struggle of an entire age to grow toward the mature vision of hope held out by Vatican II?

Thomas Merton and Dorothy Day

In my opinion there are two such persons, Thomas Merton (1915-1968) and Dorothy Day (1897-1980). If Vatican II is the culmination of a process moving toward the reconciliation of Church and world and spirit and matter (as Teilhard described in his writings on the level of theory), then we can say that Merton and Day epitomize in their lives the practical implementation of that process.

Merton and Day had much in common. Both were spiritual seekers, converts to Catholicism after a brief and adolescent flirtation with communism. Both were independent spirits, determined to find authentic existence in a world devoted to sham and superficiality. Each parented a child born out of wedlock—Merton in his student days at Cambridge, Day in her early career as a free-lance journalist in New York City. Both chafed under the stilted and pompous paternalism often associated with life in the institutional Catholic Church, but both were hopelessly in love nonetheless with the true soul of Catholicism—its call to prayer and service, its demand for a complete surrender of the self to Christ in a life lived for his people. Until the end of their lives, both Merton and Day proclaimed the Catholic Church as the highest hope for a world lost in despair and illusion.

As similar as they were in temperament and instinct, they chose two different paths by which to express their Catholic faith. Merton became a Trappist monk, cloistered away from the world in a monastery in Gethsemane, Kentucky (although, as his writings gained popularity, he later made many forays into the active world). Day lived most of her life in a poor neighborhood in New York City where she devoted herself to the Catholic Worker movement that she cofounded with Peter Maurin in 1933.

Merton, then, was principally a contemplative, whose insights into the interior life of prayer, solitude and silence influenced many Catholics to rediscover the great treasure of medieval Catholic spirituality. Day, on the other hand, lived her life in the tradition of apostolic service best represented by the mendicant movement of the 13th century (see *The People of the Faith*, p. 97). Merton can thus be thought of as having resurrected the spirit of such spiritual fathers as Bernard of Clairvaux (see *The People of the Faith*, p. 84), while Day epitomized the spirit of Francis of Assisi.

Yet Merton and Day cannot be defined in terms of antithetical distinctions, and in that lies their precise relevance and importance for the Vatican II Church. In other words, we should not think of Merton as a monk locked away from the world, unaware of the real concerns of ordinary people; nor should we think of Day as a social activist with no spiritual depth. Merton and Day are significant to the era of Vatican II precisely because they each harmonized the inner and the outer, the life of contemplation and the life of action, the interior call of the spirit and the demand of the gospel to give one's life for others. We could thus say that while Merton was a "contemplative activist," Day was an "active contemplative."

Through his writings Merton spoke as a prophet, calling the world to abandon its illusions and falsehood and to turn within to the only authentic life—the life of the inner spirit, on which all authentically human work and activity must be based. His denunciation of racism and the Vietnam War, for example, were spoken in the prophet's voice, a voice tempered in prayer and solitude and in great personal struggle toward holiness.

When Merton spoke, the world heard a human being speaking to them. They heard a man who had walked through the dark valley of trial and temptation, a man who was aware of his smallness and weakness but who, out of his own sense of "woundedness," would teach all the more authoritatively that only in Christ can the world be healed of its hatred and strife. Merton's readers heard reflected in his spiritual struggle the world's struggle in miniature, and for that reason they could heed his call to seek authentic existence by turning within, where the deep life of the spirit leads the soul to conversion and healing.

Dorothy Day, on the other hand, was involved in virtually every form of Christian activism—from running Catholic Worker soup kitchens and shelters for transients, to standing on picket lines with migrant farm workers in California, to being arrested with antiwar protesters during the Vietnam era. Yet she never for a moment let her coworkers forget that Christian activism was authentic only if based on a life of prayer and asceticism.

One of the most telling examples of Day's synthesis between action and contemplation in her service of the Church is recalled in her response to Pope John XXIII's announcement of Vatican II. At the time, Day was heavily involved in a busy ministry of service to the poor and constantly needed for advice and leadership by the Catholic Worker centers around the country. She was acutely aware of the need for more and more *work* on behalf of justice. But she nonetheless dropped everything, flew to Rome, rented a cheap apartment near the Vatican and fasted and prayed for the success of the Council. Like Thomas Merton, Dorothy Day knew and practiced authentic Christianity—a Christianity that harmonizes contemplation and action, that brings not just human energy but the Spirit's own power to bear in transforming the world into the new age which Teilhard saw dawning.

We could devote an entire book to a study of the writings of these two contemplative-activists, but let's quote just two excerpts from their writings. The first is from Dorothy Day, the mystic-in-the-world who, for half a century, spent nearly 16 hours every day actively involved in the problems of the poor. Yet, as her *modus vivendi*, she urged not frenetic activity but a life lived spontaneously from the level of prayer:

> I believe we must render most reverent homage to Him who created
> us and stilled the sea and told the winds to be calm, and multiplied
> the loaves and fishes. He is transcendent and He is immanent. He is
> closer than the air we breathe and just as vital to us....Let us do the
> same thing [as the communists]. Let us canvass blocks, factories,
> schools, form groups to study, not Marxism, but the encyclicals of
> the popes—the writings of the Church on social questions as well as
> on the liturgy. The two should go together. There should be daily
> Mass, a community act, as well as the individual work which we
> must each do. We believe in the Communion of Saints; we know that
> in the act of the Mass we are associated with a great body, the Church
> militant, the Church suffering, the Church triumphant.[8]

And now listen to Merton the monk speak of the life of Christian activism:

The requirements of a work to be done can be understood as the will of God. If I am supposed to hoe a garden or make a table, then I will be obeying God if I am true to the task I am performing. To do the work carefully and well, with love and respect for the nature of my task and with due attention to its purpose, is to unite myself to God's will in my work. In this way I become His instrument. He works through me. When I act as His instrument my labor cannot become an obstacle to contemplation, even though it may temporarily so occupy my mind that I cannot engage in it while I am actually doing my job. Yet my work itself will purify and pacify my mind and dispose me for contemplation....In any case we should always seek to conform to the *logos* or truth of the duty before us, the work to be done, or our own God-given nature. Contemplative obedience and abandonment to the will of God can never mean a cultivated. indifference to the natural values implanted by Him in human life and work. Insensitivity must not be confused with detachment. The contemplative must certainly be detached, but he can never allow himself to become insensible to true human values, whether in society, in other men or in himself. If he does so, then his contemplation stands condemned as vitiated in its very root.[9]

The writings and the lives of Thomas Merton and Dorothy Day, well represent that "faith enrichment" which the future Pope John Paul II saw as the essence of Vatican II's teaching. The Vatican II Catholic is a contemplative-in-action—someone who, like Merton and Day, harmonizes the traditional Catholic spirituality of interiority, self-abnegation and prayer with the call to active service on behalf of the gospel. If any trend can best summarize the development of post-Vatican II Catholicism, it is found in the lives of Catholics who emulate Merton and Day—monks in the world, contemplatives in action, Christians rooted in the Church's life of prayer and saturated at the same time in the Church's social apostolate.

We have touched here on simply a few of the most observable trends in post-Vatican II Catholic life. In the next chapter we turn to some developing theological trends as we continue to define the shape of the renewed Church bequeathed to us by Vatican II.

CHAPTER FIFTEEN

THE VATICAN II CHURCH AND HUMAN LIBERATION

An Overview of Recent Theology

Before Vatican II the Church was like a phalanx of soldiers being led into war by the pope, bishops, priests and religious, with the laity trooping behind as infantry. Since the conclusion of Vatican II, this image has changed drastically. Nowadays the Church is more like a group of pilgrims passing through a desert, all seeking the best way to express their understanding of post-Vatican II Catholicism, all seeking a higher degree of union with their fellow pilgrims.

And one of the ways these pilgrims communicate with each other is through theology. In this chapter, then, we will examine some prominent theological expressions that have emerged since Vatican II and discuss their significance for the Church's effort to implement the conciliar renewal.

FROM PAUL VI TO JOHN PAUL II

Toward the end of his pontificate, Pope Paul VI seemed to many observers to be losing his grip on the leadership of the Church. He died a saintly but troubled man, vexed by the refusal of many in his pluralistic flock to obey or, perhaps, even to understand what he was trying to say.

On August 26, 1978, the Conclave of Cardinals elected as Paul's successor the well-liked and affable patriarch of Venice, Albino Luciani, a man who had sat through every session of Vatican II without once expressing a public opinion. Choosing the name John Paul I, the new pope cautioned his audience that, despite the reverence his choice of name displayed for both of his predecessors, he possessed neither John XXIII's simple wisdom nor Paul VI's erudition.

John Paul I was pope for only 33 days, endearing the world to himself by his spontaneous and loving smile, and charming it by the publication of his "open letters," written to various magazines under such pseudonyms as Pinocchio and Mickey Mouse. With his untimely death, the faithful in Rome whispered to each other that God had not wanted as pope such a gentle and kindly figure. Their words perhaps filtered into the electoral conclave; for the cardinals this time chose a man whose ecclesiastical career had been forged in the crucible of persecution, war and totalitarian oppression.

John Paul II is at once the most simple to understand and the most complex of persons. He is simple to understand in that his entire being is inspired and motivated by an innate sense of Catholic tradition. He is, as it were, a walking representation of that tradition. Yet he is also a complex man. As we came to realize in Chapter Twelve, there is doubtless no one in the world who is as ardent a champion of and as informed a spokesman for Vatican II's renewal. In matters involving the Church's institutional structure, however, John Paul could just as easily be living in the 19th century. A staunch advocate of obedience to hierarchical authority, he relies heavily on the curial bureaucracy in his day-to-day management of the Church and resists all appeals to open the ordained priesthood to women or married persons.

At the same time, John Paul II deals with his fellow bishops as equal partners, listens attentively to their words at synods and encourages them to write their own synodal documents. Even Catholics opposed to his stands on certain issues have never been able to accuse John Paul II of personal animosity, bitterness or smallness. When he takes a stand on a controversial issue, John Paul never speaks out of insecurity or fear, as did Pius IX and Pius X. On the contrary, if there is one word which epitomizes John Paul II, it is *security*. He is certain of where he stands and where he is going, and he always speaks out of reasoned principle.

John Paul's Principles

If John Paul II is a principled pope, what principles best epitomize his approach to papal leadership? We could say that he is motivated first and foremost by the principle of *sacralization*—that is, by the desire to make the world, as the focal point of God's action, *holy*. And as a subsidiary to this key principle, we could say that John Paul II is motivated by the desire to restore humanity to its lost dignity.

John Paul's vision is thoroughly colored by his experience as a young man growing up in Poland. His brother, mother and father all died in his formative years, and his days as a young seminarian in the Diocese of Krakow coincided with the Nazis' occupation of Poland. When his seminary was closed down, it went underground, and thus Karol Wojtyla pursued his priestly studies while moving from house to house—in much the same fashion as did English priests in the 16th century during the heyday of Catholic persecution under Queen Elizabeth I. Further, as Polish Jews were rounded up and shipped to Auschwitz (located in Wojtyla's own diocese), Karol participated in sheltering hundreds of persecuted Jews.

No sooner did the Nazi horror end, however, than a similar one replaced it—the establishment in Poland of a Stalinist puppet State inimical to democracy, Polish autonomy and religious freedom. As bishop (1958) and then archbishop (1963) of Krakow, Wojtyla learned to practice the delicate art of survival in a Communist State. For the Church to survive in Poland, Wojtyla realized, it needed leaders fearless enough to resist Communist bullying and prudent enough not to push the Communists into open violence against the Church.

Perhaps it was his skill at negotiating between these two extremes which motivated the cardinals on October 16, 1978, to elect Wojtyla pope. In his first address to his new Roman parishioners, John Paul II succinctly summarized the two chief elements in his upbringing: "The cardinals have summoned a new bishop of Rome," he said. "They have called him from a far country; far, yet close, because of our communion in the traditions of the Church."

Anyone who wishes to understand John Paul II must take into account his Polish background. It is easy for American critics to speak of John Paul as inflexible and conservative when they have never had to experience life under the constant harassment of a Communist dictatorship. The Poles literally struggle every day with a totalitarian regime just for the privilege to worship God in public. In comparison, our American Church debates can seem petty and trivial.

In a totalitarian dictatorship like Poland, unity among Christians is the sole bulwark of religious freedom. And, from John Paul's perspective, the Church's traditions are the best safeguard against Communist annihilation. One can imagine the disastrous consequences if Polish Catholics were as divided as American Catholics, bickering endlessly about every issue under heaven.

John Paul's Catholicity
Yet, despite John Paul's Polish upbringing, he is a man uniquely qualified to head a universal Church. Well traveled even as a bishop,

John Paul has seen and been seen by more Catholics than any other pope in history. With doctoral degrees in both theology and philosophy, and fluent in half a dozen languages, John Paul can discuss the issues of the day both from the scholar's and the pastor's perspective.

John Paul's catholicity—his universal perspective and outlook—can best be seen in the great task of his pontificate: his effort to sacralize the world and to restore humanity to a state of dignity. Growing up in a country dominated first by Nazis and then by Communists, John Paul experienced firsthand the war which totalitarianism wages against both humanity and religion. In June 1979 the Pope traveled to Poland and preached a blunt message right under the noses of uneasy party bosses. "Christ," he proclaimed, "cannot be kept out of the history of man in any part of the globe. The exclusion of Christ from the history of man is an act against man."[1]

This statement is the basis of the Pope's Christian humanism. For John Paul II, human history cannot be considered apart from the participation of God in that history. Further, one cannot know God and worship him unless one first proclaims the nobility and dignity of human nature. "Man," the Pope wrote in his encyclical *Dives in Misericordia* ("Rich in Mercy," 1980), "cannot be manifested in the full dignity of his nature without reference to God, not only at the level of a concept but also in an integrally existential way."[2]

John Paul's Christian Existentialism

John Paul II is fond of the word *existential*. He used it frequently in *Sources of Renewal* and in his other writings to refer to the entire context of a person's life and vocation—family background, gender, cultural environment, socioeconomic status, the political system under which the person lives and so on. For John Paul II, one cannot answer the question "What is man?" apart from the unique contexts in which individual persons live. For him, each person is a unique focal point of divine action. Christ lives not just in abstract humanity, but in the lives of individual men and women in their unique existential situations.

For this reason the Pope eschews any classist analysis of history. Contrary to Marxist teaching, the Pope says, human beings do not have value as members of a class (which, as a totality, is of more importance than its constituent members). Rather, individual human beings are noble and of value in and of themselves, despite their class, race or party. "Every man," the Pope proclaimed, "by virtue of being man, has a right to social advancement in the framework of his community."[3]

For John Paul II only Christ and his redemption of humanity can satisfy the longing of the human heart; only in Christ does humanity find its dignity. Because of humanity's dignity as the head of redeemed creation, the Pope distinguished in *Dives in Misericordia* between justice and mercy.

Whereas Marx's appeal "...to overthrow all circumstances in which man is humiliated, enslaved, abandoned and despised"[4] is a call to justice, the gospel of Jesus Christ, the Pope said, is a call to mercy and love as well as to justice. The Pope wrote, "The experience of the past and of our own time demonstrates that justice alone is not enough, that it can even lead to the negation and destruction of itself, if that deeper power which is love is not allowed to shape human life in all its dimensions."[5]

John Paul's Position on Contemporary Issues

The Pope sees his own calling to sacralize the world as a mission to return humanity's focus to "that deeper power which is love." For that reason he resists any tendency which smacks of secularization. His antipathy to women's ordination and to the ordination of married persons must be seen in this light. For John Paul II, the ordination of women and of married persons runs counter to the Church's mission to make the world holy: in reference to women, because he believes priests must come from the same group of people whom Jesus called as apostles (males); and in reference to married persons, because he believes that the single man can most efficiently attend to the task of resacralization.

On this issue the Pope's critics charge him with contradicting himself. If, the critics argue, human beings are of value because of their redeemed status as persons who are in Christ, separate and apart from their membership in the group or class, why then are the two classes of females and married persons excluded by the Pope in his definition of priestly ministry? Why cannot women and married persons sacralize the world as competently as celibate males? As the Pope wrote in his own encyclical, *Redemptor Hominis*: "In the mystery of the Redemption man becomes newly 'expressed' and, in a way, is newly created. He is newly created! 'There is neither Jew nor Greek, there is neither slave nor free, there is neither male nor female; for you are all one in Christ Jesus.'"[6]

Some observers see the Pope's views on qualifications for the priesthood as the necessary adjunct to his catholicity—specifically, his desire to unite the Roman Catholic Church to the Greek Orthodox Church. Since the latter body is adamantly opposed to female priestly ordination (although it tolerates married males as priests), the Pope is said to have sacrificed consistency for ecumenism. This argument is somewhat dubious since John Paul has allowed married Episcopal priests to become Catholic priests—wives and all.

Whatever his motives, the Pope has steadfastly resisted pleas to expand the ordained ministry to encompass women and married persons, even though in some areas of the world, such as Latin America, laypersons are the only "priests" some Catholics see for months on end. When the Pope in 1979 at Puebla, Mexico, denounced "all forms of humanism imprisoned within a strictly economic, biological or psychological view of man,"[7] some observers perhaps winced at mention of the word "biological."

In other respects, the Pope's views on how to sacralize the world and to restore humanity's dignity have met with more support. During his 1979 trip to Ireland, for example, the Pope decried the use of violence as a means to achieve otherwise justifiable social reforms. "Peace," he said, "can never flourish in a climate of terror, intimidation and death."[8]

And the Pope has consistently condemned the materialism of capitalist countries as vigorously as he has condemned Marxist materialism. In his 1979 trip to the United States, he criticized "wealthy and surfeited people" who ignore "radical injustice." In his Yankee Stadium homily of October 2, he bluntly accused rich America of hoarding the world's resources to itself, thereby treating underdeveloped countries in the same way that the rich man treated Lazarus (Luke 16:19-21):

> The poor of the United States and of the world are your brothers and sisters in Christ. You must never be content to leave them just the crumbs from the feast. You must take of your substance, and not just of your abundance in order to help them. And you must treat them like guests at your family table.

Whereas secularization is an inherent tenet of the totalitarian State, in the capitalist West, the Pope says, secularization arises from unbridled greed and hedonism. "The life of pleasure," he preached, "is the new slavery."[9] In both Communist and capitalist states, the same temptation threatens to destroy civilization: "...that man should be persuaded into believing himself alone."[10]

Finally, everywhere he has traveled the Pope has consistently condemned what he regards as the single greatest sign of humanity's loss of self-respect—legalized abortion:

> If a person's right to life is violated at the moment in which he is first conceived in his mother's womb, an indirect blow is struck also at the whole of the moral order, which serves to ensure the inviolable goods of man.
>
> Among these goods life occupies the first place. The Church

172

defends the right to life not only in regard to the majesty of the Creator, who is the first giver of this life, but in respect too, of the essential good of the human person.[11]

OTHER THEOLOGICAL PERSPECTIVES

The media often gives the impression that John Paul is constantly at loggerheads with Catholic theologians. With several notable exceptions, this is not the case. In actuality the Pope and most contemporary theologians share the same starting point: the belief that individuals in their existential situations are the focal points of God's ongoing relationship with humanity—and the related belief that Christianity is most authentic when it strives to empower individuals to reach their full human potential in Christ.

Both John Paul II and other contemporary Catholic theologians elaborate upon this theology of Christian humanism by emphasizing the goodness and dignity of material creation and of human work. In post-Vatican II theology, the modern world, as the meeting point between God and human beings, is seen as good so long as human existence is submitted to the divinizing action of the Redeemer. As John Paul expressed it in *Redemptor Hominis*, "the God of creation is revealed as the God of redemption, as the God who is 'faithful to himself,' and faithful to his love for man and the world, which he revealed on the day of creation."[12]

We could perhaps summarize the central theme of contemporary Catholic theology by saying that God and human beings are seen as united in Christ for the purpose of bringing the world to holiness, to the revelation of God's goodness now manifested in creation only partially and incompletely. In short, Catholic theology today stands for the proposition that the world, God and humanity are all united in an embrace of love in which each of the partners seeks only the best and highest for his beloved.

This idea was at the core of Teilhard's writings, as when he wrote:

All over the earth at this moment, at the heart of the new spiritual atmosphere created by the appearance of the idea of evolution, there flow the currents of love of God and faith in the world, the one current highly sensitive to the other.[13]

Contemporary theology, as expressed in Teilhard's writings and in *Redemptor Hominis*, represents in effect the Church's last word on the goodness of God's creation and, in particular, the last word on the unique dignity of redeemed human nature. This optimistic outlook has only recently triumphed within the halls of Catholic theology.

As we have seen in the three preceding volumes in this series, Christianity has waged a nearly constant civil war over the question of the value and worth of matter, sometimes denigrating matter and the human body to such an extent that only "spirit" was seen as good and worthy of God's love. Especially with Teilhard and now at the highest level of the Church's *magisterium*, Catholicism has put its final stamp of approval on the words of Genesis, "God looked at everything he had made, and he found it very good" (1:31).

Karl Rahner

Although Teilhard may be thought of as one of the principal exponents of the new Catholic theology, it is not entirely accurate to classify Teilhard as a theologian. As we saw in Chapter Eleven, his interests were so varied and universal that it is really impossible to place a single tag on his writings. The title of 20th-century Catholic theologian par excellence belongs instead to the German Jesuit, Karl Rahner (1904-1984). In terms of his output, influence and creativity, Rahner deserves to be ranked among the greatest of Catholic theologians, on a par with Thomas Aquinas.

Rahner served as a *peritus* (theological adviser) to the bishops at Vatican II and established himself as one of the leading conciliar spokesmen for renewal. As a professional theologian and confidant of Cardinal Franz Konig of Vienna, Rahner was not looked upon with suspicion as Teilhard had been, and he was thus able to move freely within the corridors of power. Although he developed his theology independently of Teilhard, Rahner and Teilhard shared many of the same ideas and, like Teilhard, Rahner also had much in common with John Paul II.

Like Pope John Paul II in his early philosophical essays, Rahner focused on what he called "theological anthropology"—the belief that the human person in the fullness of his or her existential situation is the focal point of God's action on earth. Only by understanding our humanity, Rahner wrote, can we understand God's ongoing revelation, because it is only through our humanity that we encounter God. God is God to *us* only because there is an "us" to start with, an ostensibly self-evident truism which is often overlooked. Out of this divine-human encounter—indeed, *only* through this divine-human encounter—can human beings become free and autonomous beings.

For Rahner, the answer to the question "What is humanity?" is best found in Jesus Christ. It is Jesus who best tells us what God is like, and likewise it is Jesus who best tells us what humanity can

174

become. Only in Jesus can the divine-human relationship be fully understood. Yet Jesus should not be thought of as an unattainable model. Like Teilhard, Rahner saw humanity growing organically into Christ—being "transformed" into Christ—through the progressive evolution of our humanity as it is inspired by grace.

Rahner completely overhauled the previous Catholic understanding of grace as a quantifiable "thing" and replaced it with the understanding of grace as a *relationship* with God. Grace, for Rahner, is God's self-communication to creation. There is no separation between God's grace and nature, since all nature as created by God is either "graced" or existentially oriented toward grace. In this graced universe, all creation is in evolution toward completion in Christ. Rahner summarized this aspect of his thought as follows:

> Theology has been too long and too often bedeviled by the unavowed supposition that grace would be no longer grace if it were too generously distributed by the love of God! Our whole spiritual life is lived in the realm of the salvific will of God, of his prevenient grace, of his call as it becomes efficacious: all of which is an element within the region of our consciousness, though one which remains anonymous as long as it is not interpreted from without by the message of faith. Even when he does not "know" it and does not believe it,... man always lives consciously in the presence of the God of eternal life.[14]

Rahner's teaching on grace led him to speak of "anonymous Christianity." Since human nature is graced and transformed by God's self-communication, anyone who accepts and authentically expresses his or her true human nature is a Christian, even if that person is not linked to the institutional Church. Although the empirical Roman Catholic Church is, for Rahner, the supreme sacrament of salvation—"the historical manifestation" of God's redeeming grace—it is grace rather than institutional identity which is the key ingredient in salvation. So long as one is authentically human, so long as one's "fundamental option" is toward God rather than away from God, Rahner argued, anyone—even if he or she is not specifically Christian—will be saved. Such is the majesty and power of grace.

This was a far cry from the Church's former belief that only someone incorporated into the institutional Church could be saved (see, for example, *The People of the Faith*, p. 102). For Rahner, "...the fundamental mystery of human existence is the Christian mystery, and it is anonymously or explicitly present wherever human life is lived authentically, no matter what words are used to define and describe it."[15]

Rahner's theology, like that of Teilhard, is principally a theology of hope. In an age when all human life on earth can be snuffed out in an hour, Rahner optimistically pointed humanity toward triumph. As Teilhard believed, so too did Rahner believe that human beings are "auto-evolvers": They move toward the future with the eternal destiny of the universe in their own hands. The salvation of the universe—its ultimate fulfillment and completion in Christ—is already seen dimly through the powers of hope. "And hoping for what we cannot see means awaiting it with patient endurance" (Romans 8:25).

This, Rahner believed, is a principal task of human beings today—to exercise the virtue of hope, to live as if we are victors in Christ rather than victims of evil. And wherever victims throw off oppression and become victors—wherever God's self-communication is more visibly manifested on earth—there one finds hope and triumph—"the glorious freedom of the children of God" (Romans 8:21).

Jürgen Moltmann

This relationship between freedom and hope has been explored by other contemporary theologians. The German Protestant theologian, Jürgen Moltmann (b. 1926), in his book *Theology of Hope*, stated that the "practice of hope" is central to Christian theology. Moltmann's thesis helped to develop a major theme of contemporary theology, summarized by the word *praxis*, which we could define as the act of reflecting theologically on human action. In other words, through praxis we start with the actual context of human existence and reason backward to theory, rather than constructing a theory first and then trying to impose our theory on people's actions, as theology has traditionally done (see pp. 152-153).

Looked at in this way, Moltmann's theology of hope becomes intricately involved with people's day-to-day existence, particularly the political conditions under which they live. Thus the theology of hope becomes, for Moltmann, "political theology." "Political theology," he said, "sinks its roots in the theology of hope."[16] Unless theology becomes praxis, unless it is applied to people's real-life political situations, Moltmann says, theology will simply be irrelevant to modern life. Thus, for Moltmann, theology can encourage the practice of hope only if it encourages political freedom at the same time. Only people who are or who can become free can hope. Hope, then, is not so much the source of freedom as the result of a life lived in pursuit of freedom.

Edward Schillebeeckx

The Dutch Catholic theologian Edward Schillebeeckx (b. 1914) likewise pursued this theme of the relationship between freedom and hope: "God's saving activity means the emancipation from oppression of all kinds, and the theologian needs to name both where that has been happening and where salvation still needs to happen."[17] Like Teilhard, Rahner and Moltmann, Schillebeeckx is a theologian of hope. The central themes of his theology are: "the utter graciousness of God's leading humanity forward to completion; God's commitment to humanity, especially in suffering; and the enduring significance of God's revelation in Jesus Christ."[18]

It is this latter theme—God's revelation in Jesus Christ—that has gotten Schillebeeckx into hot water with Vatican officials. Schillebeeckx believes that Scripture can only be understood in the cultural-historical context in which it was written. If we are to apply Scripture to today's problems, we can do so only by first acknowledging what the authors of Scripture intended their words to mean in their own day. It is erroneous to impose our 20th-century values on the Bible. It is equally erroneous to impose 19 centuries of Church tradition and cultural conditioning onto the Jesus of first-century Palestine.

Schillebeeckx's Christology has been challenged by Rome because he sees the Church's traditional description of the Jesus in the early creeds as retroactively superimposed on the Jesus of the Gospels. Rome suspects that Schillebeeckx denies the divinity of Christ by seeking too diligently to define Jesus' humanity within the context of the historical milieu. Schillebeeckx has stated his own case in this way: "I do not deny that Jesus is God, but want to assert that he is also man, something that has been overlooked. But when you say that, you are suspect."[19]

Hans Küng

Schillebeeckx's German counterpart, the priest-theologian Hans Küng (b. 1928), has likewise questioned traditional Christology, as in his book *On Being a Christian*:

> Can we have less of a Christology in the classical manner, speculatively or dogmatically "from above" but—without disputing the legitimacy of the older Christology—more of a historical Christology from "below," in the light of the concrete Jesus, more suited to modern man?[20]

On December 15, 1979, Küng's teachings were censored by the Vatican, and shortly thereafter the German bishops revoked Küng's license to teach as a Catholic theologian at the University of Tubingen. Pope John Paul II, in a letter written on May 15, 1980, commended the bishops for taking the action:

Does a theologian who no longer accepts completely the doctrine of the Church still have the right to teach in the name of the Church, and on the basis of a special mission received from her? Can he himself still wish to do so, if some dogmas of the Church are contrary to his personal convictions? And under these circumstances can the Church, in this case her competent authority, continue to oblige him to do so?[21]

Gustavo Gutierrez and Liberation Theology

Both Moltmann and Schillebeeckx have emphasized the necessity of situating theology within the context of the struggle for human freedom. Each has stressed that salvation is not simply a theological concept but a call to action on behalf of those oppressed by injustice.

Beginning in Latin America in the 1960's, theologians began to apply the insights of European theologians like Moltmann and Schillebeeckx to their own Churches. Basing their theology on praxis (see p. 176), they wrote that action on behalf of the oppressed precedes the writing of theology—indeed it even precedes understanding the gospel. Only by entering into the life of poverty and oppression which the "anonymous of history" suffer, only by experiencing life from the point of view of those to whom Jesus himself preached the gospel, these theologians said, can one really know what the Gospels are trying to say.

This theology came to be called "liberation theology" because its main objective is to liberate the oppressed from unjust domination and empower them to live authentically human lives. The most well-known and prolific liberation theologian is a Peruvian priest, Gustavo Gutierrez (b. 1928).

Gutierrez received a classical European theological education but returned to Peru to live in the slums of Lima, where he became convinced that European perspectives were inadequate to address the problems of Latin America. He eventually rejected his European training altogether and formulated a more radical view of liberation theology.

Liberal European theology such as Moltmann's, Gutierrez says, is inadequate for Latin America because it has grown out of the very European tradition which is responsible for Latin American colonialism. In other words, it is written from the perspective of oppressors rather than of the oppressed.

Such liberal theologies as Moltmann's, Gutierrez says, "gave more attention to the demands of bourgeois society (than traditional metaphysical theology), but ended by accepting the place that society assigned them—the sphere of the private."[22] In other words, Gutierrez is saying, liberal theologians did not actually enter vigorously into the political sphere and confront unjust structures of oppression with the gospel. Only liberation theology can do this, Gutierrez says, because it alone is a theology that comes from the poor and oppressed themselves, rather than from middle-class theoreticians who speculate about what is best for the poor without actually living in poverty themselves.

Gutierrez's message is both blunt and challenging. He does not disguise the fact that he uses Marxist methods to construct his theology. This, however, did not subject him to hierarchical criticism, because Pope Paul VI himself, in a papal letter entitled *Octogesima Adveniens* (1971), declared that Marxism as a form of social analysis (as opposed to a philosophy of history and political movement) could, if used prudently, be applied to theological method.

In the same letter the Pope declared that a socialism which does not exclude Jesus Christ in its worldview may be reconciled with Christianity, thereby taking the sting out of Leo XIII's condemnation of socialism (see p. 57). Paul VI also condoned a limited type of "utopianism"—that is, belief in a perfectible human society on earth—so long as such utopianism simply provokes criticism of unjust social structures and inspires people's hope in the future, without denying that true human perfection comes only in heaven.

We mention these three aspects of Pope Paul VI's teaching because they were each part of Gutierrez's original formulation of liberation theology and, thus—at least as theoretical premises—consistent with the magisterium's teaching. Whether Gutierrez's entire theology actually squares with official Church teaching, however, becomes another question. Like the theology of Schillebeeckx and Küng, that of Gutierrez (and other liberation theologians such as Leonardo Boff) has continued to cause anxieties in Rome.

The reason for this lies principally in Gutierrez's reliance on the Marxist concept of history as a class struggle (recall our discussion on pp. 61-64 ff.). Anyone, Gutierrez believes, who is still a part of the *bourgeoisie* is an oppressor. And since only the oppressed can truly understand the gospel, only their view of theology is accurate. As members of the oppressor class, then, the middle classes of Europe and America cannot, to Gutierrez's way of thinking, construct or teach a true theology.

This classist view of history and society is in conflict with John Paul II's views as stated above (p. 170). Further, critics of Gutierrez's view of liberation theology question that his classist perspective is represented in the New Testament. Jesus, they say, confined his teaching and ministry not to classes, but to individuals, especially to individuals despised by other Jews of his day as belonging to the wrong "class" (for example, the Syro-Phoenician woman of Mark 7:24-30). And while it is true that Jesus saw his ministry as proclaiming "liberty to captives" (Luke 4:18), he did not exclude anyone—not even "bourgeois Pharisees"—from the ranks of those who were "captives." In other words, Jesus admitted anyone into his company (and into his Kingdom), regardless of the person's class affiliation.

Gutierrez's reaction to this critique would perhaps be to say that, as middle-class oppressors, his critics simply cannot understand what Jesus' intentions really were. Only if one becomes poor and oppressed can one know the truth. But this approach accomplishes little more than excluding Gutierrez's critics from entering into any realistic dialogue with him.

Further, it is unclear why no one in the middle class can be considered oppressed (or, to put it the other way, why everyone in the middle class is an oppressor). By Gutierrez's own line of reasoning, if one cannot understand life in the lower class unless one becomes a member of the lower class, can Gutierrez truly understand middle-class life if he does not first enter into the middle class?

Another aspect of his theology which causes problems for him in Rome is Gutierrez's call for the elimination of private property and the establishment of socialism. At Puebla in 1979, Pope John Paul II urged the Latin American bishops to establish reforms which "have the goal of enabling all to have access to property, since property in some respects constitutes the indispensable condition for man's liberty and creativity, enabling him to rise out of obscurity and alienation."[23]

If Gutierrez intends by his theology to establish a collectivist society, he perhaps first needs to explain how such a society would avoid the pitfalls of previous socialist experiments. Specifically, how would he avoid the evolution of the very type of totalitarian State with which Karol Wojtyla was intimately acquainted as bishop of Krakow? One sees the negative side of liberation theology in the example of the Sandinista regime in Nicaragua. While liberating many of the poor from oppression, this regime has denied freedom of the press and other basic rights to its citizens, and harasses Church leaders who disagree with its policies.

During his visit to Rio de Janiero in July 1980, John Paul II took note of liberation theology's devotion to the concept of class struggle by saying, "...the class struggle is not the path of social order; it brings with it the risk of reversing the roles of those who engage in it, and creating new situations of injustice."[24]

Perhaps Latin American liberation theologians could profit from the Pope's Polish experience, just as he and those of us from the

180

European cultural tradition could learn from Gutierrez and other Third World theologians. These theologians unquestionably speak sincerely and with Christian love on behalf of the "nonpersons" of Latin America, defined by Gutierrez as "the poor, the exploited, the ones systematically and legally despoiled of their humanness, the ones who scarcely know they are persons at all."[25]

The Puebla Conference

Whatever critique one might make of liberation theology, one cannot deny that Gutierrez and other Latin American liberation theologians paint an accurate picture of the oppression and injustice suffered by the Third World's poor at the hands of the wealthy countries.

The Latin American Bishops Conference ("CELAM"), meeting at Puebla, Mexico, in 1979, appropriated many of the insights of liberation theology and came out squarely in favor of "A Preferential Option for the Poor" (as their principal conference document was entitled), as did John Paul II in his own homilies:

> Viewing it in the light of faith, we see the growing gap between rich and poor as a scandal and a contradiction to Christian existence (cf. Paul VI, *Populorum Progressio*, 3). This is contrary to the plan of the Creator and to the honor that is due him. In this anxiety and sorrow the Church sees a situation of social sinfulness, all the more serious because it exists in countries that call themselves Catholic and are capable of changing the situation.[26]

> Analyzing this situation more deeply we discover that this poverty is not a passing phase. Instead it is the product of economic, social, and political situations and structures, though there are also other causes for the state of misery. In many instances this state of poverty within our countries finds its origin and support in mechanisms which, because they are impregnated with materialism rather than any authentic humanism, create a situation on the international level where the rich get richer at the expense of the poor, who get even poorer. (Opening Address, III, 3)[27]

Liberation theology, along with the other theological perspectives discussed in this chapter, are but the natural outgrowth of Vatican II's call for Catholics to Christianize the world by working in the world as servants of the gospel. Today's theology—whether written by John Paul II, Rahner or Gutierrez—demands positive action. Gone are the days when "fasting and praying" for the poor were enough. Today from every corner of the Catholic world we hear restated Jesus' own words, "Why do you call me 'Lord, Lord,' and not put into practice what I teach you?" (Luke 6:46).

CHAPTER SIXTEEN

THE UNFINISHED AGENDA

Issues for an American Church

In this chapter we will look at issues of significance to the American Church, with a view to answering the question which ended the last chapter: "Why do you call me 'Lord, Lord,' and not put into practice what I teach you?" (Luke 6:46). We will identify these issues which call American Catholics to put their faith into *practice* by examining recent teachings of the American bishops.

Fifty years ago American Catholics unhesitatingly followed the dictates of their bishops. The bishops, in turn, first looked to Rome before teaching their flocks anything of a substantive nature. Now all that is changed. Today the bishops think for themselves, and so do their flocks. Many American Catholics pick and choose which of the bishops' teachings they will follow. Whether this situation should be characterized as "healthy pluralism" or "disintegrating disobedience" is a matter on which one could find a wide variety of opinions.

The bishops themselves acknowledge that not every jot and tittle of their pastoral statements are to be accepted as dogma. For example, in their pastoral letter on war and peace (1983), they wrote, "...not all statements in this letter have the same moral authority. At times we state universally binding moral principles found in the teaching of the Church; at other times the pastoral letter makes specific applications, observations and recommendations which allow for *diversity of opinion*..."[1] (emphasis added).

At the same time, however, the bishops "expect Catholics to give our moral judgments *serious consideration* when they are forming their own views on specific problems"[2] (emphasis added). Somewhere between this "diversity of opinion" and "serious consideration" lies the norm of Catholic orthodoxy in the Church of the United States.

Notice that the bishops have abandoned the triumphalistic language of yesteryear in which every maxim was followed by an anathema. Today the bishops are treating their fellow Catholics as adults. In their statement *Called and Gifted: The American Catholic Laity* (1980), the bishops wrote, "One of the chief characteristics of lay men and women today is their growing sense of being adult members of the Church."[3] While adulthood suggests freedom from childlike subservience, it also suggests mature responsibility. As the bishops put it, "Adulthood implies knowledge, experience and awareness, freedom and responsibility, and mutuality in relationships" (PL*418).

In other words, the bishops are saying, "We're willing to enter into mature dialogue with our flocks." The question then becomes whether the laity are willing to do their part—to become informed enough on the issues of today to become responsible partners in dialogue with their bishops.

THE PASTORAL LETTERS

If one wants to align oneself with the Catholic Church in the modern world in its particular American setting, the place to start is the pastoral statements of the National Conference of Catholic Bishops (NCCB). What follows them, is a sampler of the more significant issues addressed by the NCCB.

Feeding the Hungry: Toward a U.S. Domestic Food Policy (April 16, 1975)
The debate over American food policy must be seen in a larger context. Hunger and malnutrition flow from basic failures in our society's social and economic structures. (PL 52)

Pastoral Plan for Pro-Life Activities (November 20, 1975)
Programs of service and care should be available to provide women with alternate options to abortion. (PL 85)

The Economy: Human Dimensions (November 20, 1975)
Government must play a role in the economic activity of its citizens. Indeed, it should promote in a suitable manner the production

---

* PL refers to the *Pastoral Letters of the United States Catholic Bishops, Vol. IV: 1975-1983*, followed by the page number.

of a sufficient supply of material goods. Moreover, it should safeguard the rights of all citizens, and help them find opportunities for employment. (PL 94)

The Right to a Decent Home: A Pastoral Response to the Crisis in Housing (November 20, 1975)

It is not enough for us to point to the reality of poor housing and recommend that government and other institutions take appropriate action. We must also reflect on our own responsibilities and opportunities for action. We call on individual Catholics, dioceses, and parishes, as well as other Catholic organizations, to join us in a new commitment to those who suffer from poor housing. (PL 113)

Pastoral Responsibility: Reflections on an Election Year (February 12, 1976)

In summary, we believe the Church has a proper role and responsibility in public affairs flowing from its Gospel mandate and its concern for the human person and his or her rights. We hope these reflections will contribute to a renewed sense of political vitality in our land, both in terms of citizen participation in the electoral process and the integrity and accountability of those who hold and seek public office. (PL 136)

Society and the Aged: Toward Reconciliation (May 5, 1976)

Many of the needs of the elderly will only be met adequately when the needs of others are met through a national policy guaranteeing full employment, a decent income for those unable to work, equitable tax legislation, and comprehensive health care for all. (PL 144)

To Live in Christ Jesus: A Pastoral Reflection on the Moral Life (November 11, 1976)

If we can acknowledge selfishness as folly and self-sacrifice as victory, if we can love enemies, be vulnerable to injustice and, in being so, still say that we have triumphed, then we shall have learned to live in Christ Jesus. (PL 195)

To Do the Work for Justice (May 4, 1978)

We pray and we trust that God's love, alive in the hearts of our people, will fire their imaginations and enkindle in them a desire for a more simple way of life, free from dependency on luxuries mistaken for necessities; that it will liberate them from prejudgments about others which are an obstacle to sharing the faith with them; and will enable them to view with an objective eye the deleterious effects on human beings of unjust social structures and to strive with courageous hearts to change these for the better.... (PL 254)

Brothers and Sisters to Us (November 14, 1979)
Racism is a sin; a sin that divides the human family, blots out the image of God among specific members of that family, and violates the fundamental human dignity of those called to be children of the same Father. (PL 344)

Pastoral Letter on Marxist Communism (November 12, 1980)
All too often Christians are faulted with a certain indifference toward earthly projects, as if one could not fully count on us for radical social reform. The charge may be unfair, but the danger is real enough. Our hope in another life must not be allowed to seduce believers into neglecting our task in the present one. (PL 392-393)

Called and Gifted: The American Catholic Laity (November 13, 1980)
We are convinced that the laity are making an indispensable contribution to the experience of the People of God and that the full import of their contribution is still in a beginning form in the post-Vatican II Church. (PL 423)

Reflections on the Energy Crisis (April 2, 1981)
[A]ll people of good will have a positive duty to conserve energy and to use energy efficiently under the conditions prevailing in the nation and the world. Those who have adopted simple styles of life deserve praise for their courage and commitment. (PL 446)

The Challenge of Peace: God's Promise and Our Response (May 3, 1983)
Offensive war of any kind is not morally justifiable....

The arms race is one of the greatest curses on the human race; it is to be condemned as a danger, an act of agression against the poor, and a folly which does not provide the security it promises....

We do not perceive any situation in which the deliberate initiation of nuclear war, on however restricted a scale, can be morally justified....

Peacemaking is not an optional commitment. It is a requirement of our faith. We are called to be peacemakers, not by some movement of the moment, but by our Lord Jesus.[4]

Economic Justice for All: Catholic Social Teaching and the U.S. Economy (November 13, 1986)

The basis for all that the Church believes about the moral dimensions of economic life is its vision of the transcendent worth—the sacredness—of human beings. The dignity of the human person, realized in community with others, is the criterion against which all aspects of economic life must be measured.[5]

A 'THEORY' OF THE CHURCH

Within the broad parameters of the bishops' pastorals, we find what could be called a consistent *theory* of the Catholic Church in the United States. Like every theory, the bishops' theory of the Church still needs testing and application. Yet it could be argued that precisely by putting the bishops' theory to the test the American Catholic Church will find its true post-Vatican II identity.

Something Albert Einstein once wrote will perhaps illustrate how the new post-Vatican II theory of the Church will come into recognizable shape:

> ...[C]reating a new theory is not like destroying an old barn and erecting a skyscraper in its place. It is rather like climbing a mountain, gaining new and wider views, discovering unexpected connections between our starting point and its rich environment. But the point from which we started out still exists and can be seen, although it appears smaller and forms a tiny part of our broad view gained by the mastery of the obstacles on our adventurous way up.[6]

By applying the model of Einstein's "mountain" to the post-Vatican II Church, we come to realize that the "old barn" of Catholic tradition has not been exchanged for a new Vatican II "skyscraper." Rather, since Vatican II we have all been progressing up a mountain, some of us climbing to dizzying new heights, some of us still milling around base camp. Those who are ensconced at rarefied levels can encourage those still concerned about possible oxygen starvation to come up and enjoy the view. As the American bishops have told us in their pastorals, there is a lot of mountain left to be climbed.

We end our story of the Church in the modern world here— abruptly, inconclusively. That is because the story is still being told. None of us knows for sure how it goes from here.

Since we ourselves are characters in the story, we are all engaged in the process of building the "finished product" of the Church in the modern world. And, as the American bishops tell us in their pastorals, there is a considerable unfinished agenda. There is much work still to be done. Thus, as People of Hope, we must always turn our eyes toward the future, toward the Church-in-formation we have all been commissioned to build.

CONCLUSION

The New Synthesis: Uniting the Church to the World

I mentioned Albert Einstein in the last chapter for a reason. The modern world referred to in Vatican II's document *The Church in the Modern World* is largely the Einsteinian world. Gone forever is the static worldview of an earlier science in which things operate according to fixed laws and are capable of precise observation and measurement. Instead, in the Einsteinian universe time decreases as velocity increases; one's observation of subatomic particles causes them to alter their position and momentum; all of creation becomes a unified continuum of space and time; and energy and matter are simply different observable conditions of the same unknowable force.

Like all of humanity's discoveries, Einstein's portended both excitement and danger, the possibility for unimaginable progress or the most heinous of crimes. No one could have foreseen that Einstein's $E = mc^2$—his formula for the interchangeability of matter and energy—would lead human beings to construct bombs that could destroy all life on earth. Such power in the hands of a race that has known little else but warfare is a stupefying prospect, making the question of our age the same as that asked by the psalmist,

> What is man that you should be mindful of him,
> or the son of man that you should care for him? (Psalm 8:5)

As Einstein himself once ruefully observed, mentally we are grown-ups possessed of frightening power, while spiritually and emotionally we are still children, relating to each other aggressively and suspiciously, insisting on hoarding our possessions and defending them from others. This combination of adult minds and infantile emotions in a race possessed of nuclear weapons makes the practice of hope extremely difficult, and in fact we see despair all around us today.

A SPIRIT-MATTER FUSION

Yet Einstein's discoveries themselves can be an occasion for hope—but only if the scientist's hunger for knowledge is submitted to the force of love. When the modern scientific mind is joined to a heart which loves, we have found someone who is uniquely qualified to speak to us about the future. That is why in the preceding pages I relied so heavily on the vision of Teilhard.

In an Einsteinian universe, as Teilhard repeatedly told us, we can no longer separate our "spiritual" selves from our "everyday" selves. In today's world, the scientist and the lover, the activist and the monk, the everyday laborer and the seeker after God must be one and the same person. The schizophrenic compulsion to steer our lives in two separate directions—one marked "earth" and the other "heaven"—must end. If we are to survive the peril our minds have created, we must once again heed the cry of our hearts for peace, unity, forgiveness and reconciliation.

What is needed today, and what Teilhard and the bishops at Vatican II pointed us toward, is a radically new synthesis of the spiritual and the material, the heavenly and the earthly, the Church and the world, the lover and the scientist. Jesus Christ came into *this* world, the Einsteinian space-time continuum, and redeemed it. Thus there is nothing to fear in our new universe so long as we embrace it, humanize it and submit it to the divinizing energy of the Resurrection.

In the new synthesis of the Vatican II Church, the boundary line between the scientist and the lover—like the boundary line between matter and energy in Einstein's universe—is incapable of being firmly fixed. We are now called to be, not scientists one minute and lovers the next, but constant scientist-lovers. We are called, as Teilhard put it, "ever to be faithful to earth." And who is most faithful to earth? The Christian-worker, the monk-activist, the spiritual-materialist—*we*, the Church-in-the-world, the People of Hope.

Just as Thomas Aquinas seven centuries ago provided humanity with a new synthesis of grace and nature, faith and reason, and religion and philosophy which worked and made sense in his world, so too does *our* new synthesis—the one outlined by Teilhard, Vatican II, Karl Rahner, John Paul II and liberation theologians—explain the

20th-century world to us and give us hope for the future. The true Christian today is one who dares to hope in the goodness of humanity, the earth and tomorrow. The Christian is one who can proclaim confidently that *Emmanuel* means "God is with us," or, perhaps more to the point, "God is with us *still*." In short, the Christian is one who gives birth to hope in others.

THE CHURCH OF THE PEOPLE OF HOPE

Let's turn back for a moment to the four diagrams of the Church-world dichotomy that we considered in the Introduction (pp. 2-3). We are now ready for a diagram to express the new synthesis between the Church and the world.

The synthesis to be achieved by the People of Hope will be an integrated worldview in which there is no longer a disparity between the Church and the world, so long as all of our human endeavors are submitted to the redemptive work of Jesus Christ. Diagramatically, therefore, we can conceive of the new Christian synthesis simply in terms of one unified set, as follows:

The Worldview of the People of Hope
Here there is no disparity between the Church and the world, so long as human effort is submitted to the redemptive work of Jesus Christ.

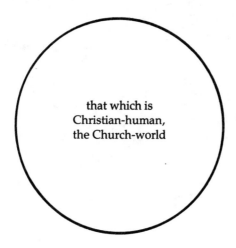

that which is
Christian-human,
the Church-world

This new synthesis is still being fabricated. The world is yet to be united to the gospel. Science still needs to be captured by love. But here and there it is happening, in thousands of untold stories and forgotten examples of love and sacrifice performed by the People of Hope.

Let's close with some words of hope found in a letter written by a Christian of our own day. Shortly before she was murdered in El Salvador on December 2, 1980, Maryknoll missioner Sister Ita Ford wrote these words to her niece, words which express in a sense the prayer of the entire Church from its earliest days to now:

> I hope you come to find that which gives life a deep meaning for you. Something worth living for—maybe even worth dying for—something that energizes you, enthuses you, enables you to keep moving ahead.

APPENDIX

The Documents of Vatican II

LATIN TITLE AND ABBREVIATION	ENGLISH TITLE
Apostolicam Actuositatem (AA)	Decree on the Apostolate of Lay People
Ad Gentes Divinitus (AGD)	Decree on the Church's Missionary Activity
Christus Dominus (CD)	Decree on the Pastoral Office of Bishops in the Church
Dignitatis Humanae (DH)	Declaration on Religious Liberty
Dei Verbum (DV)	Dogmatic Constitution on Divine Revelation
Gravissimum Educationis (GE)	Declaration on Christian Education
Gaudium et Spes (GS)	Pastoral Constitution on the Church in the Modern World
Inter Mirifica (IM)	Decree on the Means of Social Communication
Lumen Gentium (LG)	Dogmatic Constitution on the Church

Nostra Aetate (NA)	Declaration on the Relation of the Church to Non-Christian Religions
Orientalium Ecclesiarum (OE)	Decree on the Catholic Eastern Churches
Optatam Totius (OT)	Decree on the Training of Priests
Perfectae Caritatis (PC)	Decree on the Up-to-Date Renewal of Religious Life
Presbyterorum Ordinis (PO)	Decree on the Ministry and Life of Priests
Sacrosanctum Concilium (SC)	The Constitution on the Sacred Liturgy
Unitatis Redintegratio (UR)	Decree on Ecumenism

NOTES

Introduction

1. Carl Becker, *The Heavenly City of the Eighteenth-Century Philosophers* (1932), in *Theology Today*, Vol. XLII, No. 3 (October 1985), p. 283.

Chapter One

1. Hubert Jedin, ed., *History of the Church*, Vol. VII (The Crossroad Publishing Co., 1982), p. 56.
2. "Le Catechisme Imperial" (1806), *ibid.*, p. 72.
3. John Tracy Ellis, *Documents of American Catholic History*, 151, *ibid.*, p. 176.

Chapter Two

1. Jedin, *ibid.*, p. 273.
2. *Ibid.*, p. 233.
3. Felix Dupanloup, "Letter to Cardinal de Rohan," *ibid.*, p. 283.
4. Jedin, *ibid.*, p. 284.
5. *Ibid.*, p. 283.
6. *Acts of Gregory XVI*, 169-174, *ibid.*, p. 287.
7. *Ibid.*
8. Jedin, *ibid.*, p. 291.
9. *Ibid.*, Vol. VIII, p. 5.

Chapter Three

1. *Ibid.*, Vol. VII, p. 59.
2. *Ibid.*, p. 88.
3. *Ibid.*, p. 124.

Chapter Four

1. *Ibid.*, Vol. VIII, p. 215.
2. L. Scheffezyk, *ibid.*, p. 242.
3. Justo Gonzalez, *A History of Christian Thought*, Vol. III. (Abingdon Press, 1983), p. 367.
4. *Pastor Aeternus, ibid.*, p. 363.

Chapter Five

1. Jedin, *op. cit.*, Vol. IX, p. 9.
2. *Ibid.*, p. 20.
3. *Acts of Leo XIII*, 115, *ibid.*, Vol. VII, p. 85.

Chapter Six

1. Jedin, *ibid.*, Vol. XI, p. 384.
2. *L'Abbé Lemire, ibid.*, p. 385.
3. E. Renard, *Le Cardinal Mathieu, ibid.*, p. 386.
4. Jedin, *ibid.*, Vol. IX, p. 388.
5. *Ibid.*, p. 404.
6. *Ibid.*, p. 409.
7. *Ibid.*, p. 416.
8. *Ibid.*, p. 418.
9. *Acts of Leo XIII*, 274, 279, *ibid.*, Vol. VII, p. 308.
10. Jedin, *ibid.*, Vol. IX, p. 320.
11. S. V. Gibbons, "Micropedia," *Encyclopedia Brittanica*, 15th ed. (Encyclopedia Brittannica, Inc., 1983), Vol. IV, p. 529.
12. Jedin, *op cit.*, Vol. IX, p. 334.
13. *Ibid.*, p. 434.
14. *Ibid.*, p. 442.
15. Friedrich von Hugel, *Letters to a Niece*, 60 (1921), *ibid.*, p. 444.
16. Jedin, *ibid.*, Vol. IX, p. 452.
17. Pius X, "Letter to Msgr. Bonomelli" (1911), *ibid.*, p. 471.
18. From newspaper *Vigie* (December 5, 1912), *ibid.*, p. 468.

Chapter Seven

1. *L'Osservatore Romano* (May 16, 1929), *ibid.*, Vol. X, p. 60.
2. Jedin, *ibid.*, p. 79.
3. *Ibid.*
4. *Ibid.*, p. 87.
5. Konrad Repgen, "Foreign Policy of the Popes in the World Wars," *Ibid.*, p. 92.
6. *Rotta Report* (March 20, 1942), *ibid.*, p. 95.
7. L. Salvatorelli (1955), *ibid.*, p. 78.
8. "Church Pronouncements," *The Jerome Biblical Commentary* (Prentice-Hall, Inc., 1968), Chapter 72, sec. 6, p. 625.

Chapter Eight

1. John Jay Hughes, "The Council and the Synod: A Tale of Two Popes," *St. Anthony Messenger* (October 1985), p. 16.
2. *Ibid.*
3. Jedin, *op. cit.*, Vol. X, p. 99.

4. Hughes, *op. cit.*, p. 17.
5. *Ibid.*
6. *Ibid.*, p. 18.
7. Jedin, *ibid.*, Vol. X, p. 145.

Chapter Nine

1. Richard R. Niebuhr, "Friedrich Schleiermacher," *A Handbook of Christian Theologians*, Martin E. Marty and Dean G. Peerman, eds. (Abingdon Press, 1984), p. 18.
2. Friedrich Schleiermacher, "Letter to Friedrich H. Jacobi," *ibid.*, p. 25.
3. *The Christian Faith, ibid.*, p. 31.
4. Martin J. Heinecken, "Søren Kierkegaard," *ibid.*, p. 128.
5. Søren Kierkegaard, *The Attack Upon Christendom, ibid.*, p. 135.
6. Martin J. Heinecken, "Søren Kierkegaard," *ibid.*, p. 141.
7. Bernard E. Meland, "Rudolf Otto," *ibid*, p. 173.
8. Rudolf Otto, *The Idea of the Holy, ibid.*, p. 180.
9. *Ibid.*
10. *Ibid.*, p. 182.
11. Adolf von Harnack, *The History of Dogma*, "Adolf von Harnack," Wilhelm Pauck, *ibid.*, p. 99.
12. Wilhelm Pauck, "Adolf von Harnack," *ibid.*, p. 103.
13. George B. Caird, "C. H. Dodd," *ibid.*, p. 328.
14. Rudolf Bultmann, *Jesus and the Word*, "Rudolf Bultmann," John Macquarrie, *ibid.*, p. 446.
15. Daniel Jenkins, "Karl Barth," *ibid.*, p. 398.
16. *Ibid.*, p. 404.
17. Hans Hofmann, "Reinhold Niebuhr," *ibid.*, p. 356-357.
18. Reinhold Niebuhr, *Does Civilization Need Religion?*, *ibid.*, p. 358.
19. Reinhold Niebuhr, *The Nature and Destiny of Man, ibid*, p. 369.
20. Dietrich Bonhoeffer, *The Cost of Discipleship*, "Dietrich Bonhoeffer," Franklin Sherman, *ibid.*, p. 466.
21. *Prisoner for God, ibid.*, p. 481.
22. *Ibid.*, p. 482-483.
23. Walter Liebrecht, "Paul Tillich," *ibid.*, p. 487.
24. *Ibid.*, p. 490.
25. *Ibid.*, p. 491.

Chapter Ten

1. Maurice de Wulf, *An Introduction to Scholastic Philosophy*, 194, *Twentieth-Century Religious Thought*, John Macquarrie (Charles Scribner's Sons, 1981), p. 282.
2. Karl Adam, *The Spirit of Catholicism*, 69, *ibid.*, p. 292.
3. Macquarrie, *ibid.*, p. 293.
4. Pope John XXIII, *Mater et Magistra* (May 15, 1961), Jedin, *op. cit.*, Vol. X, p. 231.

5. Pope Pius XII, "Address to College of Cardinals" (February 26, 1946), *ibid.*, p. 233.
6. *Gaudium et Spes*, 44, 2, *ibid.*, p. 236.
7. Pope John XXIII, *Pacem in Terris*, 9, *ibid.*, p. 237.
8. Pope Pius XII, "Berlin Address" (August 10, 1952), *ibid.*
9. Pope Pius XI, *Quadragesimo Anno*, 79-80, *ibid.*, p. 238.
10. Pope John XXIII, *Mater et Magistra*, 65, *ibid.*, p. 240.

Chapter Eleven

1. Pierre Teilhard de Chardin, *The Divine Milieu* (Harper and Row, 1960).
2. *Ibid.*, *The Heart of the Matter* (Harcourt, Brace and Jovanovich, 1978), p. 214.
3. *Ibid.*, *Christianity and Evolution* (1971), p. 220.
4. *Ibid.*, *Writings in Time of War* (Harper and Row, 1968), p. 237.
5. *Ibid.*, p. 243.
6. *Ibid.*, p. 244.
7. *Ibid.*, p. 246.
8. *Ibid.*, *Science et Christ* (Editions du Seuil, 1956), p. 112.
9. Pierre Leroy, *Letters From My Friend Teilhard de Chardin*, (Paulist Press, 1980), in *America*, Vol. 144, No. 20, May 23, 1981, "A Remembrance of Pierre Teilhard de Chardin," p. 418.
10. *Ibid.*, p. 419.
11. *Ibid.*
12. *Ibid.*

Chapter Twelve

1. Hughes, *op. cit.*, p. 20.
2. Karol Wojtyla, *Sources of Renewal: The Implementation of Vatican II* (Harper and Row, 1980).
3. All quotations from the Vatican documents are taken from *Vatican Council II: The Conciliar and Postconciliar Documents*, Austin Flannery, O.P., gen. ed. (Costello Publishing Co., 1975; rev. ed., 1981).

Chapter Thirteen

1. "Message to the People of God" in *Our Sunday Visitor* (December 7, 1985).

Chapter Fourteen

1. Stephen Duffy, "Catholicism's Search for a New Self-Understanding," Gerard M. Fagin, S.J., *Vatican II: Open Questions and New Horizons* (Michael Glazier, Inc., 1984), p. 34.
2. *Ibid.*, p. 35.
3. *Ibid.*

4. Pope John Paul II, *Redemptor Hominis* "Redeemer of Man"; United States Catholic Conference, March 4, 1979, p. 53.
5. Jay P. Dolan, *The American Catholic Experience* (Doubleday, 1985), p. 437.
6. Francine Cardman, "'The Church Would Look Foolish Without Them': Women and Laity Since Vatican II," Fagin, *op. cit.*, p. 127.
7. Dolan, *op. cit.*, p. 435.
8. *Dorothy Day: Meditations*, selected and arranged by Stanley Vishnewski (Paulist Press, 1970), pp. 25-26, 83.
9. Thomas P. McDonnell, ed., *A Thomas Merton Reader* (Doubleday Image Books, 1974) pp. 429, 430.

Chapter Fifteen

1. Paul Johnson, *Pope John Paul II and the Catholic Restoration* (Servant Books, 1981), p. 75.
2. *Ibid.*, p. 81.
3. *Ibid.*, p. 77.
4. Karl Marx, *Critique of the Hegelian Philosophy of Law, ibid.*, p. 77.
5. Pope John Paul II, *Dives in Misericordia, ibid.*, p. 83.
6. *Redemptor Hominis, op. cit.*, p. 28 [See Chapter 14, n. 4].
7. Johnson, *ibid.*, p. 95.
8. *Ibid.*, p. 99.
9. *Ibid.*, p. 106.
10. *Ibid.*, p. 107.
11. *Ibid.*, p. 110.
12. Pope John Paul II, *Redemptor Hominis, op. cit.*, p. 26.
13. Teilhard de Chardin, *The Heart of the Matter, op. cit.*, p. 102.
14. Karl Rahner, *Theological Investigations,* Vol. IV (Seabury, 1974), pp. 180-181.
15. Anne E. Carr, "Karl Rahner," Marty and Peerman, *op. cit.*, p. 535.
16. Jürgen Moltmann, "Faith and Politics," *The Power of the Poor in History*, Gustavo Gutierrez (Orbis Books, 1984), p. 185.
17. Robert J. Schreiter, "Edward Schillebeeckx," Marty and Peerman, *op. cit.*, p. 637.
18. *Ibid.*, p. 638.
19. Johnson, *op. cit.*, p. 157.
20. *Ibid.*, p. 160.
21. *Ibid.*, p. 162.
22. Gutierrez, *op. cit.*, p. 184.
23. Johnson, *op. cit.*, p. 102.
24. *Ibid.*, p. 101.
25. Gutierrez, *op. cit.*, p. 57.
26. Pope John Paul II, "Address to the Indians of Oaxaca and Chiapas," #29, Gutierrez, *ibid.*, p. 135.
27. Pope John Paul II, "Opening Address at Puebla," III, 3, *ibid.*, p. 133.

Chapter Sixteen

1. *The Challenge of Peace: God's Promise and Our Response*, Summary, (United State Catholic Conference, May 3, 1983), p. 3.
2. *Ibid.*, p. 4.
3. National Conference of Catholic Bishops, *Called and Gifted: The American Cathlolic Laity* (November 13, 1980), *Pastoral Letters of the United States Catholic Bishops, Vol. IV: 1975-1983* (United States Catholic Conference, 1984), p. 418.
4. *The Challenge of Peace, op. cit.*, pp. 5-7, 9.
5. *Economic Justice for All: Pastoral Letter on Catholic Social Teaching and the U.S. Economy* (United States Catholic Conference, 1986), p. 15.
6. Albert Einstein and Leopold Infeld, *The Evolution of Physics* (Simon and Schuster, 1938), p. 31.

INDEX

Americanism, 68-69
Anti-Catholicism, in Europe, 9-10, 36, 39, 58-61, 169; in U.S., 37-38
Antonelli Giacomo, Cardinal, 32
Assumption of Mary, 87
Attack on Christendom, The (Kierkegaard), 99
Auto-evolution, 119, 120
Baptism in the Holy Spirit, 157
Barth, Karl, 103-104
Bauer, Ferdinand, 45
Benedict XV, Pope, 75, 77-78
Bergson, Henri, 71
Bible, 86, 101; after Vatican II, 148, 179-180; historical-critical method, 68, 69-70, 101-104, 177; and liberation theology, 179-180; historical studies of, 102-103, 177
Biblical scholarship, Catholic, 69-70, 86, 148; Protestant, 101-104
Birth control, 160-161
Blondel, Maurice, 71
Bolivar, Simon, 16-17
Bonald, Louis, Count, 24
Bonaparte, Napoleon, 8, 10-11
Bonhoeffer, Dietrich, 105-106
Bosco, John, 42
Bourgeoisie, 61, 179
Bultmann, Rudolf, 102-103
Canon Law, Code of (1917), 66
Carrera, Rafael (Guatemala), 40
Carroll, John, 17
Catholic Action, 24, 82
CELAM, 181-182
Celibacy, 155, 171-172
Charismatic Renewal, 156-159
Charles X (France), 19-20
Chateaubriand, François, 23
Christian Faith, The (Schleiermacher), 96-97
Church, changing concepts of, 3, 91, 132, 134-137, 139, 147, 161-163, 169, 187-188; and

democracy, 17-18; in Africa, 162; in Austria, 35-36; in England, 36-37; in France, 8-10, 15, 34-35, 59; in Germany, 16; in Holland, 162; in India, 163; in Italy, 15-16, 56, 82; Latin America, 16-17, 39-40, 161-162; in Poland, 169; in Prussia, 35; in Spain, 39-40; in United States, 17, 37-38, 68-69, 172, 183-184, 187; and Liberalism, 2-3, 20-22; and Modernism, 54, 70-73; rise of national Churches, 161-163, 169; and totalitarianism, 79, 82-83; and working class, 36-37, 56-59, 63-64, 80-81, 153-154; and world, 2-5, 42-44, 54, 70-73, 80-81, 86, 114-116, 135-136, 147-148, 152, 191; and World War I, 77; and World War II, 84-85
Church Dogmatics (Barth), 103
Church in the Modern World, The (Vatican II). *See Gaudium et Spes*
"Civil Constitution of the Clergy" (France), 9
Clergy, 42; in France, 8-9, 15, 21, 26, 34, 60-61; and French Revolution, 9-10; elsewhere in Europe, 36, 57, 58; and laity, 18, 24, 35, 136-137, 146-147, 154, 162; and liberalism, 9, 14-16, 21, 70-71; and priest shortage, 154-156, 171-172; and reforms, 41-42, 67; and theology, 45-46, 70-71; in U.S., 18, 183-184; role of, 139, 147, 154-155, 160; after Vatican II, 136-137, 139-140, 154, 160, 161-162, 171-172, 183-184